*Serving Gifted Learners Beyond the Traditional Classroom*

The *Critical Issues in Equity and Excellence in Gifted Education* Series

# Serving Gifted Learners Beyond the Traditional Classroom

## A Guide to Alternative Programs and Services

Edited by

**Joyce L. VanTassel-Baska, Ed.D.**

Prufrock Press Inc.
Waco, Texas

a service publication of

NATIONAL ASSOCIATION FOR
**Gifted Children**

Library of Congress Cataloging-in-Publication Data

Serving gifted learners beyond the traditional classroom : a guide to alternative programs and services / edited by Joyce L. VanTassel-Baska.
      p. cm. — (The critical issues in equity and excellence in gifted education series)
   ISBN-13: 978-1-59363-211-3 (pbk.)
   ISBN-10: 1-59363-211-8 (pbk.)
   1.  Gifted children—Education. 2.  Alternative education.  I. VanTassel-Baska, Joyce.
   LC3993.S47 2007
   371.95—dc22
                                    2006024717

Copyright © 2007 Prufrock Press Inc.
Edited by Lacy Elwood
Cover and Layout Design by Marjorie Parker

ISBN-13: 978-1-59363-211-3
ISBN-10: 1-59363-211-8

Printed in the United States of America.

At the time of this book's publication, all facts and figures cited are the most current available. All telephone numbers, addresses, and Web site URLs are accurate and active. All publications, organizations, Web sites, and other resources exist as described in the book, and all have been verified. The authors and Prufrock Press Inc. make no warranty or guarantee concerning the information and materials given out by organizations or content found at Web sites, and we are not responsible for any changes that occur after this book's publication. If you find an error, please contact Prufrock Press Inc.

Prufrock Press Inc.
P.O. Box 8813
Waco, TX 76714-8813
Phone: (800) 998-2208
Fax: (800) 240-0333
http://www.prufrock.com

To the memory of Julian C. Stanley and his pioneering work
in developing alternative programs and services.

# Contents

# List of Tables

# List of Figures

# Acknowledgments

I would like to acknowledge the support of Dr. Susannah Wood in the final preparation of this manuscript. Her careful proofing and formatting work was deeply appreciated.

—Joyce VanTassel-Baska

# CHAPTER 1

# Introduction and Overview
# of the Issues

*Joyce L. VanTassel-Baska*

## Introduction

This book is conceived to be a unique contribution to the field of gifted education in its focus on alternatives to traditional public schooling as we know them for gifted students. The authors explore a selected number of services and programs that have gained reputation and credibility in the field as appropriate and beneficial opportunities for gifted students and their families for investment of time and resources. The book also has as its purpose to raise critical issues about such delivery mechanisms, especially as they impact the inclusion of groups from underrepresented populations, as they take resources from school-based programs, and as they promote alternative learning environments that change the fundamental character of schooling in this country.

This book represents more than 2 years of planning in respect to its conceptualization. It began as an idea among a group of scholars and mushroomed into a full-blown book project, augmented by many voices from around the world. It is my special pleasure to see it come to fruition. The audience for the book consists of parents and educators, as well as researchers and community leaders who care deeply about the development of talent within our society.

This book presents self-standing chapters that address different program and service models found to be effective with gifted learners in contexts beyond school. These chapters delineate the nature of opportunities, the research base for these opportunities, and some of the issues associated with each particular type of program. The authors represent veterans in the field with longstanding involvement in these program prototypes. Others are fresh faces and voices, new to formal gifted education circles. Two of the authors bring an international perspective to the volume, allowing us to see the extent to which these programs and services are global, not just national in scope. Yet, each author has an important story to tell about the opportunities that gifted students can access in the larger community and the variety of those opportunities in respect to their area of talent.

In the second chapter that follows, Olszewski-Kubilius begins with the myriad of reasons for the proliferation of out-of-school academic opportunities, including unmet academic needs, specialized interests, and lack of supportive parents or having a peer group. She then describes the talent search programs that now represent the most comprehensive national orientation to talent development that we have—the search; the programs during the summer and academic year and online; and the outreach services that include seminars, counseling, tutorials, and other opportunities for students and families. The Olszewski-Kubilius chapter also reviews the research on the impacts of special out-of-school programs for the gifted, including issues of self-concept, academic development, and evidence of future aspirations and performance. Special note is made of the effects of such opportunities on girls and minority students. Issues of school acceptance of students' work in these programs are discussed in some detail, suggesting schools' lack of willingness to acknowledge gifted students' documented accomplishments even now.

The Kitano chapter highlights well the issues of such types of program opportunities for diverse students. This chapter describes the plight of these underserved students in respect to out-of-school programs, suggesting that issues of ethnic group identity, peer group relationships, and use of leisure time may mediate the positive impact of such experiences. Moreover, biculturalism and bilingualism remain important considerations in building academic performance and social adjustment in these students. Issues of marginalization and alienation ("fewness") are described as critical to these students' adjustment in such settings.

The Johnsen, Feuerbacher, and Witte chapter illustrates the problems of ensuring representation of low-income and minority students in university-based offerings and retaining them over time, even as the trend to attract such populations increases. This chapter presents a study conducted on a university-based program that deliberately sought to enhance the participation and retention of minority and low-income students through the following: providing mentors, special classes that addressed strengths and interests, teachers who were trained to work effectively with such students, parent education, and peer support activities. Findings from a sample of cases of both those students who were and were not retained suggest that these students require strong social support in addition to positive self-perceptions to ensure that they will both participate and return to such program settings. The chapter raises issues of the extent of need for monitoring personal and social adjustment variables for these students if university-based experiences are to be as fruitful as intended.

The Cross and Miller chapter provides a comparison of residential high school models as a form of education that is public, but separate from traditional high school programs, and outlines their common and unique features. Model I schools focus on the development of scientific talent, Model II on the development of talent in the arts, and Model III on early college entrance opportunities, regardless of talent areas, revealing key distinctions among the schools described. High on the list of common features, however, is the presence of a cohort of students with similar interests and aptitudes who find each other and benefit from interactions, both in and out of the classroom.

Benefits common to students attending these schools include academic and peer support, as well as the opportunity to have a foreshadowing of the competition and lifestyle of college. The authors are even-handed in suggesting some liabilities associated with these schools as well, raising issues of who the schools are best designed for among the gifted population, the evenness in the quality of the curricular experiences provided, and the potential impacts on more traditional high schools.

The Coleman chapter builds on his earlier work: an ethnographic study he conducted at one of the residential schools described in Chapter 5. The chapter discusses in greater detail the issues that gifted students face during the adolescent years as they embark on a more serious track of talent development. The author outlines carefully the social context variables of these schools that facilitate the development of talent and comments on ways that these contexts differ from others offered in society at large, suggesting their critical role in developing high-level talent. He presents 11 central insights that he gleaned from his work in one residential high school about the interaction effect of the school and its students.

The Brody chapter addresses the need for highly gifted students to experience personalized services in their talent development process. These services include guidance and counseling on psychosocial, academic, and college and career areas. The author describes an array of these services currently available to highly gifted students through the Julian Stanley Study of Exceptional Talent (SET) at Johns Hopkins University and suggests that issues of level of aptitude in certain domains coupled with personal predispositions activate the decisions that adolescents are likely to make in critical areas of program and college selection, even with the personal guidance of a professional. She also provides a description of resources central to assisting highly talented students with academic counseling.

The Riley and Karnes chapter chronicles the importance of contests and competitions for the gifted and lays out the negative issues associated with emphasizing student involvement in these enterprises. The chapter raises the issue of competitions as an important way to develop excellence and group dynamic skills, as well as questions the extent to which competitions are equitable, especially with respect to who can participate if schools remain rigid gatekeepers in respect to eligibility. Facilitation of competition participation by schools is discussed, noting the importance of integrating competitions into overall curricular emphases for the gifted.

The Adams and Olszewski-Kubilius chapter delineates the history of distance learning opportunities for the gifted over the past several decades, noting the exponential growth of opportunities in this area as technologies become more sophisticated and accessible for learning purposes. The authors also discuss several successful models of distance learning, involving large numbers of students annually. The paucity of data on the impact of distance learning on the achievement and long-term learning of gifted students is acknowledged by the authors, raising several issues associated with the easy access of technology and the difficulty in understanding what types of gifted students will benefit and under what conditions of support.

The Feng chapter discusses the nature of premiere mentorship experiences in the United States and Singapore, including the Research Science Institute (RSI) and the newer Olympiad programs in the subject areas of discrete sciences including physics, chemistry, and biology, mathematics, and computer science. The author contends that these programs provide a crystallizing experience for students fortunate enough to be selected for them and further the development of elite scientific talent in the United States and abroad. Data on student views of mentor programs suggest the key role of teachers in activating and sustaining student interest in science areas, while existing science programs in schools are perceived as lacking in meaningful experimentation and real science activities. The chapter also explores the key research-based components in developing successful mentor programs.

The Chee chapter explores in great detail the current landscape of service learning opportunities for gifted and other learners throughout the world and provides a sound rationale for exposing gifted students to such opportunities throughout their school years. She carefully demonstrates the important linkage between the development of leadership and service learning opportunities, noting that the two emphases are rarely conjoined to benefit gifted learners. The chapter delineates different modes and types of service learning that have proven effective with such learners and ends with a suggested model for such activities. The chapter raises important issues about the need for a systematic way to instill altruistic behaviors in the gifted through connected learning to the larger community.

The final chapter by VanTassel-Baska explicates the issues raised in the earlier chapters and chronicles the relative contributions of research and development of each type of alternative program or service. It suggests a new model for gifted programming in this century, one that creates institutional and agency networks to promote talent development outside the traditional public schools as a viable answer to societal calls for educational excellence, shortages in key fields of human endeavor, and the need for high-level scientific talent to be competitive worldwide. She suggests that there is a need to put our energy into alternative approaches that exhibit ostensible and measurable outcomes. Instead of creating islands of excellence, we need to create systems of talent development in every state that offer an array of opportunities to these learners at different stages of development. By seeking alternative solutions to direct services beyond the schoolhouse doors, we open up the avenues of learning more consistently to what we know is effective with the best learners.

## Core Issues in Offering Alternative Programs and Services

So, what are the issues associated with offering alternative programs and services for gifted populations? Is this something we should be concerned about or applaud? I would argue there are 10 aspects to the situation that bear commentary.

*1. Alternative programs tend to weaken school-based opportunities.*
One reason to be concerned about the proliferation of these opportunities is their tendency to flatten or even depress the

services available to gifted students in schools. While all such services require cooperation of the schools in order to participate, the involvement of schools in most university and community-based programs is minimal, thus fragmenting the system of service delivery. School districts many times claim these services as their own for funding and mandate purposes such that it appears the outside alternative opportunities are more connected than they really are. Moreover, in several states, funding for gifted programs is bifurcated by funding for special statewide or regional opportunities, which tend to grow more than allotments for local district programs, setting up a situation of local district underfunding for gifted resources. In many school districts, the politics of No Child Left Behind (NCLB; 2001) further play into this scenario as resources are deployed more broadly to enhance learning for all, leaving targeted direct instruction to the gifted by the wayside.

*2. Alternative programs lack integration with school-based options.*

Another concern to have about these alternative options for the gifted is the implication for greater fragmentation in the way gifted students are served. With the exception of the residential or full-day school model employed in several states, there are few of these offerings that represent a fulltime placement for gifted students over even a few years. Even when out-of-school programs can carefully document student proficiency in an area (see the Olszewski-Kubilius chapter), schools can deny access to the next level course and/or refuse to give credit for the coursework taken. Students then may inadvertently suffer a lack of articulation of services that exacerbates their overall sense of being "held back." Moreover, the likelihood of creating a viable program of studies on anything other than an individual model becomes obsolete as geography, different agencies, and different models vie for student involvement.

*3. Alternative programs do not reach sufficient numbers of low-income and minority students who are gifted and may not provide the support structures necessary for success.*

Because such programs reside outside of school, the public school contexts that these students have available to them often do not avail themselves of offering high-powered programs nor of providing support for their students to attend alternative programs. Therefore, these students are left without monetary and parental support mechanisms to participate in the alternative programs that may best meet their needs. Although foundations like Jack Kent Cooke are attempting to address this issue on a small scale, there is a real need for greater attention to these promising learners nationwide in order to ensure their involvement in alternative programs and services.

*4. Most alternative programs are costly, even for middle-income families, and scholarships are scarce.*

Alternative program costs also put an additional burden on parents who want their children to seize these opportunities when they are offered. Parental involvement then becomes a precursor to student access in many of these options, putting at risk the working family without adequate resources to provide their children with these opportunities. The sheer cost of taking a course in a summer program can run $2,000 for 3 weeks and taking an online course can be more than $1,000. For high-income families, these charges are insignificant, but for other families they are prohibitive, even though the benefits accrued from such participation can be outstanding for the prospective student. How do we reconcile our need for such programs and services with the reality of who is left behind?

*5. Alternative programs and services take local gifted programs off the hook in respect to appropriate education of the gifted.*

In most school districts across America, gifted students are not a priority when it comes to resource allocation in respect to personnel or funding (VanTassel-Baska & Feng, 2004). This situation is further exacerbated by what the priorities are: the implementation of a massive federal initiative to increase annual yearly progress for all learners, the rigid implementation of a standards-based curriculum, and the mindless focus on high-stakes but low-level state assessments that tend to blur the distinctions around what real learning is. This problem of neglect in the development of high-level ability and talent is a central one in schools right now that enhances the allure of out-of-school options as schools can claim connection and participation in them while continuing to ignore the presence of these students each day during compulsory seat time.

*6. Alternative programs are dependent on schools as gatekeepers in respect to student access.*

Running successful alternative programs means that you can advertise your products and services to a targeted audience. For the most part, this audience is reachable only through local district personnel and public appeals in relevant media. Schools vary tremendously in the extent to which they deliberately provide information to students and families about out-of-school opportunities. If a school does not have a gifted coordinator or has one with other responsibilities, the likelihood of communicating such opportunities is diminished. There is no direct line from the sponsoring agency to the student for making the optimal match of student need to alternative program opportunities. As such services continue to proliferate, it may be the best marketing model that prevails, rather than the best services, given the problems associated with access.

*7. Alternative programs and services create a separate environment for educating gifted children that threatens public schools' ability to retain and serve these learners.*

Perhaps nowhere is this debate more clearly defined than in the residential school contexts described by Cross and Miller in Chapter 5. Even though a very small percentage of any school district's students would attend these state academies, the public schools in each state worry about the "brain drain" on their test scores and their average daily attendance figures. Yet, the schools do not respond to this threat in a proactive way by beefing up programs and services to this population. Hypothetically, the presence of a residential program in a state should elevate the offerings to gifted students statewide through the dissemination of models that work and can be implemented in all schools, the diffusion of teaching techniques found to be effective with gifted adolescents, and the sharing of important insights about identification and counseling, areas in which residential schools have demonstrated expertise. Yet, this is not the reality, even as these schools have engaged in numerous outreach strategies over the years.

*8. Alternative programs and services often are not viewed by educators as central to the education of gifted learners.*

In some educators' minds, only what happens in a traditional public school counts in respect to the education of the gifted. If the local school district cannot take credit for the educational impact, then the program that deserves it will remain unrecognized. Talent search programs, for example, have worked for more than 25 years to engage schools in using off-level test data for internal identification and for setting up special school-based options for learners identified to be in need of them within the schools. Detailed narrative and quantitative reports of student progress and mastery attainment routinely go to schools to arrange appropriate placement and credit for students accelerating through given areas of the curricula. Yet, the majority of school districts do not use the data provided by the alternative programs, and worst of all, may force students to repeat classes in which they have already mastered the material.

*9. Alternative programs and services for the gifted have attracted the for-profit sector.*

As these programs and services become more market-driven and more bottom-line oriented, the cost of programs goes up and the quality of services may be compromised. Not all alternative programs offer the same benefits—yet parents, anxious to see their child receive value-added opportunities, respond positively to the marketing campaigns that tout brand-name higher education institutions as sites for programs, even if there is no specialist in gifted education guiding the design and development of the offerings. What protection do we have for ensuring the quality of such offerings? How will parents be able to judge what works and what doesn't in a sea of alternatives? Who will provide consumer protection for such services?

*10. Alternative programs are gifted education in the current climate.*

Because many local school districts' gifted programs have either been eliminated, reduced in funding and personnel time, or neglected due to issues associated with the impact of NCLB, these students' need for challenging out-of-school opportunities has grown. Even as the face of gifted education in public schools is diminished, if not absent from the landscape of public education, the types of programs noted in this book are increasing, with healthy enrollments and waiting lists of students who want to participate. The evaluations of these programs suggest that students benefit in more powerful ways from their participation in such opportunities than they do in school-based options, even when the options are comparable, such as Advanced Placement and honors courses. Flexible time frames, intensive learning opportunities, and having an authentic peer group all contribute to that situation.

Many school districts list out-of-school opportunities as the core of their gifted program, even to the point of having a scheduled class during school time focused on the "rules of competition" for the Future Problem-Solving Program or the problem sets for the Math Counts competition. Thus, competitions often become the core curriculum for gifted learners rather than the substantive learning that supports them.

## Conclusion

These issues and many others pervade the landscape of providing services to gifted children in alternative settings. It is hoped that such issues can form the basis for fruitful discussion about the needs of gifted children in schools, laboratories, museums, and libraries throughout our country. If alternative programs and services are the wave of the future for gifted education, then we need to ensure that they have supplanted local school district options for clear and good reason, that they offer a superior alternative, and that they can become widespread enough to become a viable alternative nationally.

The best of all possible worlds, however, would be for public schools to wake up to the needs of the gifted and provide the needed resources to serve them adequately in day-to-day settings and link those students in greatest need, including the poor and minority along with the highly gifted, to the optimal alternatives available in the larger community. Partnerships between schools and outside agencies providing talent development resources founded on similar beliefs and values and shared resources could create the optimal climate for the talent development so desperately needed in this country.

## References

No Child Left Behind Act, 20 U.S.C. § 6301 (2001).

VanTassel-Baska, J. T., & Feng, A. X. (Eds.). (2004). *Designing and utilizing evaluation for gifted program improvement.* Waco, TX: Prufrock Press.

# The Role of Summer Programs in Developing the Talents of Gifted Students

*Paula Olszewski-Kubilius*

## Introduction

There is a history in the United States of cultural institutions offering academic programs for children who live in their communities. These include museums and arts organizations, among others. Generally, these programs are geared for children of all ability areas. However, increasingly, special programs that occur outside typical school hours are being developed for academically gifted students, especially by universities and colleges.

## Why Special Programs?

One important question is why special programs should exist for gifted learners. Are they needed? If so, why? Many individuals believe that outside of school, educational programs are absolutely necessary for gifted children because of their special learning needs (Olszewski-Kubilius, 1989). Typically, these programs provide a level of challenge and a pace of learning that are more suitable to the intellectual capabilities of gifted students and are very different from what they encounter in school. There are more opportunities for independent inquiry, in-depth study of a topic, and accelerated learning. For many gifted children, this is the first time they are placed in a learning situation that requires study and concentrated work. In short, it is often the first time students are truly engaged in learning and truly being challenged.

Another reason for summer programs is that the talent development process may require additional intensive instruction beyond what schools can or are willing to provide—even very good schools (Bloom, 1985). It is well known and widely accepted that developing musical or athletic talent to a high level requires lessons, special teachers, and long hours of devoted study over a period of years. In these areas, school programs (with the exception of special schools for the arts) typically provide only initial exposure to the talent field and an arena for identification of talent by coaches or teachers. Parents expect to supplement their children's learning and development through outside programs and lessons. Similarly, research has indicated that gifted scientists, writers, and others spent considerable time learning in their talent area from parents and mentors or from tinkering and studying on their own (Piirto, 1992; VanTassel-Baska, 1995). A great deal of learning takes place outside of school, independently and informally (Olszewski-Kubilius & Lee, 2004b). As with musical and athletic talent, however, parents may not be knowledgeable enough to instruct their child in the talent area beyond a certain point or to provide appropriate educational materials. Even in the best schools, the amount of instruction in an area for a gifted child may not be sufficient to develop the talent or to satisfy the child's hunger for learning (Thompson, 2001).

Even if a parent or mentor is capable of providing additional instruction, academically gifted children need to have friends and interaction with intellectual peers. Most academically gifted children spend little of their time in school in homogeneous classes with other gifted children (Archambault et al., 1993; Cox, Daniel, & Boston, 1985). The emphasis in most schools is on grouping children according to age, not ability. However, classes with other gifted children are more likely to foster friendships based on common interests and priorities and provide general social support for educational pursuits and talent development (Olszewski-Kubilius, Grant, & Seibert, 1993). In addition, these settings can offer a greater degree of intellectual stimulation and challenge.

Another reason out-of-school programs for gifted children are needed is that schools often simply fail to provide for these children, especially for special subgroups such as underrepresented and/or underachieving minorities (Alamprese, Erlanger, & Brigham, 1988; Ford, 1996; VanTassel-Baska, Patton, & Prillaman, 1991) and the highly gifted. Reasons include lack of funds or other resources, lack of qualified teachers, too few students to set up classes in rural settings, and needs that cannot be met in the local school's gifted program. Parental demand for special opportunities has often fueled the development of out-of-school programs.

Finally, special programs for some academically gifted children may be necessary to save them from a pattern of underachievement or poor study habits that can result from "easy" or "boring" classes (Rimm, 1991) and lack of peer support for academic achievement. Thus, special out-of-school programs have become a vital part of the education of gifted youths.

Moreover, special programs for gifted students have proliferated with the advent and growth of the regional talent search programs in the U.S. Programs such as Northwestern University's Center for Talent Development, Duke University's Talent Identification Program, Johns Hopkins University's Center for Talented Youth, Denver University's Rocky Mountain Talent Search, and others conduct regionally based academic talent searches using off-level testing for elementary and middle school students. These programs and others in various countries have contributed to the growth of summer programs for gifted students by providing an efficient and economical identification system involving more than 250,000 students annually. These programs produce directories of available summer programs and make them available to talent search participants, thereby increasing knowledge about and access to such out-of-school opportunities.

## General Issues With Special Programs

Regardless of who sponsors special programs or their content, there are some general issues that result from their existence.

### Relationship to In-School Programs

A frequent concern of educators is the articulation between in-school programs and out-of-school programs. While many extraschool educational programs offer enrichment-type courses only, some programs enable gifted students to take courses they would normally take in school (e.g., algebra) in special summer and Saturday programs or through a distance learning program. When students accelerate themselves in a content area at the seventh or eighth grade through a special program, there can be both immediate and long-term consequences. Immediate consequences include how the student should respond to the course just completed and in what kind of course the student should now be placed. Long-term consequences include how to accommodate a high school junior who has completed all of the mathematics courses that the high school has to offer. Schools may actively discourage students from participating in special programs because of these articulation issues or they may indirectly discourage them by not responding appropriately after the experience. Research has shown that students who complete high school coursework in summer programs often do not receive credit for such work and many are not even appropriately placed in the content area (Olszewski-Kubilius, Laubscher, Wohl, & Grant, 1996), despite the fact that research has consistently documented that such students are well prepared for subsequent courses and, in fact, succeed in them (Kolitch & Brody, 1992; Mills, Ablard, & Lynch, 1992). Some students even have to repeat the courses they take during the summer in their home schools (Olszewski-Kubilius, 1989). Nothing is more demoralizing to a good student, especially one who seeks challenging courses in special programs, than being required to retake a course or not being allowed to go on to the next course in the sequence.

## Access to Special Programs

Institutions of higher education most often sponsor special summer and Saturday programs. Most charge tuition. As a result, many are simply out of reach for academically gifted children who are economically disadvantaged. Minority children are less likely to be identified as gifted and, therefore, less likely to be placed in special programs within their schools (Alamprese et al., 1988; VanTassel-Baska et al., 1991). They are also underrepresented in talent search testing and other out-of-school educational programs. But, gifted minority students, especially those who are economically disadvantaged, are in dire need of the services provided by these special programs. The costs of residential summer programs are often too high for even moderate-income families, and commuter programs may be too distant, especially in more rural areas. Thus, although special summer and Saturday programs are increasingly seen as vital to talent development, access to them is too often limited to the more economically advantaged gifted students and those in resource-rich geographic locations.

Distance learning programs are becoming increasingly available in our technologically oriented society, particularly Web-based courses, but these also typically involve tuition costs that make them inaccessible to many of the same students (Adams & Cross, 1999/2000).

## Instructional Models and Program Types

Summer and Saturday programs vary on many dimensions, such as content, duration, intensity, sponsorship, and overall purpose. There are many different program and instructional models. Program attributes are important because they determine the type of student for whom the experience is most appropriate. Summer programs that offer intensive accelerated courses are a better match for very able students with good study skills and an ability to learn independently (Bartkovich & Mezynski, 1981; Benbow & Stanley, 1983; Lynch, 1992; Olszewski-Kubilius, Kulieke, Willis, & Krasney, 1989). These programs typically use techniques such as telescoping or curriculum compacting to reduce the amount of time students spend on a course by as much as 50%. Programs that offer students an opportunity to study a single subject in great depth are more suited to students with intense, focused interests (VanTassel-Baska, 2006) and specific talent areas. Programs can give students the chance to sample several different courses (e.g., students take one class in the morning and one in the afternoon). Some Saturday programs are single-shot events that have career awareness as the primary focus or introduce students to a field of study, while other summer programs include this as a small component of their academic classes. Some programs offer typical elementary, high school, or college classes with the goal of accelerating students in the content area, while others offer enrichment types of classes that generally pose fewer articulation problems for local schools (Feldhusen & Sokol, 1982). Programs can consist of mentorships, internships, or shadowing of an adult professional on the job. Some summer programs even offer study abroad opportunities (Limburg-Weber, 1999/2000).

### Meeting Social and Emotional Needs

Summer and Saturday programs meet the intellectual needs of children and also their social/emotional needs (Olszewski-Kubilius & Lee, 2004a). For some children, the desire for an intellectual peer group may be the most important reason for pursuing summer or Saturday programs. However, summer programs that are residential and at least 2 weeks in duration, and Saturday programs that offer 8 to 10 weeks of contact, will best provide a social context for the development of sustained peer relationships and friendships.

### Study Abroad

Study abroad during the summer or the academic year is also an option for high-school-aged students. School year programs are organized as stay-at-home programs with attendance at a local school and special foreign language classes (Limburg-

Weber, 1999/2000; Olszewski-Kubilius & Limburg-Weber, 2003). Summer programs typically consist of travel combined with study of the host country's culture and language. The benefits of study abroad programs include increased facility with another language and broadened cultural perspectives (Olszewski-Kubilius & Limburg-Weber). These programs are most appropriate for students desiring to learn a foreign language and seeking a broader worldview.

Some programs attempt to serve gifted students with a wider range of above-average abilities; others focus on a more homogeneous group, for example, highly gifted students. These latter types of programs typically use off-level testing as a way of discerning high levels of talent within an area. Some programs target students typically underrepresented in gifted programs, such as minority or economically disadvantaged students or females (Brody & Fox, 1980; Fox, Brody, & Tobin, 1985; Haensly & Lehmann, 1998). Characteristics of special programs are important to educators who often must respond to the students' experience at the local school level, to parents who are seeking programs that will further their child's talent development, and to gifted students who desire suitable, supportive, and enjoyable learning environments.

### Research-Based Benefits of Out-of-School Programs

Organizers of special programs believe that gifted students benefit greatly from them. Research evidence exists regarding some of these purported benefits, and this body of research will be reviewed in the next section. The benefits include (Olszewski-Kubilius, 1989):

- perceptions of increased social support for learning and achievement due to homogeneous grouping with other gifted students and support from teachers and counselors;
- positive feelings due to being in a learning situation that presents a more appropriate match between the student's intellectual abilities and the challenge or rigor of a course;
- development of study skills as a result of immersion in an intellectually challenging course;

- development of independence and enhancement of general living skills in residential programs because of living away from home on one's own;
- increased knowledge about university programs and college life;
- raising of expectations and aspirations for educational achievement as evidenced by higher educational and career aspirations due to success in a challenging learning environment;
- reinforcement for risk taking as evidenced by seeking other academically challenging environments as a result of extending oneself both intellectually and socially;
- growth in acceptance of others, knowledge of different cultures, and an enhanced worldview as a result of living and socializing with a more diverse group of students; and
- self-testing of abilities due to placement in an intellectually challenging situation and subsequent reevaluations and goal setting that can further a student's progress in attaining excellence.

### Research on the Effects of Special Programs

Parents, educators, and researchers are interested in the effects of special programs on gifted students' self-concepts, self-esteem, and self-perceptions. Students and parents seek out these programs because they believe they will provide a better and more appropriate environment—socially, emotionally, and academically. In general, the research suggests that they are positive experiences for most students.

Previous research has shown that gifted children tend to have higher scores on global self-concept measures when compared to nongifted children (see Hoge & Renzulli, 1993, and Olszewski, Kulieke, & Willis, 1987, for reviews of this literature). Thus, while giftedness per se is not associated with reduced levels of self-esteem, the question is whether placement in a special program for gifted students results in changes in self-esteem or self-perceptions. As Olszewski et al. (1987) noted, a change in environment, which involves a change in friends, social climate, and/or academic rigor or challenge, can impact self-perceptions. Such changes result from a reevaluation of one's competence in a particular area based on a new reference group—in this case, one that consists of true intellectual peers. This is often referred to as the big-fish-little-pond effect (BFLPE), coined by researcher Herbert Marsh (Marsh & Hau, 2003). Marsh and colleagues conducted a large sample, cross-cultural study of the BFLPE and found that there was a ubiquitous negative effect of participation in academically selective schools on academic self-concept.

Delcourt, Loyd, Cornell, and Goldberg (1994) obtained similar results for some gifted program models—specifically, lower perceptions of academic competence among students in homogeneous gifted classes or schools compared to students in other program types. However, students in all program types studied reported that they felt comfortable with the number of friends they had in their own school and their popularity. Rogers and Span (1993), in reporting on the results of a meta-analysis of studies on ability grouping, concluded that ability grouping, whether for regular instruction or for enrichment, has little impact on gifted students' self-esteem. They found a slight decrease in self-esteem when full-time grouping starts, but in special programs for the gifted, no such decline was observed reliably. A small but positive increase in self-esteem was found for enrichment programs.

Studies specifically conducted on children enrolled in special summer or Saturday programs also show varied results. Kolloff and Moore (1989) measured the self-concepts of 5th–10th graders attending three different 2-week summer residential programs. Their results indicated that students' self-concepts were more positive at the end of the program than at the beginning, as measured by two separate instruments. Changes however, were small to moderate on average. The authors speculate that an enhanced self-concept is the result of a more appropriate academic setting and greater peer acceptance.

VanTassel-Baska and Kulieke (1987) found an increase in self-esteem for seventh through ninth graders enrolled in a summer program designed to foster scientific talent development. However, these findings were not replicated in a second summer when results showed no pre- to postprogram changes on an instrument that measured global self-worth. Olszewski et al. (1987) used an instrument that assessed various domains of self-concept with seventh- through ninth-grade students participating in two summer residential programs. Students were measured before the program, and on the first and last days of the programs. Results showed declines in academic self-concept over time, an initial decline then increase in social acceptance, and positive changes for physical and athletic competence over the course of the 3-week programs.

Cooley, Cornell, and Lee (1991) report that African American students who attended a predominantly White university summer enrichment program were accepted by other students and were comparable in self-concept and academic self-esteem as assessed by teachers. These authors concluded that even summer programs for gifted students that are predominantly White could provide a supportive environment for gifted Black students.

In summary, although the research results are mixed, it appears that negative effects of placement in special summer or weekend programs on self-esteem, self-concept, and self-perceptions, due to a higher level comparison group, do occur, but are generally slight to moderate in size and probably transitory.

### Effects of Fast-Paced Summer Programs

One instructional model that is used extensively in summer programs across the United States involves fast-paced courses. These programs emerged subsequent to the creation of the regional talent searches for seventh and eighth graders, which began more than 30 years ago. Fast-paced summer courses are typically open to students scoring at levels on the ACT or SAT comparable to college-bound seniors. They offer an array of honors-level high school courses that students seek to complete in a reduced time frame (150 hours of in-school instruction is reduced to 75 hours of instruction during the summer). The summer courses also encourage excellence, hard work, and a positive attitude toward academic accomplishment.

Research has shown that the SAT scores used as cutoffs for entrance into these types of programs are valid and help select students who will succeed academically (Olszewski–Kubilius, 1998; Olszewski–Kubilius et al., 1989). Research has also shown that student achievement is high. On average, students complete two courses in precalculus mathematics within 50 hours of instruction (Bartkovich & Mezynski, 1981) and perform higher on standardized tests than students who spend an entire year in similar mathematics classes (Stanley, 1976). Similar achievement levels have been found for fast-paced science classes (Lynch, 1992). Better performance in such classes, especially in mathematics, is associated with well-developed, independent study skills (Olszewski–Kubilius et al., 1989), which can compensate for somewhat lower initial SAT entry scores.

The evidence regarding how schools respond to fast-paced classes is equivocal. The percentage of students who get credit for fast-paced classes varies across studies, with reports of 80% for subsets of students who specifically ask for credit (Lynch, 1990) versus 50% for students who achieve proficiency in the subject as measured by performance on standardized tests (Olszewski–Kubilius, 1989). It is easier for summer students to get appropriate placement subsequently in their local schools than credit for summer coursework (Lynch, 1990; Olszewski–Kubilius, 1989). Additionally, credit rates vary by subject area and were higher for cumulatively organized subjects such as algebra or Latin, and lower for verbal classes such as writing or literature (Olszewski–Kubilius, 1989).

The awarding of credit by schools for summer courses is facilitated by accreditation of the summer program by an outside educational agency (Olszewski–Kubilius et al., 1996). Lee and Olszewski–Kubilius (2005) reported that after a summer program at a major Midwestern university had been accredited by the North Central Association of Colleges and Schools, and thus was able to award credit to middle and high school students who successfully completed high school courses, the percentage of summer students whose schools honored the credit increased significantly from 28% preaccreditation to 64% eight years postaccreditation.

Research has shown that fast-paced, accelerative summer programs can significantly influence many aspects of students' academic careers, occupational choices, and aspirations. Documented effects include taking AP calculus earlier in high school, taking more college courses while still in high school, pursuing a more rigorous course of study in mathematics, and entering more academically competitive colleges than equally talented students who do not participate in a summer program (Barnett & Durden, 1993). Females who participate in fast-paced classes seem to benefit particularly, especially those who take mathematics in the summer (Olszewski-Kubilius & Grant, 1996). These female students subsequently accelerated themselves more in mathematics, earned more honors in math, took more AP classes of any type in high school and more math classes in college, participated more in math clubs, more often majored in math or science in college, and had higher educational aspirations. A summer program designed specifically for mathematically talented females helped them to keep even with mathematically talented boys in terms of accelerating themselves in math through high school (Brody & Fox, 1980; Fox et al., 1985). Finally, additional effects of the summer program for girls include a greater commitment to consistent full-time work in the future and higher educational aspirations (Fox et al.). See Olszewski-Kubilius (1998) for a summary of research on fast-paced summer programs.

Why do summer programs impact students in these ways and gifted females particularly? It is likely that when students succeed in challenging accelerated coursework such as fast-paced summer classes, their confidence in their abilities is bolstered, enabling them to select other challenging educational opportunities.

Several outside-of-school programs reported in the literature focus on particular groups of gifted students considered in need of special services because they are underrepresented in school-based gifted programs. For example, Lynch and Mills (1990) provided Saturday and summer classes to sixth-grade, low-income, minority students. The classes provided instruction in mathematics and language arts. Results showed that students made greater gains on standardized tests in mathematics (although not in reading), compared to a group of similar students who did not receive special instruction. The authors reported that as a result of the gains students made, some qualified for their in-school gifted programs.

Confessore (1991) reported on a longitudinal follow-up of students who participated in a university-based summer arts program 10 years prior. The students were adolescents at the time of participation and took college-level classes in art, music, dance, theater, or creative writing. Results of surveys showed that, in general, students had remained active in the arts subsequent to the program, and 83% stated that the program helped them confirm their identity as artists. Participants also reported that contact with other artistically talented adolescents was a major benefit of the program. Like academically oriented programs, special out-of-school programs in the arts can have positive long-term effects for gifted students.

## Negative Effects of Out–of-School Programs

Although it is clear that there are many benefits of out-of-school programs for gifted students, there are some downsides, as well. The main problem with these experiences is that they cannot, nor should they, substitute for or replace a challenging in-school program or curricula. Gifted children need an education that is matched to their learning and social and emotional needs all of the time, not just for several weeks in the summer or on weekends. The danger in relying on out-of school programs as the only venue for appropriate educational opportunities for gifted students is the potential that students will not develop their talents fully nor acquire the motivation and study habits required to achieve excellence if they only have sporadic opportunities to do so. They will not have an articulated program that leads them to ever more complex, challenging courses in their talent areas. And, they will not have sustained access to peers who can stimulate their thinking and support their efforts.

Although it is ultimately beneficial for educators to be knowledgeable about out-of-school opportunities for gifted students so that they can help students obtain them, there is also the danger that schools will come to view this as their only or primary obligation to serve gifted students, which ultimately reinforces the belief held by some that gifted children will succeed without special efforts or attention to their needs by schools. Additionally, many out-of-school opportunities involve fees, which can greatly tax family resources and generate resentment among parents who wonder why their children's educational needs are not being met in public schools.

### How Educators Can Utilize Summer Programs

Educators who work with gifted students can assist them by being knowledgeable about the different types of summer programs so that they can help students find one that is matched to their learning needs and characteristics.

There are several good guides to summer programs available (see the resources listing at the end of this chapter). The following guidelines will help educators develop or find the right kind of program for a particular student.

- Assess the degree to which the program is accelerative in terms of content and pacing. A fast-paced class that compresses a full year of high school coursework into 3 weeks and 75 hours of instruction is appropriate for more highly gifted students, who are capable of working several years above grade level.
- Assess the degree to which the program offers students opportunities to explore topics in depth versus sample a variety of topics. Programs that allow students to focus on one subject or discipline will meet the needs of students with domain-specific talents and intense, well-developed interests.
- Assess the degree to which the program will provide opportunities for significant interactions with intellectual

peers. Residential programs of at least 2 weeks duration and commuter programs of at least 3 weeks duration will provide enough time for students to form friendships and significant new peer relationships.

- Assess the degree to which the program will enable a student to get credit for summer courses by providing written documentation of a student's progress and performance in the program and/or because the program is accredited. (This will be especially important for students who are seeking to substitute a summer course for a course in their regular school programs or desire credit or advanced placement subsequent to their summer courses.)

## The Future of Special Programs

It is likely that the demand for summer programs for gifted students will increase. Summer and Saturday programs have become vital to the talent development of academically gifted students, but the educational models they embody, including fast-paced instruction or problem-based learning, need to become an essential part of the local school curricula, as well.

Also, as the number of summer and extraschool programs for gifted students rises, the articulation between these programs and in-school programs and curricula will likely become more of an issue. The increases in the variety of different types of supplemental programs, the number of institutions that offer them, and the number of students who participate in them, have had some negative consequences for students. Rather than deal with the myriad of programs and make decisions about student credit and placement based on evaluations of their quality, schools sometimes opt for general blanket policies that do not allow credit for any "outside" courses or programs. However, with a growing number of states instituting legislation to support dual enrollment and the growing number of programs seeking accreditation, the precedent is set to accept credits from outside institutions, particularly institutions of higher education. Special summer and Saturday programs for gifted students have the potential to link schools and universities and other institutions in significant, important ways. The most important component, however, is educators' knowledge about out-of-school program opportunities and their openness to having students both participate in them and be rewarded for their documented achievements.

## References

Adams, C. M., & Cross, T. L. (1999/2000). Distance learning opportunities for academically gifted students. *Journal of Secondary Gifted Education, 11*, 88–96.

Alamprese, J. A., Erlanger, W. J., & Brigham, N. (1988). *No gift wasted: Effective strategies for educating highly able, disadvantaged students in math and science* (Vols. 1–2; USOE contract #300-87-0152). Washington, DC: Cosmos Corporation.

Archambault, F. X., Jr., Westberg, K. L., Brown, S. W., Hallmark, B. W., Emmons, C. L., & Zhang, W. (1993). *Regular classroom practices with gifted students: Results of a national survey of classroom teachers.* Storrs: The National Research Center on the Gifted and Talented, University of Connecticut.

Barnett, L. B., & Durden, W. G. (1993). Education patterns of academically talented youth. *Gifted Child Quarterly, 37*, 161–168.

Bartkovich, K. G., & Mezynski, K. (1981). Fast-paced precalculus mathematics for talented junior-high students: Two recent SMPY programs. *Gifted Child Quarterly, 25*, 73–80.

Benbow, C. P., & Stanley, J. C. (Eds.). (1983). *Academic precocity: Aspects of its development.* Baltimore: Johns Hopkins University Press.

Bloom, B. S. (Ed.). (1985). *Developing talent in young people.* New York: Ballantine.

Brody, L., & Fox, L. H. (1980). An accelerative intervention program for mathematically gifted girls. In L. H. Fox, L. Brody, & D. Tobin (Eds.), *Women and the mathematical mystique* (pp. 164–178). Mahwah, NJ: Lawrence Erlbaum.

Confessore, G. J. (1991). What became of the kids who participated in the 1981 Johnson Early College Summer Arts Program. *Journal for the Education of the Gifted, 15*, 64–82.

Cooley, M. R., Cornell, D. G., & Lee, C. C. (1991). Peer acceptance and self-concept of Black students in a summer gifted program. *Journal for the Education of the Gifted, 14*, 166–170.

Cox, J., Daniel, N., & Boston, B. O. (1985). *Educating able learners. Programs and promising practices.* Austin: University of Texas Press.

Delcourt, M. A. B., Loyd, B. H., Cornell, D. G., & Goldberg, M. D. (1994). *Evaluation of the effects of programming arrangements on student learning outcomes.* Storrs: The National Research Center on the Gifted and Talented, University of Connecticut.

Feldhusen, J., & Sokol, L. (1982). Extra-school programming to meet the needs of gifted youth: Super Saturday. *Gifted Child Quarterly, 26,* 51–56.

Ford, D. Y. (1996*). Reversing underachievement among gifted Black students.* New York: Teachers College Press.

Fox, L. H., Brody, L., & Tobin, D. (1985). The impact of early intervention programs upon course-taking and attitudes in high school. In S. F. Chipman, L. R. Brush, & D. M. Wilson (Eds.), *Women and mathematics: Balancing the equation* (pp. 249–274). Mahwah, NJ: Lawrence Erlbaum.

Haensly, P. A., & Lehmann, P. (1998). Nurturing giftedness while minority adolescents juggle change spheres. *Journal of Secondary Gifted Education, 9,* 163–178.

Hoge, R. D., & Renzulli, J. S. (1993). Exploring the link between giftedness and self-concept. *Review of Educational Research, 63,* 449–465.

Kolitch, E. R., & Brody, L. (1992). Mathematics acceleration of highly talented students: An evaluation. *Gifted Child Quarterly, 39,* 78–96.

Kolloff, P. B., & Moore, A. D. (1989). Effects of summer programs on the self-concepts of gifted children. *Journal for the Education of the Gifted, 12,* 268–276.

Lee, S. Y., & Olszewski-Kubilius, P. (2005). Investigation of high school credit and placement for summer coursework taken outside of local schools. *Gifted Child Quarterly, 49,* 37–50.

Limburg-Weber, L. (1999/2000). Send them packing: Study abroad as an option for gifted students. *Journal of Secondary Gifted Education, 11,* 43–51.

Lynch, S. J. (1990). Credit and placement issues for the academically talented following summer studies in science and mathematics. *Gifted Child Quarterly, 34,* 27–30.

Lynch, S. J. (1992). Fast-paced high school science for the academically talented: A six-year perspective. *Gifted Child Quarterly, 36,* 147–154.

Lynch, S. J., & Mills, C. J. (1990). The Skills Reinforcement Project (SRP): An academic program for high potential minority youth. *Journal for the Education of the Gifted, 13*, 364–379.

Marsh, H. W., & Hau, K. (2003). Big-fish-little-pond effect on academic self-concept: A cross-cultural (26 country) test of the negative effects of academically selective schools. *American Psychologist, 58*, 264–276.

Mills, C. J., Ablard, K. E., & Lynch, S. J. (1992). Academically talented students' preparation for advanced-level courses after an individually-paced precalculus class. *Journal for the Education of the Gifted, 16*, 3–17.

Olszewski, P., Kulieke, M. J., & Willis, G. B. (1987). Changes in the self-perceptions of gifted students who participate in rigorous academic programs. *Journal for the Education of the Gifted, 10*, 287–303.

Olszewski-Kubilius, P. (1989). Development of academic talent: The role of summer programs. In J. VanTassel-Baska & P. Olszewski-Kubilius (Eds.), *Patterns of influence on gifted learners: The home, the self and the school* (pp. 214–230). New York: Teachers College Press.

Olszewski-Kubilius, P. (1998). Research evidence regarding the validity and effects of talent search educational programs. *Journal of Secondary Gifted Education, 7*, 134–138.

Olszewski-Kubilius, P., & Grant, B. (1996). Academically talented females in mathematics: The role of special programs and support from others in acceleration, achievement, and aspiration. In K. D. Noble & R. F. Subotnik (Eds.), *Remarkable women: Perspectives on female talent development* (pp. 281–291). Cresskill, NJ: Hampton Press.

Olszewski-Kubilius, P., Grant, B., & Seibert, C. (1993). Social support systems and the disadvantaged gifted: A framework for developing programs and services. *Roeper Review, 17*(3), 20–25.

Olszewski-Kubilius, P., Kulieke, M. J., Willis, G. B., & Krasney, N. (1989). An analysis of the validity of SAT entrance scores for accelerated classes. *Journal for the Education of the Gifted, 13*, 37–54.

Olszewski-Kubilius, P., Laubscher, L., Wohl, V., & Grant, B. (1996). Issues and factors involved in credit and placement for accelerated summer coursework. *Journal of Secondary Gifted Education, 8*, 5–15.

Olszewski-Kubilius, P., & Lee, S. Y. (2004a). Parent perceptions of the effects of the Saturday Enrichment Program on gifted students' talent development. *Roeper Review, 26*, 156–165.

Olszewski-Kubilius, P., & Lee, S. Y. (2004b). The role of participation in in-school and outside-of-school activities in the talent development of gifted students. *Journal of Secondary Gifted Education, 15*, 107–123.

Olszewski-Kubilius, P., & Limburg-Weber, L. (2003). *Designs for excellence: A guide to educational program options for academically talented middle & secondary students.* Evanston, IL: The Center for Talent Development, Northwestern University.

Piirto, J. (1992). *Understanding those who create.* Dayton: Ohio Psychology Press.

Rimm, S. (1991). Underachievement and superachievement: Flip sides of the same psychological coin. In N. Colangelo & G. A. Davis (Eds.), *Handbook of gifted education* (3rd ed., pp. 424–434). Needham Heights, MA: Allyn & Bacon.

Rogers, K. B., & Span, P. (1993). Ability grouping with gifted and talented students: Research and guidelines. In K. A. Heller, F. J. Mönks, & A. H. Passow (Eds.), *International handbook of research and development of giftedness and talent* (pp. 585–593). Oxford, England: Pergamon.

Stanley, J. C. (1976). Special fast mathematics classes taught by college professors to fourth through twelfth graders. In D. P. Keating (Ed.), *Intellectual talent: Research and development* (pp. 132–159). Baltimore: Johns Hopkins University Press.

Thompson, M. (2001). *Developing verbal talent.* Retrieved June 23, 2006, from http://www.ctd.northwestern.edu/resources/talent-development/verbaltalent.html

VanTassel-Baska, J. (1995). The talent development process in Emily Bronte and Virginia Woolf. *Roeper Review, 18*(1), 14–18.

VanTassel-Baska, J. (2006). Curriculum design issues in developing a curriculum for the gifted. In J. VanTassel-Baska & T. Stambaugh (Eds.), *Comprehensive curriculum for gifted learners* (3rd ed., pp. 17–30). Needham Heights, MA: Allyn & Bacon.

VanTassel-Baska, J., & Kulieke, M. J. (1987). The role of community-based scientific resources in developing scientific talent: A case study. *Gifted Child Quarterly, 31*, 111–115.

VanTassel-Baska, J., Patton, J., & Prillaman, D. (1991). The nature and extent of programs for the disadvantaged gifted in the United States and territories. *Gifted Child Quarterly, 34*, 94–96.

## Resources for Summer Program Opportunities

*National Association for Gifted Children Summer Program Index*
http://www.nagc.org/index.aspx?id=1103
Articles on choosing and researching summer programs.

*Duke University's Guide to Educational Programs*
http://www.tip.duke.edu
A publication of Duke's Talent Identification Program to help
students find future educational programs.

*Summer Opportunities for Kids & Teenagers*
http://www.petersons.com/books/
summeropportunitieskidsteens.asp
Produced annually by Peterson and Thompson, this guide is a
basic directory to summer programs.

*Midwest Academic Talent Search's (MATS) Educational Program
Guide*
http://www.ctd.northwestern.edu/mats
This guide is produced annually and available to all MATS
participants for free.

*Imagine . . . Opportunities and Resources for Academically Talented
Youth*
http://cty.jhu.edu/imagine
Published by Johns Hopkins University Press and Center for
Talented Youth, this newsletter often publishes information
about educational opportunities for youth.

# The Value of Out-of-School Programs for Gifted Youth From Diverse Backgrounds

*Margie K. Kitano*

## Introduction

Given the relatively few hours students spend in formal schooling each day, the impact of out-of-school activities on academic and social behavior has generated increased interest. Out-of-school programs serve a range of populations with a variety of purposes, creating a broad literature base. Organized out-of-school activities are seen as having potential for improving life outcomes, particularly for students at risk for academic underachievement, dropping out, teen pregnancy, substance abuse, or delinquency (Kahne et al., 2001). Moreover, enrichment programs organized outside of school are perceived as vehicles for developing talent and extending academic pursuits. Given their range of income and socioeconomic status levels, gifted students from culturally and linguistically diverse backgrounds may be found in both types of programs. Research supports the positive effects of out-of-school activities on educational attainment, especially for students placed at risk by poverty (Olszewski-Kubilius & Lee, 2004b).

Out-of-school activities have been more widely studied among higher rather than lower socioeconomic status students (Jordan & Nettles, 2000). Little of the extant research has focused specifically on gifted students (Olszewski-Kubilius & Lee, 2004b), and even less has focused on gifted students from culturally and linguistically diverse or economically disadvantaged backgrounds. The need to promote participation and achievement of diverse students among top performers (Miller, 2004) supports consideration of out-of-school activities beneficial to diverse gifted students. Gifted students of color frequently find themselves a numerical minority in classrooms and programs, and their "fewness" itself may have implications for social and emotional development not faced by their majority peers. This chapter examines the value of out-of-school programs for gifted students from culturally and linguistically diverse backgrounds, with emphasis on dilemmas related to fewness: ethnic identity development and interaction with similar peers. Issues are discussed within the context of opportunities and options provided by the family, school, and community. A "synthesis" framework combining the models presented by Jordan and Nettles (2000) and Valentine, Cooper, Bettencourt, and DuBois (2002) organizes the discussion.

## The Framework

Valentine and colleagues (2002) identified six mutually exclusive categories of nonschool activities of high school students: homework, employment, school-sponsored extracurricular activities (e.g., athletics and clubs), structured (adult-supervised) out-of-school activities (e.g., church or scouting activities, music lessons), unstructured time alone and with family and peers (e.g., watching TV, using the Internet) and sleeping. Reviewing extant theory and research, they present a model describing the relationship between out-of-school activities and achievement. The major principles of their model can be summarized as follows: Out-of-school activities across these six categories vary with respect to (a) academic relatedness and (b) the extent to which they promote identification with school. These two variables directly or indirectly affect achievement as measured by school grades and standardized tests. Direct effects occur when the activity (e.g., homework) involves students in practicing academic skills or in applying academic content. Activities can indirectly influence achievement by working on self-beliefs—including self-esteem, self-efficacy, and coping strategies—and motivation, which has a reciprocal relationship with achievement. Based on the model and research reviewed, Valentine et al. hypothesize that activities consistent with academic needs that promote identification with school and occur in groups are likely to benefit achievement. The effect may occur directly or indirectly, by supporting students' positive self-beliefs.

The Valentine et al. (2002) model acknowledges but does not directly address the contributions of ethnicity, culture, or economic status. Jordan and Nettles (2000) analyzed data from the National Educational Longitudinal Study of 1988 within a previously developed model describing relationships between school contexts (urban/rural, racial composition, size) and individual characteristics (e.g., SES, gender, race, prior achievement, and self-concept) and student investment in out-of-school activities. Their framework suggests that school context and student background characteristics affect educational outcomes directly and indirectly with student investment in out-of-school activities as a mediator. Outcomes investigated were participation in extracurricular school activities, depth of leadership, preparedness for class, perception of life chances, and achievement in math and science at grade 12.

Analyses of student background characteristics and participation in out-of-school activities at grade 10 supported the model in predicting grade 12 outcomes. Students from higher socioeconomic status (SES) backgrounds reported greater participation in school clubs than their lower SES peers; females and students with higher reading test scores participated in extracurricular activities more at grade 12. Tenth-grade reading test scores correlated with depth of participation in group activities 2 years later. Student involvement in structured activities, time spent with adults, and involvement in religious activities in 10th grade appeared to contribute to outcomes in 12th grade. Time spent alone was positively related to most outcome variables, especially math and science achievement. Hanging out with peers was negatively related to most outcome variables. While the direction tended to be negative, hours spent working showed no significant relationship with outcomes.

A synthesis and elaboration of the two models (see Figure 3.1) offers greater explanatory power for considering issues related to diversity and out-of-school activities for the gifted and talented. This combined framework suggests that characteristics of the school, individual, family, and community influence choice of and investment in out-of-school activities. Across type of activities, the degree to which they support students' interests, talents, and desire for challenge also affects learning either directly or indirectly. The extent to which activities promote students' positive ethnic identity—and the degree to which that ethnic identity embraces school values—may influence self-beliefs, motivation, and achievement, as well as social/emotional adjustment, an end in itself. The next sections review research relevant to the combined model in describing relationships among components for gifted and talented students, especially those from diverse backgrounds.

### Challenge, Interests, and Talents

The elaborated model suggests that students' talents and interests contribute to their investment in and selection of out-of-school activities. Recent research supports this relationship. Milgram (2003) reported that pursuit of challenging activities in a talent domain (e.g., art, drama, dance, leadership) during the school years leads to adult creative accomplishments in that domain. Moreover, for both gifted and typical students, out-of-school activities predict adult vocational domain (Milgram). Many talented adolescents report that participation in talent activities provides opportunities for developing close friendships and for enhancing social skills in general (Patrick, Ryan, & Alfeld-Liro, 1999).

Olszewski-Kubilius and Lee's (2004b) survey of students attending a university-based summer enrichment program indicated that gifted adolescents are involved in a range of school- and community-based programs and engage them-

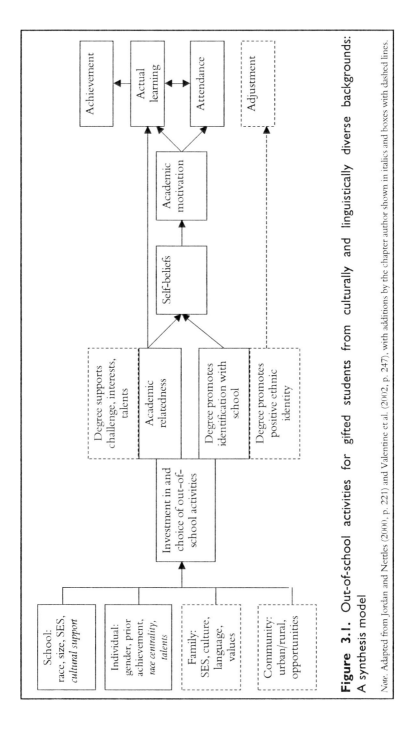

**Figure 3.1.** Out-of-school activities for gifted students from culturally and linguistically diverse backgrounds: A synthesis model

*Note.* Adapted from Jordan and Nettles (2000, p. 221) and Valentine et al. (2002, p. 247), with additions by the chapter author shown in italics and boxes with dashed lines.

selves in independent talent development activities at home. The researchers found consistency between students' interests, abilities, and motivation for challenge and their selection of summer courses and extracurricular activities. These studies involved primarily White, middle-class students.

Schweigardt, Worrell, and Hale (2001) examined course selection among academically talented students from a range of ethnic backgrounds attending a nonresidential, university-based summer enrichment program. They found that academically talented female students tended to cross traditional gender boundaries in terms of course selection, while males were more likely to enroll in traditionally male courses. Asian American students' enrollment in traditionally male and traditionally female subjects was more balanced than for non–Asian Americans. The authors noted that one implication of these findings may be that talent programs not affiliated with students' home schools may encourage exploration across traditionally gendered subjects, especially for females and Asian American students.

Bucknavage and Worrell (2005) recently surveyed academically talented middle and high school students, including students of color, on their participation in extracurricular activities. The students were attending a university-based summer program. The researchers found that minority students reported higher participation rates in ethnic and cultural clubs than did White students, with minority females having the highest rates. African American and Hispanic students reported lower rates than White and Asian American students in playing musical instruments, a finding possibly due to differences in economic status. These studies support the critical role of student interest in selection and commitment to out-of-school activities.

### Individual and School Characteristics

Recent analyses of achievement data suggest that African Americans, Latinos, and Native Americans are underrepresented among the highest levels of achievement across socioeconomic groups (College Board, 1999; Miller, 2004). Miller uses the term *fewness* to describe the relatively small numbers of students from these groups among top students at all levels of education. Fewness produces problems at both lower and upper/middle economic status levels, affecting participation in out-of-school enrichment activities.

Schools serving economically disadvantaged communities may have small numbers of high-achieving and identified gifted students and aim their curricula and limited fiscal resources at the larger number of students at risk for underachievement. These schools are unlikely to offer a variety of advanced courses or supplementary programs to meet the needs and interests of the few high achievers (Miller, 2004). Olszewski-Kubilius and Lee (2004b) noted that out-of-school programs can provide recognition to talented students not formally identified as gifted by the schools. Nevertheless, limited access to gifted services in the schools reduces access to out-of-school programs appropriate for gifted students, which necessarily serve even fewer students. While identified or unidentified gifted students may participate in out-of-school programs designed for at-risk students, such programs are not likely to challenge them. Furthermore, families with limited financial resources tend to provide fewer structured out-of-school opportunities for their children (Jordan & Nettles, 2000).

Saturday school provides one potential option for serving high-achieving students in economically disadvantaged communities. In California, for example, the state reimburses school districts for Saturday enrollment and attendance, supporting the cost of a half-day of school operation (Parmet, 2005). Some districts advertise the free service open to all students as a "bonus." While some schools target students who need extra academic assistance, others use the time for special projects, with teachers taking advantage of the opportunity to work with students in smaller groups. Saturday school also can benefit students whose parents are unable to assist with academic work.

Even when economically disadvantaged gifted students receive special support for attending out-of-school enrichment programs, fewness is a hypothesized deterrent to participation. Worrell, Szarko, and Gabelko (2001) examined factors related to the return rate of underrepresented African American and

Hispanic students participating in a summer program for academically talented youth. These students received financial support, transportation, mentoring/tutoring, and counseling. Their return rate was comparable to the return rate for students who did not receive special support services. However, the researchers viewed the return rate as low relative to supports provided. Retention was not significantly related to grade point average, achievement test scores, summer program grades, attendance, or SES. The authors hypothesized that other summer opportunities and potential social isolation may have reduced the return rate for underrepresented students, who comprised only 5% of summer program participants.

The number of high-achieving underrepresented students from middle- and upper-socioeconomic groups attending schools in more affluent neighborhoods may also be relatively small. While more of these schools may offer advanced courses and enrichment programs, fewness may make finding peer groups difficult for studying and socializing (Miller, 2004). Nevertheless, given the opportunity, underrepresented students do participate in enrichment activities designed to meet their needs for challenging experiences that address their specific interests and talents. Olszewski-Kubilius and Lee (2004b) reported that of 1,469 primarily higher socioeconomic status 4th- through 11th-grade students attending an enrichment and accelerative university-based summer program, 51.4% were White, 37.1% were Asian or Pacific Islander, 3.5% were African American, 2.1% were Hispanic, and 3.9% were multiracial. The authors did not indicate the extent to which these percentages are proportionate to students identified as gifted in the relevant population. Nevertheless, the figures suggest that at least some students of color will avail themselves of available enrichment opportunities, despite expectations of fewness.

### School and Community Contexts

In addition to the proportion of diverse gifted students comprising school enrollments, perceived support for diversity may contribute to student choices of out-of-school activities. Based on a survey of 125 African American 6th- through 10th-grade students in Chicago, Kahne et al. (2001) found that students, especially African American male students, rated afterschool programs as providing significantly more attractive affective contexts than those offered during the school day. Students were enrolled in programs focused on entrepreneurship and personal responsibility, arts, or community service. Youth participating in community-based afterschool programs perceived these programs as preferable to the school day in terms of affective context, support for youth development, and opportunities to be engaged as resources to others. The authors suggest that some African American students may experience community contexts as safer, more respectful, and more motivating than the formal school environment.

Being gifted does not ensure a supportive school environment for students of color. Harmon's (2002) qualitative study of the experiences of six gifted, inner city, elementary-age African American students participating in a desegregation program presents a case in point. Bussing to a school serving middle- to upper-SES students resulted in daily name-calling and harassment from White students, with little intervention from adults responsible for their safety. Taunting also occurred on the school grounds, with the result that the study participants chose friends among the minority students at the new school. For both gifted and typical students, school climate with respect to diversity may contribute to students' choices regarding school-based versus community-based out-of-school activities.

### Family Interests and Community Opportunities

Family values also contribute to the type and venue for out-of-school activities chosen. Recent research (Dunn, Kinney, & Hofferth, 2003) with Midwestern middle-class parents indicates that they perceive out-of-school activities as tools for transmitting values to their preadolescent children, as well as providing opportunities for social interaction and discovering their talents. Similarly, youth of color may seek or be guided by their family to out-of-school experiences that support the development of ethnic identity and provide opportunities for socialization with peers from similar backgrounds. Such opportunities may be particularly important for high-achieving youth of color facing fewness in schools or those attending schools that encourage assimilation, do not support students' ethnic identity development, or disparage students' home cultures or languages.

Even where schools are neutral or supportive of students' diverse cultural backgrounds, families may encourage their high-achieving children's participation in community-based activities designed to preserve culture of origin by passing it on to newer generations of children and youth. Lu's (2001) interview study of 35 parents of children and youth ages 4 to 13 attending a Chinese language school in Chicago revealed the families' desire for cultural preservation and bicultural identity development. The majority of parents and children attending the school were born in the United States. Through Sunday and summer classes, the school offered reading, writing, and speaking in Chinese; Chinese culture; martial arts; dance; mathematics; English; art; and computer skills. Special classes were held for adopted Chinese children. Interviewees described positive effects of their children's increased pride in being Chinese and becoming bilingual/bicultural. Lu concluded that the emergence of Chinese schools across the country challenges assumptions about middle-class Asian Americans' desire to assimilate and suggests that biculturalism may serve as a better predictor of positive adjustment for immigrant families.

Ethnic communities frequently sponsor organizations and activities that provide opportunities for youth, including the gifted, to learn and pass on the home culture and language. In a retrospective study of high-achieving Latinas (Kitano, 1998), 4 of 15 women interviewed volunteered that they had participated in "queen" competitions (e.g., Miss Fiesta), which proved invaluable in attaining social and leadership skills. Informal family gatherings and oral storytelling also provide additional opportunities to pass on family history and culture to younger generations. Research on Native American youth indicates that their participation in cultural activities, strong feelings of

belonging to the Native community and family, and appreciation of elders, parents, and extended family support school success (Strand & Peacock, 2002). Native American professional
organizations sponsor school-related and out-of-school programs for students talented in science and engineering that offer
culturally supportive opportunities to pursue their interests
(e.g., see American Indian Science and Engineering Society,
2006).

Perry (2003) calls on schools, community organizations,
churches, and families to organize group activities for African
American youth that share African American history and its traditionally strong achievement motivation, support intellectual
pursuits (e.g., literary or prelaw societies; study groups), and
encourage the valuing of biculturalism and African American/
standard English bilingualism. Perry traces the strong achievement orientation of African Americans over time and their
successful strategy of developing "counterhegemonic" communities to build a collective Black identity as literate and achieving.
She attributes the lack of success of U.S. schools in promoting African American achievement to the fact that they are not
intentionally designed to foster an African American identity of
achievement (e.g., sharing history and literature illustrating the
African American philosophy of achievement), to buffer students against racism, to develop hope and optimism, or to pass
on coping strategies needed to respond successfully to racism
in a modern society that views itself as open and integrated.
Out-of-school activities sponsored by the community could
support students' understanding of African Americans' historically strong valuation of education and achievement, development of positive racial identity, and the use of effective coping
strategies.

The nature of the community in respect to urban or rural
location and size of ethnic populations affects availability and
range of opportunities for pursuing interests related to family culture and language, as well as students' talent areas and
interests. While gifted students in rural areas may experience more individualized treatment (Burney & Cross, 2006),
fewness could be problematic for those from culturally and

linguistically diverse backgrounds. Moreover, appropriate out-of-school activities may require extended travel time and financial resources (Burney & Cross). Online courses and programs can increase access for rural gifted students (Belcastro, 2002; Olszewski-Kubilius & Lee, 2004a), provided that schools, families, or community centers offer computer facilities, fee assistance as needed, and knowledgeable guidance. Networked classrooms, e-mail, and chat rooms related to online programs also have potential for mitigating issues related to fewness in rural communities.

### Identity Development

Fewness of African American, Latino, and Native American students among the highest achieving students across economic groups may present challenges to gifted adolescents of color who are struggling to establish ego identities that will ground them for further development. The literature raises two issues in this regard: whether strong ethnic identity development supports achievement and whether development of a positive identity requires interactions with similar peers (i.e., gifted students from the same ethnic background). These issues constitute important considerations in designing the purposes and content of out-of-school activities inclusive of gifted students from diverse backgrounds.

Erikson (1968) described the major psychosocial task of adolescence as defining a strong identity. This task may be more complex for those with multiple identities differing from the "norm" based on ability/disability, ethnicity, religion, language, or sexual orientation. According to Erikson, adolescents must integrate and synthesize their experiences and qualities of the self to develop ego identity. Quintana (1998) described children's growing understanding of race and ethnicity based on cognitive developmental theory and interviews with some 500 Latino, African American, Korean, Mexican, Brazilian, Guatemalan, and Colombian children across the United States and Latin America.[1] Consistent with Erikson's task of identity development, Quintana suggests that adolescents move from a passive, objectively defined ethnic status (e.g., ethnicity as defined by heritage), to a more actively expressed ethnic identity. Additionally, adolescents develop ethnic group consciousness, using "we" and "us" more often than do younger children. Also, relative to younger children, they may increase their use of stereotypes to describe majority group members. Given adolescents' growing ethnic group consciousness, Quintana suggests that programs attempting to de-emphasize ethnic differences and build on similarities may be ignoring adolescents' needs to express their developing identities in constructive ways. As ethnic differences become salient, youth need support to become biculturally competent so they can participate effectively across contexts.

Rumbaut's (2000) study of children of immigrants corroborates the critical nature of ethnic identity development in school achievement, particularly for Latino and Asian students from immigrant families. His Children of Immigrants Longitudinal Study (CILS) followed the progress of a large sample of youth representing 77 nationalities in San Diego and Miami/Fort Lauderdale. Some 2,063 youths ages 14–15 were interviewed in 1992 (T1) and again in the 1995–1996 school year (T2) during their final year of high school. In-depth interviews of a stratified sample of parents supplemented the survey data. The San Diego sample included a range of socioeconomic status levels and families from Mexican, Filipino, Vietnamese, Laotian, and Cambodian backgrounds, with smaller numbers from Chinese, Japanese, Korean, and Indian backgrounds and from Central and South America and the Caribbean. Among Rumbaut's findings was that identification with U.S. racial-ethnic minorities (e.g., Chicano, Black) in junior high school correlated with lower GPAs, higher dropout and suspension rates, and lower aspirations in high school. However, this effect was not found for other types of ethnic self-identities such as

---

1   Quintana describes the development of children's ethnic and racial cognition across racial groups based on theories of social cognitive development and perspective taking and is thus distinguished from group-specific models of ethnic identity development, such as Cross' (1991) on Black identity.

American, mixed, or national origin. Rumbaut interprets these data as supporting the theory that some adolescents adopt oppositional identities that consider achieving in school as acting White. According to regression analyses, choosing as close friends peers who had dropped out of school or had no college plans negatively predicted GPA, whereas best outcomes were associated with having college-bound friends. Rumbaut's findings indicate that developing a positive ethnic identity, inclusive of academic values, and having achieving friends may contribute to positive educational outcomes of students from immigrant families.[2]

Consistent with Lu's (2001) hypothesis about the value of bilingualism, Rumbaut (2000) reported that English learners who achieved English fluency by T1 demonstrated higher achievement and lower dropout and suspension rates than students who spoke English only, corroborating other studies showing a positive relationship between fluent bilingualism and school achievement. Having limited English proficiency at T1 was associated with lower achievement, higher dropout rates, and lower aspirations at T2. Consistent with Valentine et al.'s (2002) predicted relationship between academic relatedness of out-of-school activities and achievement, Rumbaut found that the number of daily homework hours proved the strongest single predictor of GPAs, while the number of hours spent watching TV daily was significantly associated with lower GPAs. Academic outcomes at T2 also correlated with gifted identification and achievement test scores at T1.

Research on resilience and school success of American Indian and Alaska Native students, including the National Longitudinal Study of Adolescent Health, supports the benefits of biculturalism for Native people (Strand & Peacock, 2002). Native youth report that comfort with interacting in both Native community and mainstream schools enhances school success. Further, bicultural adults appear better adjusted (e.g., report less depression) than those classified as assimilating, tra-

---

2   Other research identifies additional factors contributing to positive academic outcomes. For example, Carbonaro and Gamoran (2002) reported that students who receive intellectually challenging content have higher levels of achievement.

ditional, or marginal with respect to cultural identity. Other studies show links between spirituality and wellness.

Research on African American students describes the nature of racial identity development among gifted African American youth as critical and complex. Ford and Harris (1997) note that Black students experience more barriers to racial identity development than do White students and that gifted Black students may experience more psychological and emotional problems than Black students not identified as gifted. In a study of 152 gifted and average Black students in grades 6–9, Ford and Harris found that these students in general tended to evidence strong, positive racial identities. Female and achieving students evidenced more positive and multicultural racial identities than did male and underachieving students. Students identified as gifted held more positive racial identities than students not identified as gifted. An investigation of the role of ethnic identity among White and Black at-risk and not-at-risk adolescents (Yasui, Dorham, & Dishion, 2004) found similar levels of ethnic identity across ethnic groups, higher levels among successful adolescents, and significant correlations between ethnic identity and emotional adjustment, social adaptability, and grade point average. Belonging and positive feelings toward one's ethnic group predicted adjustment for both White and Black youth. However, pride in ethnic group membership was significantly related to adjustment for African American youth, but not for their White counterparts, perhaps because African American youth develop their identity within a context of racial stereotyping and discrimination. The results of these studies lend some support to the relationship between an ethnic identity encompassing school values and academic achievement.

In the book *Why Are All the Black Kids Sitting Together in the Cafeteria?*, Tatum (1997) eloquently explained why, despite the seemingly easy integration of children across races in childhood, adolescents cluster around racial lines during free time. She argues the need for youth to interact with others who are engaged in sorting out similar experiences such as stereotyping and racism encountered in school and the community. Sharing confirms the reality of racism, supports effective responses, and provides affirmation. Additionally, normal issues of adolescence such as sleepovers, dating, and beauty become particularly salient for gifted African American girls who are in environments characterized by fewness. Tatum asserts that race is central for youth of color because "that is how the rest of the world thinks of them" (p. 53). She describes her own and others' research suggesting that while White students begin to think about ethnic identity during middle school, Black students, especially females, engage more actively in the search for identity by that time.

Haensly and Lehmann (1998) reported from a qualitative study of bright culturally diverse youth that themes of adolescent development include giftedness and cultural identity. Their sample consisted of Hispanic and Black eighth-grade students attending a university-sponsored environmental science summer program designed to nurture mathematics and science talent. The program was designed to enable youth to experience mathematics and science enrichment activities with students of their own, as well as other, ethnic groups. Analyses of inventories, career plots, journal entries, interviews, and evaluations by staff identified themes or "change spheres" of adolescent development: biological maturation, learning process, social needs, giftedness, and cultural identity. While out-of-school programs targeting gifted youth from diverse backgrounds can address these multiple spheres of development, antiaffirmative action legislation challenges the offering of such programs.

Not all students from diverse backgrounds desire relationships with ethnically similar peers. Other literature cautions against generalizations connecting racial identity and achievement because of differences between individuals within ethnic groups and differences across the social contexts in which individuals operate. Rowley and Moore (2002) conclude from their review of research on the racial identity of African American students that relationships among racial identity, the salience or centrality of race, and achievement are highly complex and not unidirectional. The literature examined suggests that race is not important to all African Americans, that some have high self-concepts without focusing on race, that the centrality of race

depends on the individual's assessment, and that racial identity cannot be understood without examining social context.
Additionally, the authors note that more research is needed
to evaluate the assumption that African American students
want contact with other African Americans and that absence
of same-race friendships could impede identity development.
One reviewed study found that children in more integrated
schools are more aware of racial differences and more likely to
have diverse friendships than children in either predominantly
White or predominantly Black schools.

While some research support exists for the relationship
between positive racial identity and achievement, individual and
contextual variables may moderate this relationship. Individual
differences exist to the extent to which adolescents of color perceive race as central to their identity. There is increasing evidence that multicultural attitudes, as opposed to emphasis on
assimilation or separatism, may support achievement. Out-of-
school programs for gifted students from diverse backgrounds
could enhance students' development of positive biculturalism,
including valuing achievement. Activities supportive of bicultural ethnic identity may be an important link to educational
attainment for some gifted students of color, especially where
schools ignore ethnic issues.

## Case Example

The following case example helps illustrate the synthesized
framework and contributions of school, individual, family, and
community to out-of-school activities selected by culturally
diverse students. The degree to which chosen activities offer
challenge and talent development, are academically related, and
promote a positive ethnic identity inclusive of achievement
influences academic outcomes and social/emotional development.

A middle-class African American colleague's recently
shared story about her gifted son's high school education experience concretely illustrates these relationships. When her hus-
band's promotion necessitated a move from the Northeast to

the South, she planned carefully with her gifted teenage son's education in mind. The family identified the neighborhood where they would live, based on the quality of public schools. However, once relocated, they discovered that the neighborhood high school was named after a Confederate general and that the cheering squad carried Confederate flags [school climate issue]. Although the school district offered the family access to a different high school, the parents decided to place their son in a private school [family SES]. As it turned out, he was the only Black student in his class [fewness]. His teachers described him as achieving and quiet, although he was outgoing at home and among Black peers. The private school did not offer gifted programs per se, although he took advantage of before- and afterschool activities offered by the school to support test taking for college entrance exams [academic relatedness]. The parents encouraged their son's participation in community-based programs for talent development in the form of music lessons and church choir [interests and talents]. Moreover, given the problem of fewness, his parents encouraged him to participate in the nearest chapter of Jack and Jill of America, Inc., to ensure social opportunities with middle-class African American peers [family interests]. This national organization provides leadership opportunities for youth, as well as educational, cultural, civic, and social programs [community opportunities]. Both parents had grown up in Black communities and believed that their son's social and emotional adjustment would benefit from opportunities to socialize with Black peers [ethnic identification supporting adjustment]. The son did well academically in school and was reported to be well adjusted, both socially and emotionally.

## Conclusions

Several conclusions regarding out-of-school programs serving gifted students from culturally diverse backgrounds can be derived from the framework and literature reviewed. These suggestions may be applied to in-school programs, as well. However, activities outside of school tend to have more flexibility, particularly in addressing low-incidence primary language and social/emotional development.

- A range of options is required to accommodate differences in economic status, talents and interests, centrality of race, and family values among diverse gifted students. Differences across and within cultural groups in talents, resources, interests, and desire to affiliate with members of the same group does not permit one program to meet all students' needs.

- Both school and community venues should establish a climate welcoming of diversity, whether or not they have as a goal the enhancement of ethnic identity. The finding that some African American youth, for example, view the school as less safe or less respectful than community program environments is not acceptable.

- School (e.g., Saturday school) and community activities are needed to support the development of friendships and networks with high-achieving peers. Having achievement-oriented friends contributes to positive outcomes and is of particular importance where "fewness" is an issue.

- Participation of gifted youth from diverse backgrounds in culture-specific out-of-school activities (e.g., Chinese school; Jack and Jill of America, Inc.) should be interpreted as a community strength. These types of activities can support bilingualism and biculturalism, which in turn are linked to achievement and adjustment.

- Out-of-school activities not related to academics or school identification can have positive effects, such as providing students with role models or safe environments (Valentine et al., 2002). To this should be added knowledge of one's cultural history, language, and values, as well as pursuit of talent areas unrelated to the school curricula. While not directly related to academic achievement, learning in these areas may support adjustment and occupational direction.

- Additional research is needed to survey culturally and linguistically diverse gifted students regarding their experiences with school- and community-based out-of-school activities, race centrality, and peer group preferences.

# References

American Indian Science and Engineering Society. (2006). *Homepage.* Retrieved May 19, 2006, from http://www.aises.org

Belcastro, F. P. (2002). Electronic technology and its use with rural gifted students. *Roeper Review, 25,* 14–16.

Bucknavage, L. B., & Worrell, F. C. (2005). A study of academically talented students' participation in extracurricular activities. *Journal of Secondary Gifted Education, 16,* 74–86.

Burney, V. H., & Cross, T. L. (2006). Impoverished students with academic promise in rural settings: 10 lessons from Project Aspire. *Gifted Child Today, 29*(2), 14–21.

Carbonaro, W. J., & Gamoran, A. (2002). The production of achievement inequality in high school English. *American Educational Research Journal, 39,* 801–827.

College Board. (1999). *Reaching the top: A report of the National Task Force on Minority High Achievement.* New York: College Board Publications.

Cross, W. E. (1991). *Shades of black: Diversity in African American identity.* Philadelphia: Temple University Press.

Dunn, J. S., Kinney, D. A., & Hofferth, S. L. (2003). Parental ideologies and children's after-school activities. *The American Behavioral Scientist, 46,* 1359–1386.

Erikson, E. (1968). *Identity: Youth and crisis.* New York: Norton.

Ford, D. Y., & Harris, J. J., III. (1997). A study of racial identity and achievement of Black males and females. *Roeper Review, 20,* 105–110.

Haensly, P. A., & Lehmann, P. (1998). Nurturing giftedness while minority adolescents juggle change spheres. *Journal of Secondary Gifted Education, 9,* 163–178.

Harmon, D. (2002). They won't teach me: The voices of gifted African American inner-city students. *Roeper Review, 24,* 68–75.

Jordan, W. J., & Nettles, S. M. (2000). How students invest their time outside of school: Effects on school-related outcomes. *Social Psychology of Education, 3,* 217–243.

Kahne, J., Nagaoka, J., Brown, A., O'Brien, J., Quinn, T., & Thiede, K. (2001). Assessing after-school programs as contexts for youth development. *Youth & Society, 32,* 421–446.

Kitano, M. K. (1998). Gifted Latina women. *Journal for the Education of the Gifted, 21,* 131–159.

Lu, X. (2001). Bicultural identity development and Chinese community formation: An ethnographic study of Chinese schools in Chicago. *The Howard Journal of Communications, 12*, 203–220.

Milgram, R. M. (2003). Challenging out-of-school activities as a predictor of creative accomplishments in art, drama, dance and social leadership. *Scandinavian Journal of Educational Research, 47*, 305–315.

Miller, L S. (2004). *Promoting sustained growth in the representation of African Americans, Latinos, and Native Americans among top students in the United States at all levels of the education system* (Research Monograph #RM04190). Storrs: The National Research Center on the Gifted and Talented, University of Connecticut.

Olszewski-Kubilius, P., & Lee, S. (2004a). Gifted adolescents' talent development through distance learning. *Journal for the Education of the Gifted, 28*, 7–35.

Olszewski-Kubilius, P., & Lee, S. (2004b). The role of participation in in-school and outside-of school activities in the talent development of gifted students. *Journal of Secondary Gifted Education, 15*, 107–123.

Parmet, S. (2005, April 3). San Dieguito Saturday school gets an A-plus. *San Diego Union-Tribune*, B1–B2.

Patrick, H., Ryan, A. M., & Alfeld-Liro, C. (1999). Adolescents' commitment to development talent: The role of peers in continuing motivation for sports and the arts. *Journal of Youth and Adolescence, 28*, 741–763.

Perry, T. (2003). Up from the parched earth: Toward a theory of African-American achievement. In T. Perry, C. Steele, & A. Hilliard III (Eds.), *Young, gifted, and Black: Promoting high achievement among African-American students* (pp. 1–108). Boston: Beacon Press.

Quintana, S. M. (1998). Children's developmental understanding of ethnicity and race. *Applied & Preventive Psychology, 7*, 27–45.

Rowley, S. J., & Moore, J. A. (2002). Racial identity in context for the gifted African American student. *Roeper Review, 24*, 63–67.

Rumbaut, R. G. (2000). Profiles in resilience: Educational achievement and ambition among children of immigrants in Southern California. In R. D. Taylor & M. C. Wang (Eds.), *Resilience across contexts: Family, work, culture, and community* (pp. 257–294). Mahwah, NJ: Lawrence Erlbaum.

Schweigardt, W. J., Worrell, F. C., & Hale, R. J. (2001). Gender differences in the motivation for and selection of courses in a summer program for academically talented students. *Gifted Child Quarterly, 45*, 283–293.

Strand, J. A., & Peacock, T. D. (2002). *Nurturing resilience and school success in American Indian and Alaska Native students.* Charleston, WV: ERIC Clearinghouse on Rural Education and Small Schools. (ERIC Document Reproduction Service No. ED471488)

Tatum, B. D. (1997). *Why are all the Black kids sitting together in the cafeteria?* New York: Basic Books.

Valentine, J. C., Cooper, H., Bettencourt, B. A., & DuBois, D. L. (2002). Out-of-school activities and academic achievement: The mediating role of self-beliefs. *Educational Psychologist, 37*, 245–256.

Worrell, F. C., Szarko, J. E., & Gabelko, N. H. (2001). Multi-year persistence of nontraditional students in an academic talent development program. *Journal of Secondary Gifted Education, 12*, 80–89.

Yasui, M., Dorham, C. L., & Dishion, T. J. (2004). Identity and psychological adjustment: A validity analysis for European American and African American adolescents. *Journal of Adolescent Research, 19*, 807–825.

# Increasing the Retention of Gifted Students From Low-Income Backgrounds in University Programs for the Gifted: The UYP Project

*Susan K. Johnsen, Sarah Feuerbacher, & Mary M. Witte*

## Background

The goals of talent development are to help students (a) understand their own talent strengths, (b) know how to pursue and engage in the best talent development activities available, and (c) commit to the development of their talents by identifying personal and career goals (Feldhusen, 1995). Although outstanding talents are present in students from all ethnic, cultural, and socioeconomic groups, these groups are frequently underrepresented in gifted programs (Bernal, 2002; Borland & Wright, 1994; Ford, 1996; Grantham, 2003; Worrell, Szarko, & Gabelko, 2001). Largely as a result of the federal grants from the Jacob K. Javits Gifted and Talented Students Act of 1988, enrichment programs have emerged during the last 20 years with the purpose of developing the talents of these special groups and increasing the number of students from low-income and/or minority backgrounds who participate. For example, the Talent Beyond Words program (Kay & Subotnik, 1994) was designed to serve minority children and those from low-income backgrounds with potential talent in the performing arts within and outside of the school setting.

Some of the most well-known and established summer academic enrichment programs are sponsored through the national talent searches. Talent searches offer a variety of educational opportunities such as accelerated academic summer classes, commuter classes, distance learning programs, and enrichment-based residential programs. These programs have extensive longitudinal data comparing the academic achievement of students who were selected to attend the program with same-ability individuals who did not attend the programs (Benbow, Perkins, & Stanley, 1983; Center for Talented Youth, 2002; Swiatek & Benbow, 1991). Results of short-term, annual evaluations gathered from student self-reports and interviews indicate that the talent search programs assist in increasing the students' knowledge and enthusiasm for the areas studied, as well as an overall feeling of personal gain (Bourstein, Holahan, & Sawyer, 1988; Enersen, 1993; Olszewski-Kubilius, 1989). Participants reported that summer program experiences gave them a better picture of their own academic abilities and potential, helped them develop better work and study habits, and refined their educational goals (Bourstein et al.; Center for Talented Youth; Duke University, 2002; Enersen; Olszewski-Kubilius & Laubscher, 1996; University of Denver, 2003). Additional studies have shown the social benefits to participants, with gifted students having more opportunities to interact with others who have similar abilities and interests (Enersen; Olszewski-Kubilius). Although these studies show many positive effects for gifted students who are in talent search programs, none has examined the specific effects on gifted students from economically disadvantaged backgrounds when compared with others who did not participate in the program.

Worrell et al. (2001) did examine the effects of an enrichment program on gifted students from low-income backgrounds. They conducted a 9-year longitudinal study examining factors that affected the retention of 316 economically disadvantaged gifted middle and high school scholarship students. They found that grade point average, achievement test scores, final grade in the first summer of attendance, and socioeconomic status were not significant predictors of returnee status. They also reported that 44% of the students returned for a second year, which was actually comparable to the dropout rate of noneconomically disadvantaged students attending the same program. They recommended that more follow-up studies be conducted to identify possible psychosocial variables that influence retention such as the students' use of support systems within and outside the family. They added, "Researchers should conduct follow-up studies on students who return and those who do not return to hear their stories (p. 87)."

In summary, given the long-term positive effects of students who participate in summer academic enrichment programs, retaining gifted students from lower income backgrounds in these types of programs would be particularly important because of their families' limited material resources and ability to provide activities that might enhance their children's talents. Given the limited research regarding retention of this special group, we decided to evaluate the University for Young People Project (UYPP) and examine specifically the psychosocial variables that might influence these at-risk students' continued participation.

## University for Young People Project

The University for Young People (UYP) is a program at Baylor University in Waco, TX, that provides enrichment activities for gifted and talented students and is designed to develop the interests and talents of participating students. The majority of students pay tuition for experiences such as summer courses, Super Saturdays, and special conferences. Within the UYP, a special project was created to fund scholarships for gifted students from low-income backgrounds. Along with their paying peers, these UYP Project students have opportunities to attend all of the activities throughout the year.

### Project Goals

The major long-term goal of the UYP Project is to increase and retain the number of at-risk fourth-grade to high school students who participate in enrichment programs so that they have a better opportunity of attending a higher education institution. To achieve this goal, the project addresses four short-term goals:

1. to identify gifted and talented children who come from low-income backgrounds;
2. to identify children's interests and possible career goals through teachers', parents', children's, and mentors' checklists, interviews, and/or observations;
3. to integrate the children into summer enrichment classes that match these interests; and
4. to provide follow up activities for the students and their parents.

If these goals are met, it is hoped that more students will be retained in the program and attend higher education institutions in the future.

## Context

The Center for Community Learning and Enrichment (CCLE) at Baylor University directs the UYP program along with a variety of other enrichment options throughout the year for gifted and talented students. Courses are designed for students entering grades 1–12 and are taught by university faculty or teachers trained in gifted education. The younger children's program, for grades 1–4, is located at a local elementary school, while the older students' program, for grades 4–12, is located on Baylor University's campus. Although some scholarships have been available for students who want to attend the UYP classes, the majority pays tuition for each 2-week course, ranging from $75–$95 depending on laboratory fees. To be eligible for the program, students must have been identified by their local school district as gifted and talented and must submit a formal application that includes test scores, parent and teacher nominations, and performances or products. Because this is a commuter program, students primarily come from the Central Texas area.

All of the grant students are from the Waco Independent School District (WISD), an urban school district in central Texas. The district is comprised of 40% Hispanic, 38% African American, 20% White, and less than 2% Asian. The district is located in a designated Enterprise Community, which is based on the average and total income level within a particular zip code. The neighborhoods that comprise an enterprise community have few or no resources for family support, outreach, or afterschool recreation activities and contend with high poverty rates, low levels of adult education, low academic achievement rates, high dropout rates, high substance abuse rates, and youth violence. These areas are distressed economically, socially, and physically and are often disconnected from opportunities that nourish the social and academic development of children and youth, especially young at-risk adolescents. These challenges have the potential to produce a devastating effect on student retention and academic performance (McLennan County Youth Collaboration—Communities In Schools, 2001).

### Participant Criteria

Because of funding, participating project students need to meet these criteria: (a) come from low-income families as described by the U.S. Office of Housing and Urban Development; (b) be entering 4th–12th grade in the fall semester; (c) show interest in attending the enrichment program courses offered through the University for Young People; and (d) perform at least one standard deviation above the norm on tests of achievement and/or ability (84th percentile) or be identified as gifted and talented by the Waco Independent School District (WISD). The WISD uses the following assessments in its identification process: Scales for Identifying Gifted Students (SIGS; teacher and parent scales; Ryser & McConnell, 2004), Screening Assessment for Gifted Elementary Students (2nd ed.; SAGES-2; reasoning and achievement subtests; Johnsen & Corn, 2001), and classroom products and/or performances. Using a case study approach, students who perform within the top 10% on any of the quantitative instruments and/or show potential on the qualitative assessments are admitted into the gifted program.

## Program Components

To meet the long-term and short-term goals, the UYP Project includes five components: parent involvement, teacher involvement, mentor involvement, peer involvement, and academic enrichment. Specific activities are designed to address each component.

### Parent Involvement

At the beginning and end of each summer session, parents attend planned meetings to learn about the summer program, follow-up activities, the importance of rigorous courses, and resources such as college scholarship opportunities and university visits, and receive suggestions for working with school districts, guiding their students at home, and setting high expectations. Parents are invited to observe and participate in all of the enrichment activities with special activities planned for parents in conjunction with UYP Project activities. A monthly follow-up newsletter is sent to parents beyond the life of the summer enrichment programs that provides information about other enrichment options such as Super Saturdays, at-home activities, and career or higher education opportunities.

### Teacher Involvement

The director of the project meets with teachers of gifted and talented students in the Waco ISD to make them aware of the identification process and project activities. Some of these teachers of gifted and talented students also facilitate the enrichment classes and attend professional development activities through the CCLE. District teachers receive the monthly newsletter with follow-up activities that they may use with their students to enhance in-depth studies and career goal-setting. In some cases, teachers and schools are contacted to provide support to families of students who are experiencing significant economic and social challenges.

## Mentor Involvement

Mentors are primarily undergraduate and graduate students who have previous experience with children and youth and exhibit positive personal qualities and strong communication skills. All mentors are required to attend a professional development program to learn about topics such as characteristics of gifted students, talent development, cultural differences, communication, mentor characteristics, and managing behavior. Mentors work with 10–11 students who are grouped together by age or grade. While mentors are initially assigned based on interest and previous experiences with a particular age group, they may also have students in their group from the previous year who have developed a relationship with them. With the exception of a few mentors who are doctoral students, however, most are involved with the program for only 1 or 2 years—the length of time that they are upper-level undergraduate or graduate students at the university.

The mentors assist students in moving between classes, structuring social activities, and transferring students to busses or parents. During the enrichment program and throughout the year, the mentors assume a variety of roles: helping students set and achieve goals, acting as a role model, attending student activities, listening to students and functioning as a problem solver, accessing community resources, exploring opportunities for the future with students in terms of their special interests, and assisting students in interpreting their involvement in terms of success (Robins, 2003).

## Peer Involvement

During the summer enrichment program, each student is assigned a mentor and placed in a cohort with approximately nine other students from similar grade levels. As a group, the mentor and student group eat breakfast and lunch in a dormitory cafeteria, participate in recreational activities, and discuss common topics of interest. The mentor encourages the peer group to support one another's development and interests throughout the summer program and follow-up activities.

Academic Enrichment

Along with the WISD and UYP teachers, students, parents, and mentors, the UYP Project Director plans programs that match student interests and career goals. These programs provide in-depth learning in a topic of particular interest and engage students in problem solving and higher level thinking. The students are on the university campus for 4 weeks from approximately 9 a.m. to 4 p.m. each day, which includes breakfast and lunch in a dormitory cafeteria and three 90-minute courses that match their interests. UYP Project students attend classes with all of the other tuition-paying UYP students. These courses include mathematics subjects, such as algebra and geometry; engineering activities, such as rocketry, building bridges, and kite making; topics in the natural sciences, such as animal anatomy, rainforests, archeology, and paleontology; visual arts activities, such as paper maché, paper creations, photography, and calligraphy; creative writing exercises, such as designing brochures and writing stories; communications courses, such as multimedia presentations, debate, and leadership; performing arts activities, such as writing skits; and other topics, like computer science, Shakespeare, French, economics, sports heroes, physical education, inventions, cooking, and individual independent studies. Following the summer activities, the CCLE Director and the mentors plan monthly follow-up activities with the parents, students, and their teachers, which include classroom enrichment options, Super Saturdays, a creative problem solving conference, university cultural and sporting events, and at-home activities. To encourage the high school students' participation, new courses are developed for this age group with an option for the students to assume the role of a paid junior counselor. While summer courses and monthly follow-up activities are provided each year, the content varies and is based on students' evaluations and suggestions.

These five program components are intended to provide academic and social support for each of the UYP Project students. The components also reinforce one another during the year, providing ongoing contact with peer groups, dedicated teachers, and supportive mentors.

## Evaluating the Factors Influencing Retention

A cross-case study analysis was conducted to investigate the issue of retention of these at-risk learners in this university-based program. Knowing that we would be able to encourage and provide support for the students' transition to higher education settings, we wanted to learn more about the factors that might be influencing the students who did not choose to remain in the program.

### Participants

To examine these factors, we selected a representative sample of case studies (e.g., similar to the demographics of the students who attend the program). These cases included 34 current participants and 28 former participants. All of the participants needed to have attended UYP for at least 2 continuous years. Because of GEAR-UP Waco funding requirements, the majority of the students were in middle school. Demographically, the groups were quite similar with the exception of ethnicity (see Table 4.1). Hispanic males tended to be retained in the program for a longer period than other groups. In addition, 82.4% of the current students and only 25% of the former students had two parents living in the home. No differences in aptitude or achievement were found between former and current participants, which we expected because of the common application process and eligibility standards.

### Instruments

A case study containing quantitative and qualitative data is maintained for each UYP Project student. Quantitative data include application information (e.g., entering aptitude and achievement test scores) and an annual achievement test, the Iowa Test of Basic Skills, which is administered in the summer. Qualitative data include dialogue journals, reflection logs, student and parent interviews, teacher and student evaluations, and student products and performances. In the dialogue journal, the mentor asks the student about his classes and experi-

## Table 4.1

University for Young People Project Demographics

| Characteristic | Classification | Former ($n = 28$) | Current ($n = 34$) |
|---|---|---|---|
| Gender | Female | 64% ($n = 18$) | 56% ($n = 19$) |
| | Male | 36% ($n = 10$) | 44% ($n = 15$) |
| Ethnicity | African American | 46% ($n = 13$) | 35% ($n = 12$) |
| | Hispanic American | 29% ($n = 8$) | 53% ($n = 18$) |
| | White | 25% ($n = 7$) | 9% ($n = 3$) |
| | Other | 0% | 3% ($n = 1$) |
| Grade | Elementary | 14% ($n = 4$) | 15% ($n = 5$) |
| | Middle | 57% ($n = 16$) | 53% ($n = 18$) |
| | High | 29% ($n = 8$) | 32% ($n = 11$) |

ences in the program, or the mentor provides a planned prompt such as "What are three things that you like about yourself?" or "Where do you see yourself in 10 years?" The student responds to the mentor's questions or writes about other personal experiences, interests, peers, challenges, or asks the mentor questions. The mentor, in turn, responds to these student entries and the interactions continue throughout the program.

Reflection logs include daily and weekly summaries of the mentors' observations about each student's leadership abilities, relationships with other peers, relationship to the mentor, interests, career goals, and benefits from and problems with certain activities. To monitor this information, mentors take notes on their students throughout the day and summarize their notes into typewritten entries at the end of each day. At the conclusion of the week, the mentor writes a summative statement regarding changes, challenges, or progress experienced by the students.

Mentors also conduct student and parent interviews. In the case of parents who only spoke Spanish, if the mentor does not speak Spanish, then a translated interview is mailed to the parents' home. Mentors also gather data about each student's performance in the UYP classes from the program teachers. In addition, portfolios are also compiled each session, consisting of two or three student-developed products that are representative of their quality of work. All of these data provide a detailed account of the students' interests, goals, educational attainments and opportunities, and attitudes toward school and the UYPP.

## Data Coding and Analysis

In a cross-case study analysis, research occurs within each individual case and across multiple cases (Merriam, 1998). First, each student's case study was analyzed independently. The documents within the case study were compared and contrasted to formulate conceptual labels. As mentioned previously, these documents included quantitative and qualitative data: aptitude and achievement test scores, dialogue journals, reflection logs, student and parent interviews, teacher and student evaluations, and student products. Comparisons were then made across all of the current participants' case studies and then across all of the former participants' case studies. Conceptual labels were compared for similarities and grouped together into categories. Then, to examine differences between former and current participant groups, a cross-case study analysis was conducted using the software program, NVivo, which categorizes characteristics and searches for common themes that may be revealed through the case studies. Using this approach, a number of themes emerged within two major categories: personal factors, such as interests, perceptions of self, attitudes, and career goals; and environmental factors, such as relationships with enrichment program teachers, mentors, and peers, and parental attitudes and support.

### Findings

Of the identified themes, perceptions about self, relationships with peers, relationships with mentors, and perceived parental support appeared to show the greatest differences between the current and former participants (see Table 4.2).

### Perceptions About Self

Students with positive perceptions of themselves tended to have confidence in many skills and personal attributes, believed that they had achieved mastery experiences, enjoyed their individuality, wanted to be a role model for others, had specific plans for their futures, and found positive outcomes in negative situations. In contrast, students with negative perceptions of themselves tended to believe that others were not proud of them, lacked confidence, and were less likely to find something they liked about themselves. Positive and negative perceptions were formed by multiple influences. B. W., a current female elementary student, commented about a personal attribute: "The thing I like most about myself is my personality. Because without my personality, who would I be?" In contrast, M. S., a

**Table 4.2**

Differences in Themes Between Current and Former Participants

| Themes | Current ($n = 34$) | Former ($n = 28$) |
|---|---|---|
| Positive Perceptions of Self | 91.2% ($n = 31$) | 64.3% ($n = 18$) |
| Negative Perceptions of Self | 5.9% ($n = 2$) | 35.7% ($n = 10$) |
| Positive Relationships With Peers | 73.5% ($n = 25$) | 46.4% ($n = 13$) |
| Negative Relationships With Peers | 26.5% ($n = 9$) | 53.6% ($n = 15$) |
| Connected Relationships With Mentors | 73.5% ($n = 25$) | 53.6% ($n = 15$) |
| Involved Parents | 85.3% ($n = 29$) | 60.7% ($n = 17$) |
| Uninvolved Parents | 5.9% ($n = 2$) | 21.4% ($n = 6$) |
| Negative Parent Influence | 8.8% ($n = 3$) | 10.7% ($n = 3$) |

*Note.* Percentages do not equal 100 because not all students reported perceptions regarding self and/or relationships with parents

current female high school student, based her assessment on her ability in a specific talent area:

> What I think makes my mind creative would have to be my feelings toward things. Like, for example, if you really like something—well then you are going to want to express your feelings. It's like whatever you feel about things is the most creative and unique you become. . . . Also, if you don't like art well, then your work won't come out creative, only sloppy and the same as everybody else's work.

Other participants noted extracurricular activities as having a positive influence. Jo. V., a current male elementary student, wrote:

> One thing that makes me happy is playing sports. . . . Something that makes me proud of myself is when I play soccer. . . . I am the best goalie on my team. One game nobody scored on me for the first half. . . . I'm good on defense and in the front scoring the goals on the other team.

Artistic abilities were also cited as influential factors: Ja. R., a current female middle school student, wrote, "I'm special because I can sing well. I've won approximately seven talent show awards. I'm also very confident." Ag. P., a current male high school student, noted,

> Sometimes when I think of art I imagine what I am going to draw in my head or think of my favorite characters on cartoons and draw or make up characters for it. I like to draw people more than landscapes because I can draw different kinds of people.

When mentors discussed the influence of role models, M. S., a current female high school student, wrote, "Well the person I look up to the most is nobody. I like being myself and only myself." Students did note the influence of family members and friends on their positive perceptions of themselves. A. P., a current female high school student, wrote, "The best thing about being me is that I have a family that loves me and my dad always says that 'friends and other people come and go but family is forever!'" J. V., a former female middle school student, wrote, "I like to get to know people and that I like to get to know new people. . . . I think that I am easy to get along with."

In spite of difficult life situations, students with positive perceptions of themselves also tended to recognize their strengths, learn from their failures, and find positive outcomes from challenging experiences. Just as one example from many, Da. W., a current female high school student, faced challenges by being adopted, one brother's death, and another brother's incarceration; yet she made no mention of these challenges and simply focused on her strengths:

> If I didn't have my sense of humor, I wouldn't be so popular. My intelligence I think is an advantage because I am usually ahead of everyone in my class. Even in band and choir. . . . If I weren't beautiful, I wouldn't have all the boys chasing after me (ha ha). And last but not least having wonderful parents and being greatly blessed is what I thank God for everyday.

In contrast to these positive comments, students with negative perceptions of themselves wrote about perceived lack of approval from others as a dominant theme. For example, A. R., a former female high school student, wrote:

> I never finish [short stories] on paper because I prefer to tell the whole thing INSIDE first. I must learn discipline before I put them on paper. Also I fear they'll be rejected. . . . I never let anyone read my stories in writing. . . . My feelings are quite inconsequential.

Je. V., a former female middle school student, wrote in her journal, "My proudest moment was when I was born. I guess I really don't have a proudest moment. . . . It's not that I am not proud of anything, it's that I don't feel like anyone is proud of me."

Others with negative perceptions of themselves mentioned a personal lack of confidence in their talents and family struggles. For example, A. C. wrote about her interest in acting but said, "I'm not the kind of person who gives up, but I don't stand a chance."

Overall, 91.2% ($n = 31$) of the current participants expressed positive perceptions of themselves with only 5.9% or two students reporting negative perceptions. On the other hand, 35.7% ($n = 10$) of the former participants were not positive about themselves. It may be that participants who tend to continue in the program like themselves, believe in their abilities, and exhibit a positive attitude in the face of difficulties, consistent with the resilience literature on economically disadvantaged students (Katz, 1997; Shulman, 1999; Werner, 1990).

### Relationships With Peers

In addition to positive perceptions of themselves, students who were retained in the program demonstrated positive relationships with their peers. They displayed more positive behaviors, acted as leaders, were able to make connections with others for friendships, and had a healthy balance between socializing with friends and pursuing their academic interests. For example, Ag. P., a current male high school student, wrote in his first year journal, "[At] first I was nervous because I didn't know most of the people were strangers to me. . . . I've made lots of friends. . . . There's five more days to go and then I will miss everybody that I met."

Some students expressed how friendships were an important aspect of the enrichment program. For example, A. P., a current female high school student, wrote that she enjoyed the program because she could "be with all of my friends at [the program]! U [sic] can be whoever I want to be and nobody can make fun of me for it! . . . This [year] went by fast because this group was a lot better than my group last year!" K. F., a current female high school student, made similar comments.

> I am surrounded by people who are truly my friends rather than the people (at my school) who I change myself for. And in the end they only pretend to be my friends. . . . I thought about it last night and my favorite reason for coming here is that the other people here are just like me, so I don't have to change for them.

Unlike the students who exhibited positive relationships with their peers, students with negative peer relationships displayed more negative behaviors, acted as followers instead of leaders, were unable to make connections for friendships, and were more concerned with being popular than with their learning. Some students expressed that they did not enjoy their peers.

For example, A. G., a former female high school student, wrote in her journal:

> My ex-boyfriend goes to this camp. He's gotten fat and grumpy. I think he's upset because I moved on. . . . I like my classes but not my group really. . . . You say that you want us to bond! Please! It would have to be something that all not some of us want to do! UH! . . . I think [one of the students is] jealous of my hair!

Other students simply had trouble forming relationships with their peers. A mentor wrote about A. P., a current female high school student:

> [This student] is quiet as well. She does not talk during breakfast or lunch but listens to the girls and smiles. During journal time she separates herself from the group and begins to write. . . . she always seems to be either off by herself or if she is around someone, she is never talking, just standing there with them.

Finally, students with negative peer relationships often seemed not to be able to balance socializing and learning; instead, they were completely focused on being popular. D. D., a former male high school student, wrote the following statements in his journal and excluded any other discussions about his classes:

> Today I had a lot of fun with this girl. . . . I know her brother. I also had fun with a boy. . . . when I was in Brochures class, some girls were acting funny. There's something wrong with those girls, [one of them] tried to spread lies, but I got her back. . . . We just talked the whole class period . . .

In summary, peers who are interested in academic enrichment appear to have more positive peer interactions, which in turn influence their continued participation, with current participants having more positive relationships (73.5%, $n$ = 25) than former participants (46.4%, $n$ = 13).

### Relationships With Mentors

In examining the relationships with the enrichment program mentors, data were grouped into two categories. If the students ignored their mentors or journal prompts, did not journal on a daily basis, were disrespectful to their mentors, or related well with some mentors during one year and not the next, they were classified as having a disconnected relationship with their mentors. On the other hand, if they took part in daily journal discussions, wrote to their mentor about both personal issues and enrichment classes, related well with their mentors in person, and were respectful to their mentors, they were classified as having a connected relationship.

Disconnected students did not respond well to new mentors. For example, one mentor who had a disconnected relationship with R. A., a former male high school student, wrote:

> [This] student is very short in his answers to [me]. He ignores several of the questions that [I] ask him. . . . It appears that [he] has a hard time of opening up with [me]. He never wants to talk about important things in his life. [I try to do] a good job of staying positive and encouraging him to share, but he constantly refuses.

Unlike the disconnected students who did not respond well to new mentors, other students responded well to having different mentors over several years. For example, J. R., a current male middle school student, wrote about his first mentor, "[He] is a joker. He is the best counselor. I just play around with him." This student then wrote about his second year mentor, "You are the first lady counselor I've had. Well, it doesn't matter if you are a lady counselor. For a counselor you are nice. Since I can draw good I will draw you a picture. I hope you like it." Like this participant, the majority of the students seemed to have a connected relationship with their mentors. Al. S., a current male high school student, wrote to his mentor, "I'm glad you're still my counselor. . . . Thank you for saying you're glad I'm in your group." The mentor then wrote the following statement back to Al. S.

> Thanks for letting me come to your ballgame Friday. I enjoyed meeting your family and talking with your dad. And thanks for talking with me yesterday. I enjoy learning about other people's family and culture. . . . You are gifted. You work at a quicker pace and are able to do it effectively because you are so smart. Most likely you will continue to excel this way in life. People are going to respond in a number of ways—some will encourage you and cheer you on, while others will be jealous and try to slow your progress. Slow down for no one but yourself! Keep persevering my friend—the race you're running is a long one!

This mentor's statement is a key element in the development of close relationships with students in the group. Mentors who encouraged the students' positive beliefs about themselves, who became acquainted with the family, and who took a personal interest in the student's activities in all contexts (e.g., university, home, and school) were more likely to develop a close bond with the student, who consequently developed a closer bond with the UYP Project.

Although the majority of all participants had connected relationships with their mentors, the current participants exhibited more connected relationships with their mentors (73.5%, $n = 25$) than the former participants (53.6%, $n = 15$). This result may suggest that building and sustaining relationships with adults may influence the retention of students in the program.

### Perceived Parental Support

Students who were retained in the program also appeared to have strong parental support. Students and mentors frequently commented about the types of support parents provided. Parents also commented about their expectations for their children during their interviews. These comments were organized according to the degree of involvement or influence. While the majority of the parents were involved in their students' lives, current participants' parents were more involved (85.3%, $n = 29$) than former participants' parents (60.7%, $n = 17$). Current students expressed many positive feelings toward their families. For example, E. R., a middle school current female participant, wrote in her journal, "I will always have my parents and they will help me." C. R., a middle school current female participant, wrote, "The best present I ever got was my playhouse that my daddy built by himself (I helped him). The best present I ever gave is my love to my family!" One father commented about his educational philosophy and goals for his daughter, A. S., a former female middle school participant:

> I believe education is like a plant, nurture it and it will grow and mature. I think education should be gained by any means possible. Schools, campus trips, programs like [this program] are a great way to teach and expose children to different and exciting subjects. Children are like sponges. They can absorb and express with innocence. I think [this program] is great and it helps kids prepare for college. . . . She likes to learn. She waits every summer to go to UYP. She really enjoys it. [I want my daughter] to reach college and have a good job. . . . [This program is] the best program to help her get to college.

Participants identified parental support as spending time with their parents, talking about academic activities, engaging in social events, and setting goals and expectations. In spite of their limited resources, these students reported a safe, loving home environment.

A small number of former participants (10.7%, $n = 3$) and current participants (8.8%, $n = 3$) had negative experiences with their parents. For example, Je. V., a former female middle school participant, wrote in her journal to her mentor:

> It's just that yesterday on Father's Day, I didn't have any memories to share about my father and I just wish that I

had. We had a step dad but he was real mean. And I just never had a dad (real) to play with. And I just hate that. But I can't be sad. I don't want no one to see me so like that so I just act stupid.

In summary, although both groups had a few students who reported negative home influences, the current participants tended to have more positive parental involvement, which may have contributed to their retention.

## Discussion and Implications for Improving Retention

Social factors seem to strongly influence the retention of gifted and talented students from lower income backgrounds in this academic enrichment program. Relationships with peers, mentors, and parents appeared to show the greatest differences between current participants who have been retained in the program for more than 2 years and former participants who left the program after 2 years.

While studies specifically comparing returning and nonreturning economically disadvantaged participants to enrichment programs are sparse, literature does suggest that relationships are important to students in developing their talents. For example, Torrance, Goff, and Satterfield (1998) found that mentors have a positive effect on developing the interests of economically disadvantaged and/or minority gifted students. They defined mentors as

influential people who significantly help us reach our major life goals. They have the power to promote our welfare, training, learning, or careers and are usually identified as having outstanding knowledge skills, and expertise in a particular domain or area. (p. 4)

In the UYP Project program, mentors tended to be an integral part of the experiences that these students received by participating in the program. Students who continued in the program seemed to be able to build relationships with adults.

Peers also assumed an important role in talent development and retention in the UYP Project program. In this program, participants who found peers who not only became friends, but also viewed learning as important, were more likely to continue. Confirming this desire for friendship, Cox, Daniel, and Boston (1985) reported that gifted students need to work and play with other students who are similar in their interests and abilities; however, inappropriate peer groups can negatively influence the academic and extracurricular development of gifted students. Therefore, professionals who direct enrichment programs need to pay particular attention to the development of friendships that enhance academic and personal growth. The University for Young People provided opportunities for gifted students to interact socially with others like themselves.

Another major factor in the retention of students was parental support. The importance of family support has been reported in many studies (Baker, Bridger, & Evans, 1998; Diaz, 1998; Hébert, 1998; Hébert & Olenchak, 2000). Primary among these is Bloom's (1985) study that examined the family's positive influences in talent development where family members had a personal interest in the talent field and gave strong encouragement and rewards for developing talent. In the early years of talent development, the home was important for providing resources, practice sessions, and help in the child's work. While many of these UYP Project parents did not have the material resources to help their children, they realized the program's importance to their child's future and supported them in many ways by listening to their stories, setting high expectations, and creating a safe, loving environment.

The reciprocal interaction between positive self-perceptions and positive social influences most likely contributed to the current UYP Project students' retention in the program. In spite of economic difficulties, current students believed in their ability to perform well, whether it is academics or other talent areas such as art, music, or athletics. This belief might be described as self-efficacy or one's feelings of mastery or ability to succeed in a specific domain (Bandura, 1996). Bandura's (1997) research found that self-efficacy impacts one's academic performance and goals, choice of activities, effort in the activities, and *perseverance* in the activities. Unlike former students, the current students based their perceptions of themselves on their abilities in specific talent areas, noting mastery experiences gained from the enrichment classes and other programs that led them to feel successful, which in turn led them to continue in the program.

## Conclusion

One of the major concerns in gifted education is not only identifying more gifted students from lower income backgrounds but also retaining them in special programs. This program evaluation addressed this important issue by examining factors that appeared to contribute to the retention of these gifted at-risk students. Although we were limited to a small representative sample of case studies, we discovered the importance of social relationships with peers and adults in their retention. Program developers might want to consider creating an environment that includes mentors and peers with similar backgrounds and academic interests to enhance the students' perceptions of themselves, their self-efficacy, and their social relationships.

## References

Baker, J. A., Bridger, R., & Evans, K. (1998). Models of under-achievement among gifted preadolescents: The role of personal, family, and school factors. *Gifted Child Quarterly, 42*, 5–15.

Bandura, A. (1996). Multifaceted impact of self-efficacy beliefs on academic functioning. *Child Development, 67*, 1206–1222.

Bandura, A. (1997). *Self-efficacy: The exercise of control.* New York: Freeman.

Benbow, C. P., Perkins, S., & Stanley, J. C. (1983). Mathematics taught at a fast pace: A longitudinal evaluation of SMPY's first class. In C. P. Benbow & J. C. Stanley (Eds.), *Academic precocity: Aspects of its development* (pp. 51–78). Baltimore: Johns Hopkins University Press.

Bernal, E. M. (2002). Three ways to achieve a more equitable representation of culturally and linguistically different students in GT programs. *Roeper Review, 24*, 82–88.

Bloom, B. (Ed.). (1985). *Developing talent in young people.* New York: Ballantine.

Borland, J. H., & Wright, L. (1994). Identifying young, potentially gifted economically disadvantaged students. *Gifted Child Quarterly, 38*, 164–171.

Bourstein, P. J., Holahan, W., & Sawyer, R. (1988). The expectations and motivations of gifted students in a residential academic program: A study of individual differences. *Journal for the Education of the Gifted, 11*, 36–53.

Center for Talented Youth (2002). *Summer programs. Johns Hopkins University.* Retrieved February 5, 2004, from http://cty.jhu.edu

Cox, J., Daniel, N., & Boston, B. A. (1985). *Educating able learners: Programs and promising practices.* Austin: University of Texas Press.

Diaz, E. L. (1998). Perceived factors influencing the academic underachievement of talented students of Puerto Rican descent. *Gifted Child Quarterly, 42*, 105–122.

Duke University. (2002). *Duke University Talent Identification Program.* Retrieved February 17, 2004, from http://www.tip.duke.edu

Enersen, D. L. (1993). Summer residential programs: Academics and beyond. *Gifted Child Quarterly, 37*, 169–176.

Feldhusen, J. F. (1995). Talent development: The new direction in gifted education. *Roeper Review, 18*, 92.

Ford, D. (1996). *Reversing underachievement among gifted Black students: Promising practices and programs.* Teachers College Press: New York.

Grantham, T. C. (2003). Increasing Black student enrollment in gifted programs: An exploration of the Pulaski county special school district's advocacy efforts. *Gifted Child Quarterly, 47*, 46–65.

Hébert, T. P. (1998). De Shea's dream deferred: A case study of a talented urban artist. *Journal for the Education of the Gifted, 22*, 56–79.

Hébert, T. P., & Olenchak, F. R. (2000). Mentors for gifted underachieving males: Developing potential and realizing promise. *Gifted Child Quarterly, 44*, 196–207.

Johnsen, S. K., & Corn, A. L. (2001). *Screening assessment for gifted elementary students* (2nd ed.). Austin, TX: PRO-ED.

Katz, M. (1997). *On playing a poor hand well: Insights from the lives of those who have overcome childhood risks and adversities.* New York: Norton & Co.

Kay, S. I., & Subotnik, R. F. (1994). Talent beyond words: Unveiling spatial, expressive, kinesthetic, and musical talent in young children. *Gifted Child Quarterly, 38*, 70–74.

McLennan County Youth Collaboration—Communities In Schools. (2001). [McLennan County statistics]. Unpublished raw data.

Merriam, S. B. (1998). *Qualitative research and case study applications in education.* San Francisco: Jossey-Bass.

Olszewski-Kubilius, P. (1989). Development of academic talent: The role of summer programs. In J. VanTassel-Baska & P. Olszewski-Kubilius (Eds.), *Patterns of influence on gifted learners: The home, the self, and the school* (pp. 214–230). New York: Teachers College Press.

Olszewski-Kubilius, P., & Laubscher, L. (1996). The impact of a college-counseling program on economically disadvantaged gifted students and their subsequent college adjustment. *Roeper Review, 18*, 202–208.

Robins, J. (2003). A model for mentoring gifted and talented students. In *Influences: Social perspectives* (pp 26–39). Unpublished monograph, Department of Educational Psychology, Baylor University, Waco, TX.

Ryser, G. R., & McConnell, K. (2004). *Scales for identifying gifted students.* Waco, TX: Prufrock Press.

Shulman, L. (1999). *The skills of helping individuals, families, groups, and communities.* Itasca, IL: F. E. Peacock.

Swiatek, M. A., & Benbow, C. P. (1991). A ten-year longitudinal study of students in a fast-paced mathematics program. *Journal for Research in Mathematics Education, 22*, 138–150.

Torrance, E. P., Goff, K., & Satterfield, N. B. (1998). *Multicultural mentoring of the gifted and talented.* Waco, TX: Prufrock Press.

University of Denver. (2003). *Rocky Mountain Talent Search.* Retrieved February 17, 2004, from http://www.du.edu/education/ces/rmts.html

Werner, E. E. (1990). Protective factors and individual resilience. In S. J. Meisels & J. P. Shonkoff (Eds.), *Handbook of early childhood intervention* (pp. 97–116). New York: Cambridge University Press.

Worrell, F. C., Szarko, J. E., & Gabelko, N. H. (2001). Multi-year persistence of nontraditional students in an academic talent development program. *Journal of Secondary Gifted Education, 12*, 80–89.

# An Overview of Three Models of Publicly Funded Residential Academies for Gifted Adolescents

*Tracy L. Cross & Kimberly A. Miller*

## Introduction

Students with academic gifts or talents are educated in numerous types of programs across the United States. They are served in settings that can be considered as falling on a continuum from least restrictive to most restrictive. Specifically, students with gifts and talents are typically served in heterogeneous classrooms, pull-out programs, cluster groups, self-contained classes, and residential academies. Among this list of options, public residential academies represent a relatively new approach aimed at addressing the needs of gifted adolescents. While a few authors have written about residential gifted programs around the country (Boothe, Sethna, Stanley, & Colgate, 1999; Borden, 1998; Eilber, 1987; Kolloff, 2003; Sethna, Wickstrom, Boothe, & Stanley, 2001; Stanley, 1991; Stephens, 1999), to date there is no comprehensive overview detailing the similarities and differences of these schools. The purpose of this chapter is to focus specifically on three different models of public residential academies for gifted adolescents, explaining their purposes, origins, similarities, and differences. Examples of the outreach efforts of the schools are provided along with a description of common evaluation practices. The chapter concludes with an analysis of the benefits and concerns of attending one of these schools.

Students with gifts and talents require a specialized education. For many years this occurred in the context of a regular classroom environment, pull-out programs, or specialized courses within a traditional educational setting. However, for many students these options did not prove to be challenging enough (Cross, Margison & Williams, 2003), and for others in rural areas, specialized courses were not offered because the educational systems lacked the teachers with the skills and experience to teach the courses (Cross & Burney, 2005). The need for a more challenging environment to develop the abilities of gifted students spurred the creation of residential programs of gifted education. The three models of these residential programs that will be discussed were categorized as Models One, Two, and Three based on the program's focus. Model One schools are public residential high schools whose main focus is on science and mathematics. Model Two schools are public residential high schools focusing primarily on arts and humanities. Model Three schools are public residential schools that are early entrance to college programs where students obtain a high school degree and an associate's degree by taking college courses.

In addition to public residential academies that are part of this trend of states' funding particular models of residential schools, other manifestations exist. For example, a well-known program at the University of Washington, directed by the Halbert and Nancy Robinson Center for Young Scholars has existed for three decades now, and while it is quite reputable, it does not fit within the specific models discussed in this chapter. Moreover, although there are other examples of substantial residential programs sprinkled across the country, they do not represent the specific trends portrayed in this chapter.

A common issue affecting all of the residential academies is the makeup of their student bodies (representation). Representation is defined to mean different things across the schools. For some, it means drawing similar numbers of students from the various geographic regions of the sponsoring state. For others, it means representing the demographics of their state's population. Others include a broader definition of representation by establishing a goal to build as diverse a student body as possible. Three issues cut across these goals: the location of the school within each state relative to large urban centers; the relationships of the specialty areas of the schools and the numbers of the students making up the school; and the size of the student body in relationship to the number of state residents. Other factors affecting representation include whether the school is located on the campus of a college or university and the demographic makeup of the state. Whether the state has a history of boarding schools and the age of the school also affect issues of representation. These factors have been grappled with since the day of inception at each school. Many of the schools have begun summer programs for younger students to try to ensure demographic representation of their host states. The premise on which this strategy is based is that students who attend the summer programs will be more likely to attend the yearlong academy after spending time on campus. Other academies have engaged in carefully targeted recruiting efforts. Still others have customized the school settings to appeal to subgroups of children being recruited. For example, the Indiana Academy for Science, Mathematics, and Humanities pursued and received approval to create a chaplaincy program to accommodate the interest of some of its students.

Due to the significant challenge that this issue raises, funding groups such as the Sloan Foundation have offered millions of dollars to assist the residential academies in reaching their representation goals for their student bodies. As is the case in the broader field of gifted studies, underrepresentation of certain groups of students with gifts and talents also exists in the residential academies to some extent.

## Descriptions of Three Models
## of Residential Academies

*Model One Schools: Math and Science Emphasis*

The first and most well-known model was introduced with the opening of the North Carolina School of Science and

Mathematics (NCSSM) in 1980. The development of this public residential high school began in 1977 when Governor James Hunt established the school as a program to serve 11th and 12th graders who were academically gifted in science and mathematics (Eilber, 1987). Governor Hunt established the North Carolina school for three specific purposes. First, he realized that the economic growth of the state's increasing dependence on businesses focused on technology required an increased emphasis on science and mathematics training for high school students. Second, because many gifted students in North Carolina did not have access to the resources necessary to develop their talents in the field of science and mathematics, the new residential school would fill this void. Third, Hunt realized that along with the need for new opportunities for gifted students, teachers also needed new opportunities to be trained in order to provide the appropriate education for gifted students. Thus, a residential school specializing in science and mathematics could provide exceptional training for teachers in these areas.

Today, the North Carolina school continues to serve these purposes and also provides education and training to students and teachers around the state through distance education and workshops. The North Carolina school offers a top quality educational experience, and, because it is a public school, the students' only costs are personal expenses. The cost of attendance and overhead is provided by the school's $12 million dollar budget, the majority of which comes from the state legislature.

The NCSSM currently serves 580 students, split evenly by gender, and the ethnic makeup reflects some diversity (65% White, 18% Asian, 12% African American, 4% Hispanic, 1% Native American). Admittance to the North Carolina school is highly competitive and is based on test scores, transcripts, letters of recommendation, a personal essay, and an interview. Once admitted, the students are involved with an intensive curriculum that focuses heavily on the sciences and mathematics. Many of these courses are Advanced Placement courses that allow the students to test out of college classes, and all of the courses offered are taught by the school's own faculty, all of whom have master's degrees, and one third of whom have doctorates. In addition, because the

North Carolina school is affiliated with the University of North Carolina System, students have access to many of the university's academic resources. Even though the North Carolina school is heavily focused on academics, the school also provides the traditional extracurricular activities (sports, clubs, and dances) found in a traditional high school.

After the founding of the North Carolina School of Science and Mathematics, nine similar schools were established around the country between 1981 and 1995 (Louisiana, 1981; Oklahoma, 1983; Illinois, 1985; Mississippi, 1987; South Carolina, 1987; Indiana, 1988; Alabama, 1989; Arkansas, 1991; Maine, 1995; see Table 5.1). These schools are similar to the North Carolina school in gender and ethnic makeup, admittance criteria, curriculum, extracurricular activities, and outreach activities (e.g., distance education, summer workshops). Four of these schools (Louisiana, Mississippi, Indiana, and Arkansas) are affiliated with a major university, allowing students at these schools to have the extra benefit of access to university resources. Three schools (Illinois, Alabama, and Maine) also serve 10th-grade students, but only Maine admits out-of-state students (at a cost of $18,000 per year). For the Model One schools, the costs for in-state students range from only personal expenses up to $3,100 in Maine. Of these 10 schools, only 4 offer an area of academic focus in addition to science and math. The Louisiana and Arkansas schools offer arts and the Indiana and Maine schools offer humanities as an equal emphasis with science and mathematics.

### Model Two Schools: Arts and Humanities Emphasis

While the Model One schools focus primarily on math and science, with only a few offering an additional academic focus, the Model Two residential academies focus primarily on the Arts and Humanities (see Table 5.2 for a list of Model Two schools). The first school established under this model was the North Carolina School of the Arts, which opened in 1965, and like the North Carolina School of Science and Mathematics, is also administered by the University of North Carolina. Like the

**Table 5.1**
Model One Schools

| School | Opened | Web site |
|---|---|---|
| North Carolina School of Science and Mathematics | 1980 | http://www.ncssm.edu |
| Louisiana School for Math, Science, and the Arts | 1981 | http://www.lsmsa.edu |
| Oklahoma School of Science and Mathematics | 1983 | http://www.ossm.edu |
| Illinois Mathematics and Science Academy | 1985 | http://www2.imsa.edu |
| Mississippi School for Mathematics and Science | 1987 | http://www.msms.k12.ms.us |
| South Carolina Governor's School for Science and Mathematics | 1987 | http://www.scgssm.org |
| Indiana Academy for Science, Mathematics, and Humanities | 1988 | http://www.bsu.edu/web/academy |
| Alabama School of Mathematics and Science | 1989 | http://www.asms.net |
| Arkansas School for Mathematics, Sciences & the Arts | 1991 | http://asmsa.net |
| Maine School of Science and Mathematics | 1995 | http://www.mssm.org |

**Table 5.2**
Model Two Schools

| School | Opened | Web site |
| --- | --- | --- |
| North Carolina School of the Arts | 1965 | http://www.ncarts.edu |
| The Alabama School of Fine Arts | 1968 | http://www.asfa.k12.al.us |
| Texas Academy of Leadership in the Humanities | 1994 | http://dept.lamar.edu/taolith |
| South Carolina Governor's School for the Arts and Humanities | 1999 | http://www.scgsah.state.sc.us |
| Mississippi School of the Arts | 2003 | http://www.msa.k12.ms.us |

North Carolina School of Science and Mathematics, the North Carolina School of the Arts (NCSA) was established through the dedication of former Governor Terry Sanford and numerous community supporters.

The school's primary purpose has always been to professionally train talented students in the fields of music, drama, dance, and performing arts at the high school and college level. The NCSA emphasizes the performance of the arts and not academic studies of the arts. This focus was modeled after the European conservatory schools and, although a complete academic curriculum and historical perspective of disciplines is offered, the focus remains on performance. Students who attend enroll in one of five arts schools focusing on dance, design and production, drama, filmmaking, or music, and the training students receive enables the school to offer high school diplomas along with undergraduate and master's degrees. This multiple degree program is one aspect of the NCSA that makes this school unique. It is not only a residential high school for gifted adolescents, it is also an undergraduate and graduate institution for the arts, providing extensive training for students at all academic levels.

Currently, the NCSA educates students from ninth grade to graduate school and has an enrollment of 1,075 (263 are high school students) and a budget of $8,568,000 for their high school program. The ethnic makeup of the NCSA is not as diverse as the Model One schools (84% White, 5% African American, 4% Other, 3% Asian, 3% Hispanic, 1% Native American), and the NCSA serves more females than males (66% vs. 34%). Those admitted in 9th and 10th grade are students focusing on music and dance; however, the older students can focus on any of the arts. The NCSA also offers Advanced Placement courses in many areas (e.g., mathematics, science, foreign languages), providing students a rigorous comprehensive education. The NCSA does not provide opportunities to participate in athletics. The school also engages in extensive outreach (e.g., workshops, summer courses) to students and teachers around the state.

The NCSA allows out-of-state admissions, but requires that at least 50% of its students be residents of North Carolina. There is no cost for students who are residents of North Carolina, but out-of-state students pay an average of $17,000 per year to attend. Admission to the school is competitive and requires auditions, transcripts, letters of recommendation, personal interviews, essays, and a portfolio (if applicable). However, unlike the Model One schools, no formal test scores or minimum GPA is required.

The four schools that follow the model of the North Carolina School of the Arts were opened between 1968 and 2003 (The Alabama School of Fine Arts, 1968; Texas Academy of Leadership in the Humanities, 1994; South Carolina Governor's School for the Arts and Humanities, 1999; Mississippi School of the Arts, 2003; see Table 5.2). Their budgets range from $1.8 million (Mississippi) to $6.5 million (Alabama), and although they share a similar purpose, there are several main differences. All the Model Two schools have a similar ethnic makeup, but the Texas Academy is the most diverse (55% White, 20% African American, 10% Asian, 10% Hispanic, 5% Native American). Four out of the five schools serve more females than males

(North Carolina, 66% vs. 34%; Alabama, 65% vs. 35%; South Carolina, 67% vs. 33%; Mississippi, 75% vs. 25%), with the Texas Academy split evenly by gender.

The only two schools that admit out-of-state students are The Alabama School of Fine Arts and the North Carolina School of the Arts. The cost to out-of-state students in North Carolina is much higher than in Alabama (approximately $17,000 versus approximately $7,000). In addition, while the other schools charge in-state students a range of fees (from $1,700 at Alabama to more than $4,200 at Texas), the NCSA serves in-state students at no cost. The Texas Academy of Leadership in the Humanities and The Alabama School of Fine Arts are the only schools in this model that require a minimum standardized test score, and the South Carolina, Mississippi, and Alabama schools are the only schools that require a minimum GPA of a C or better for admission.

Universities administer two of the five schools in this model. The Texas Academy of Leadership in the Humanities is overseen by Lamar University, and the North Carolina School of the Arts is overseen by the University of North Carolina. While four of the schools in this model provide all academic courses on-site, the Mississippi School for the Arts only employs faculty with training in the arts, and therefore, its students must take math, science, and other courses at Brookhaven High School. Texas and Mississippi are the only two schools not currently engaged in outreach. Mississippi plans to begin an outreach program within the next few years. Alabama and the NCSA are the only two schools that do not provide opportunities for intramural or inter-scholastic athletics. Although all of the schools serve 11th and 12th graders, the North and South Carolina schools also serve 9th and 10th graders in music and dance, and the Alabama school serves students as young as 7th grade for music and dance.

## Model Three Schools: Early Entrance to College

The third model of residential academies for gifted adolescents is similar to the previous two models in academic rigor: It provides a challenging environment by having students attend

**Table 5.3**
Model Three Schools

| School | Opened | Web site |
|---|---|---|
| Texas Academy of Mathematics and Science | 1987 | http://www.tams.unt.edu |
| Advanced Academy of Georgia | 1995 | http://www.advancedacademy.org |
| Georgia Academy of Mathematics, Engineering, and Science | 1997 | http://web2.mgc.edu/natsci/games/gameshome.html |
| Missouri Academy of Science, Mathematics and Computing | 2000 | http://www.nwmissouri.edu/MASMC |
| Kentucky Academy of Mathematics & Science | N/A | http://www.wku.edu/academy |

college courses (see Table 5.3). Schools of this model began with the establishment of the Texas Academy of Mathematics and Science (TAMS) in 1987. TAMS was developed in part because the dean of the College of Education at the University of North Texas was a former high school teacher of gifted students and his experiences led him to believe gifted juniors and seniors in high school were not being sufficiently challenged. Because of this experience, he asked the university to develop an accelerated program for high school juniors and seniors. After university officials visited the North Carolina School of Science and Mathematics, they decided an all-college curriculum would be more appropriate in their state.

Dr. Julian Stanley, an eminent scholar in the field, was both an important supporter of this model and a consultant to those who developed these Model Three schools. He was invaluable to their creation, and many consider him the father of this model of gifted student education.

The Texas Academy's early entrance to college program allows students to earn both a high school diploma and an associate's degree during their first 2 years of college. Students attend courses offered by the University of North Texas faculty (all have master's degrees and the majority have doctorates), and therefore do not take Advanced Placement courses. In addition, because the University of North Texas is responsible for the students' education, the Texas Academy does not engage in outreach and has a much smaller budget than the Model One schools ($3,405,719). However, the cost to the students is much higher (approximately $7,000 per year). Although the students live on a college campus, have access to the university's resources, and can participate in intramural sports, they are housed separately from the college students, supervised closely, and have a strict curfew.

TAMS currently serves 380 students split almost evenly by gender (45% female, 55% male) and has an ethnic makeup similar to that of the Model One schools (58% White, 25% Asian, 11% Hispanic, 5% African American, 1% Native American). Admission into the Texas Academy is also similar to the Model One admission standards. All students must take either the SAT or ACT (no minimum stated for entry), provide transcripts of previous work, letters of recommendation, a written essay, and attend a personal interview.

The four schools that follow the Texas Academy of Mathematics and Science model were opened between 1995 and 2000 (Advanced Academy of Georgia, 1995; Georgia Academy of Mathematics, Engineering, and Science, 1997; Missouri Academy of Science, Mathematics and Computing, 2000; and the soon-to-be-opened Kentucky Academy of Mathematics & Science). The budgets for these schools range from $415,000 (Advanced Academy of Georgia) to $1.989 million (Missouri). All of the Model Three schools are similar with respect to admission criteria, gender makeup, and fees, but there are several differences. Only three schools (Advanced Academy of Georgia, Georgia Academy of Mathematics, Engineering, and Science, and Kentucky Academy of Mathematics & Science) admit out-of-state students (costs range from $5,800 to $7,187 per semester). The Texas Academy of Mathematics and Science has the largest out-of-state enrollment of all the schools (380). The Advanced Academy of Georgia is the only school that actively recruits international students each year from Spain (approximately 5% of enrolled students). The Texas Academy and the Advanced Academy of Georgia have a more diverse student population because they have a higher percentage of Asian students (Texas = 25%, Georgia = 12%) and Hispanic students (Texas = 11%, Georgia = 5%, from Spain) than do the other schools. Finally, like the Model One schools, two of the four Model Three schools offer an additional academic focus: the Georgia Academy offers engineering, and the Missouri Academy offers computing. Unlike the Model One and Two schools, the Model Three schools do not emphasize outreach.

## Outreach Activities in Model One and Model Two Schools

Most of the Model One and Two schools were created with expectations to extend their campuses beyond their residential communities. To that end, many engage in outreach activities. Below are examples of outreach activities engaged in by the two models of residential academies. The schools that offer the greatest array of activities and programs are noted.

### Model One Outreach Activities

All Model One schools engage in outreach activities: NCSSM has one of the most extensive outreach programs of all the Model One schools, made possible because NCSSM has set aside specific funds to hire full-time staff to run these programs (S. Adkin, personal communication, December 6, 2005). The goal of the External Programs Division at NCSSM is to "provide statewide public service and outreach efforts to improve mathematics and science education for students and teachers beyond NCSSM and to promote the use of learning technologies" (S. Adkin, personal communication, December 6, 2005). Although space does not permit a description of all NCSSM's outreach activities, several notable components will be discussed.

NCSSM began its Distance Learning Program in 1992 through a grant. Since that time, their program has continued to grow through support from other grants and state funding. Today the Distance Learning Program continues to be the state leader in K–12 educational programming for both Internet and video conferencing. This program provides credit-bearing courses for students and teachers in high school science, mathematics, and humanities, and enrichment activities that are designed to enhance course curriculum. Some examples of the courses offered are: AP Biology, Latin I/II, Advanced Functions and Modeling Mathematics, AP Physics, and AP Calculus (S. Adkin, personal communication, December 6, 2005).

In addition to distance education, NCSSM is one of 10 Mathematics and Science Education Network (MSEN) Centers whose purpose it is to strengthen K–12 science and mathematics education by improving the quality of teaching throughout North Carolina. Special programs are offered throughout the school year (with a greater number being offered during the summer) in order to assist teachers in honing their skills and learning how to effectively integrate technology into their classroom. In addition to offering specialized programming for teachers, NCSSM also hosts several summer programs for students around the state. Some examples are: Summer Ventures in Science and Mathematics, high school and elementary mathematics contests, and a mathematics fair. These programs provide younger students the opportunity to be challenged and enhance their knowledge in the field of science and math. The Summer Ventures in Science and Mathematics (sponsored by the University of North Carolina) is of particular note because it is a 4-week program where high school juniors and seniors work with university faculty on a project of their own design. This program is sponsored by the University of North Carolina with several other participating campuses (North Carolina Central University, UNC Wilmington, East Carolina University, Appalachian State University, UNC Charlotte, and Western Carolina University). Having an opportunity to work with faculty at a university exposes students to a college atmosphere, assists them in developing their research skills, and provides a mentoring relationship that may continue to serve them beyond the completion of this program.

The Illinois Math and Science Academy (IMSA) is another Model One school that provides outreach to students and faculty around the state of Illinois. IMSA has been engaging in outreach since the inception of the school and the number of programs has grown significantly since that time (K. Ciesemier, personal communication, December 7, 2005). The first goal of the Illinois school's outreach program is to increase the number of students interested and skilled in science and mathematics. The second goal is to enhance Illinois teachers' ability to effectively teach math and science curriculum. In order to meet these goals, the school provides programs throughout the year (with the majority being concentrated in the summer months) for teachers and students. Some specific examples of outreach to students include: Summer Sleuths, Science Explorer Fieldtrips, and IMSA on Wheels. The Summer Sleuths program provides students in sixth to ninth grade an opportunity to attend a 4-day workshop that involves conducting research on real-world problems and learning how to effectively present results. The Science Explorer Fieldtrips allow second through fourth graders an opportunity to engage in a hands-on, half-day science learning experience, which is facilitated by the students at IMSA. This not only provides the IMSA students the opportunity to take a leadership role, but also provides the younger students with mentors and helps to foster their interest in science. Finally, IMSA on Wheels is a mobile science theatre that provides science demonstrations to Chicago-area students in grades 3–5. It is clear that the IMSA's outreach program provides a variety of experiences that enhance young students' interests and knowledge of science and mathematics.

In addition to outreach to students, IMSA provides several programs for teachers. One of the most notable programs is the Problem-Based Learning Network for Teachers. Problem-based learning (PBL) is "an educational approach that organizes curriculum and instruction around carefully crafted situations adopted from real world issues" (Illinois Math and Science Academy, 2005, p. 1). The PBL network allows teachers to learn how to use the PBL model through "summer institutes and seminars to learn the model; classroom observations, consultations, and research to determine the effectiveness in the classrooms; and collaboration through an interactive online network with other PBL practitioners" (IMSA, p. 1). In addition to the PBL network, the Illinois school also works with teachers and school districts by providing professional development in mathematics, science, and technology curriculum and instructional methods. By enhancing the skills of teachers around the state, IMSA is able to positively impact thousands of students it would otherwise not be able to serve.

The Indiana Academy for Science, Mathematics, and Humanities (Indiana Academy) has provided extensive outreach programs for 16 years. The programs have included those that focus on faculty (Faculty Fellows Program, Monthly Workshops, Summer Workshops) and those that focus on students (Distance Education Courses, Electronic Field Trip program, and a number of summer programs for impoverished youth). The Faculty Fellows program pays the costs to bring teachers from across the state of Indiana to the Indiana Academy for an academic year to learn how to effectively teach secondary gifted students. The Fellows live in housing on the campus of Ball State University and teach classes for the Academy. They also develop curricular materials to take back to their respective high schools. During the 15 years of the program, 56 Faculty Fellows have worked and studied at the Indiana Academy.

The Indiana Academy also offers monthly workshops that provide specialized training for teachers in brief formats. For example, teachers from across the state would come to the Academy for training in using probes when conducting science experiments. Indiana Academy faculty conducts these sessions. A recent incarnation of monthly workshops was held on teaching Advanced Placement courses via distance education technologies.

The Summer Workshop program has expanded dramatically over the years to include approximately 400 teachers from across the United States and several foreign countries, who come to the Academy to learn how to effectively teach Advanced Placement (AP) courses and other rigorous courses. The training is a weeklong immersion program. To date, more than 1,000 teachers have completed this training.

Programs on behalf of students have evolved at the Indiana Academy over the years. The Distance Education program provides courses from the Academy's curriculum for students at a distance throughout Indiana and across the U.S. The technological platforms have changed over the years, from satellite, to multiple forms of Internet-based courses. High school physics is the most popular course taken, with an average of about 300 students per year. The program accommodates approximately 400 to 600 students per year in courses such as AP Calculus, AP Biology, AP Physics, Astronomy, Russian, and Japanese.

The Electronic Field Trip program (EFT) was created by the dean of Teachers College at Ball State University, Roy Weaver, to bring experiences such as attending some of the world's great museums to children from around world who otherwise would not have those opportunities. The EFT program has broadcast to millions of students from archeological digs, the Holocaust Museum, the Baseball Hall of Fame, and NASA, to name a few examples. In addition to the broadcast, curricular materials are developed and a Web site is used to coordinate activities. Because sponsors underwrite the EFT program, the cost to schools to receive the program is extremely low. According to the numbers reported by the schools that have participated in the program, each broadcast may be seen by several million students. This program grew to the point where it was moved to the Teachers College from the Academy, primarily because the programming was more appropriate for students from kindergarten to eighth grade than for high school students.

### Model Two Outreach Activities

The majority of Model Two schools also engage in outreach activities. The goals of the outreach program at the South Carolina school are to provide professional training to both students and teachers and to provide curricular consultations to schools across the state (A. Tromsness, personal communication December 13, 2005). In order to meet these goals, each department within the school (e.g., music, drama, creative writing, visual arts, and dance) provides several summer programs for students and teachers. Some of the student summer programs include Discovery, Academy, and Summer Dance programs. The Discovery program provides ninth graders with 2 weeks of intensive training in one of the four art areas (creative writing, drama, music, or visual arts). Students can also explore other art areas through attendance at workshops and master classes. The Academy program also provides the same type of intensive training in one of the four art areas, but it is designed for 10th graders and has a more nontraditional curriculum (incorporating self-directed studies, performances, field trips, etc.). The Summer Dance program invites students from around the country in grades 6–12 to attend 5 weeks of professional dance training (Vaganova method) from leading instructors around the world. These are just a few examples of the outreach programs offered by the South Carolina school; each department within the school provides specific outreach programs that are generally targeted to middle and high school students.

In addition to the outreach focused on students, the South Carolina school also offers workshops for teachers and regularly conducts curricular consultation in schools around the state. One of the most notable programs for teachers is the Arts Teachers as Artists Institutes. This program is offered to any teacher of the arts (e.g., visual arts, music, drama) and provides them an opportunity to work with master artists not only to hone their artistic abilities but also to learn how to instruct students more effectively in the arts. These courses last one week and provide the participants with three graduate and/or recertification credits. In the summer of 2006, the South Carolina school is offering courses in photography and ceramic visual arts, music improvisation and composition, and playwriting.

In addition to the educational outreach offered, the South Carolina school also hosts numerous performances that are open to the public. It is this combination of educational and community outreach that has allowed the South Carolina school to continue to foster a statewide appreciation of the arts.

A final example of a Model Two outreach program comes from The Alabama School of Fine Arts. The Alabama school's goal for outreach includes recruiting new students, sparking an interest in the arts in young students, and assisting the community at large in gaining a deeper appreciation of the arts. Some examples of their outreach programs are: Dance Excellence, Young Writers Summer Camp, and Summer Musicianship Camp (J. Northrup, personal communication, December 13, 2005). The Dance Excellence program is an intensive 2-week program for serious dancers ages 12–18. Program classes include ballet, jazz or contemporary jazz, point, male technique, pas de deux, and repertoire. However, students are also instructed in other areas (e.g., technical lighting, dance therapy) and can also participate in specialized master classes (e.g., Spanish dance, historical dance, and yoga). The Young Writers Summer Camp is a program offered to students who have a passion for writing. During the program students will learn how to create images that move readers, write descriptively without using adjective or adverbs, effectively use metaphors and similes, write meaningful dialogue, and develop scenes and dramatic arcs. The Summer Musicianship Camp is a program for students in grades 5–7 who have a desire to learn more about the fundamentals of music. The program focuses on teaching music basics that students learn through attending classes in music theory and vocal and instrumental ensemble.

The Alabama school provides curricular consultation (mainly to schools outside of Alabama that are in the process of establishing a similar arts school) and provides numerous performances for students and the community at large. In addition to these activities, the school plans to establish an ongoing relationship with local schools in order to provide assistance with curricula and to foster a greater appreciation for the arts (J. Northrup, personal communication, December 13, 2005).

## Evaluation Practices of Residential Academies

Evaluation in the public residential academies takes place in a regular and ongoing fashion and is valued by the schools' directors. However, because these schools were created for specific purposes, often drawing top students from local school districts, and because the level of support for them within a specific state is fluid, sometimes becoming quite volatile, the manner of the evaluation processes and their outcomes tend to be treated as proprietary information. For example, two of the schools (NCSM and Indiana Academy) hired professionals from outside their respective schools to conduct very thorough evaluations that led to significant changes in practices. The reports were generally used for in-house decisions. Although similar practices are engaged in more traditional public school settings, these evaluations differ in that it is generally believed that the residential academies have historically been at greater risk than other public schools for political attacks based upon evaluation data. Generally speaking, the longer the school has existed, the less vulnerable to this form of attack they have become.

Despite the possibility of attacks based upon evaluation data, the use of various evaluation efforts to improve practice is found in all of the schools. Some of the evaluation approaches are common, such as publishing certain accountability data required of all public schools, while other practices are tailored to the needs of a specific school. A few examples of each category are presented below. In addition to the required practice of publishing information about drop-out rates, attendance, and performance on state tests, including the state's high school graduation examination, the residential academies carefully monitor the quality of instruction and practices of residential employees. The processes employed to gather data ranges from traditional and mechanistic approaches, to more holistic, to somewhat informal practices of data gathering. For example, classroom observations of teachers, reviews of teaching materials and student products, reviews of the course syllabi, and student ratings of teachers are but a few of the approaches used to consider the quality of instruction. The commitment to improve instruction and other primary practices of these schools is obvious and has existed since each school began.

In addition to these common approaches, some schools consider the outcomes of instruction by analyzing standardized test scores, student products, and garnering feedback from teachers, students, and other stakeholders as to the performance of the students over time. Follow-up data are gathered from alumni that monitor their progress through postsecondary education and into their professions. The alumni also provide feedback about the effectiveness and appropriateness of the education they received while attending the school.

These less common evaluation practices are difficult to describe due to their idiosyncratic nature, and to the fact that the information gathered is typically not published. However, a few examples include those practices that attend to the categories of the three models. For example, the Model Two schools tend to emphasize the products of their students more than the Model One and Model Three schools. A second tailored practice is predictable on the basis of whether the residential academy is on the campus of a college or university. If so, then they tend to be a part of the university's expectations for ongoing evaluation. For example, the Indiana Academy complies with the Ball State University policy that all classes must be evaluated (rated) by the students who attend them. Those schools that are independent of colleges and universities tend to be more involved with their respective state departments of education and therefore tend to develop their evaluation practice with those influences in mind. The evaluation practices of the residential academies have been put into place to improve the schools and to report accountability data as required by law. These efforts have been ongoing and are used to move practice to become increasingly more effective.

## Benefits and Concerns of Attending a Public Residential Academy

The most important aspect of all the programs is that they provide an opportunity to gifted students that would not otherwise be available. All the programs offer unique environments, curricula, and challenges that could not be obtained in a traditional high school environment. The continued growth and success of these schools suggest that they are instrumental in the education of the gifted, but little research has been conducted to demonstrate the long-term benefit of these types of programs.

From his yearlong ethnographic study of a residential academy described in his book, *Nurturing Talent in High School: Life in the Fast Lane*, Coleman (2005) identifies numerous benefits to attending such a school. In a recent interview, he describes those benefits. Having high-ability, high-potential adolescents around each other 24 hours a day allows for unique interactions, exchange of ideas, and building of friendships that would otherwise not be available. This type of interaction between gifted students in a residential setting accelerates their own intellectual development and fosters the motivation for learning and creativity. Being around other adolescents to whom they are more similar than the traditional high school student allows the gifted adolescent to feel more accepted and not experience the same peer hierarchy that exists in traditional schools. Attending a residential program at a new school allows a gifted student to start anew because she does not come in with a history. Students are judged solely on their interactions at that school and not on what occurred at their home school. This allows the gifted adolescent to begin the school year on the same academic level as all of his peers. Without worrying where to fit in, creative ideas can flow more freely (see Chapter 6).

The teachers in a residential school are available the majority of the time, and because some have evening office hours, students can meet with them as soon as a problem arises or a new idea is generated. Another advantage is that the format of courses is similar to college courses, typically offering either Monday/Wednesday/Friday courses or Tuesday/Thursday courses, which prepare students for the college environment. Because the gifted students who attend these programs often come from all over the state (or country, if the school accepts out-of-state students), the gifted adolescent has the opportunity to interact with a diverse group of individuals who he would not have had the opportunity to interact with in a traditional high school. This exposure to adolescents with diverse talents and backgrounds broadens adolescents' perceptions of what being gifted means and facilitates a deeper appreciation for the various forms of ability that exist in the gifted community. Finally, residential schools have the opportunity to give their students more flexibility than would be allowed in a traditional high school. Customizing academic programs to fit the needs of each student provides more challenges and unique opportunities in order to accelerate the gifted students' intellectual growth.

Although there are many benefits to attending a residential gifted program, residential programs also have limitations. If a residential school adopts a strict Advanced Placement model, they run into the same problem as nonresidential schools: depth is sacrificed for breadth. This may be problematic because the focus is not on learning and applying the knowledge, but rather on how to pass a test to receive credit or placement in college. Although gifted residential programs provide numerous benefits not available in a traditional school, they are not appropriate for every student. Many students will not be ready to live away from home and friends, do not want to give up their other school activities, or have other needs that would be better met in a nonresidential setting. For these gifted adolescents, moving to a residential program could be less than ideal and could even have a negative effect on their educational goals. Therefore, although gifted residential programs should continue to be one of the options for the gifted adolescent, they are by no means the only appropriate option.

## Conclusion

For more than 40 years, the three models of public residential academies have offered a powerful, positive experience for many gifted adolescents, while at the same time providing outreach services for nonresidential students and teachers. The most critical aspect of the experience of attending one of these academies is an outcome of a large group of self-selected gifted students living together. This creates a special environment that cannot be duplicated without the residential component. While it is difficult to convey the power that these residential academies have in the development of their students, in a recent conversation about his year of living at a residential academy, Dr. Laurence J. Coleman declared that "Magic happens when we get highly qualified teachers who love their subjects together with academically gifted students in a residential setting."

The scope of the positive influence of the academies extends far beyond the students in residence. The outreach activities engaged in by many of the schools have extended the resources of the individual academy campus, and connected resources such as museums to students across the U.S. Tens of thousands of teachers, and hundreds of thousands of students not in residence have benefited directly from the work of the personnel who make up the residential academies.

## References

Boothe, D., Sethna, B. N., Stanley, J. C., & Colgate, S. O. (1999). Special opportunities for exceptionally able high school students: A description of eight residential early-college-entrance programs. *Journal of Secondary Gifted Education, 10,* 195–202.

Borden, M. F. (1998). Fanning the spark of exceptional creativity. *Journal of Secondary Gifted Education, 9,* 51–57.

Coleman, L. J. (2005). *Nurturing talent in high school: Life in the fast lane.* New York: Teachers College Press.

Cross, T. L., & Burney, V. (2005). High ability, rural, and poor: Lessons learned from Project Aspire and implications for school counselors. *Journal of Secondary Gifted Education 16,* 148–156.

Cross, T. L., Margison, J., & Williams, D. (2003). The Indiana Academy for Science, Mathematics, and Humanities. *Gifted Education Communicator, 34*(3 & 4), 44–46, 62–63.

Eilber, C. R. (1987). The North Carolina School of Science and Mathematics. *Phi Delta Kappan, 68,* 773–777.

Illinois Math and Science Academy. (2005). *Problem-based learning opportunities 2005.* Retrieved June 12, 2006, from http://imsa.edu/programs/pbln/institutes/sleuths/summersleuths_2005_Brochure.pdf

Kolloff, P. B. (2003). State-supported residential high schools. In N. Colangelo & G. Davis (Eds.), *Handbook of gifted education* (3rd ed., pp. 238–246). Needham Heights, MA: Allyn & Bacon.

Sethna, B. N., Wickstrom, C. D., Boothe, D., & Stanley, J. C. (2001). The Advanced Academy of Georgia: Four years as a residential early-college-entrance program. *Journal of Secondary Gifted Education, 13*, 11–22.

Stanley, J. C. (1991). A better model for residential high schools for talented youth. *Phi Delta Kappan, 72*, 471–473.

Stephens, K. R. (1999). Residential math and science high schools: A closer look. *Journal of Secondary Gifted Education, 10*, 85–92.

# Insights Into the Culture
# of a Residential High School

*Laurence J. Coleman*

## Introduction

Programs for promoting the development of talent in children are not new. All involve placing children with potential with knowledgeable adults. The definition of the terms *children with potential* and *knowledgeable adults* varies among educational programs, but successful programs honor the tacit secret of gifted education—place students with high ability and motivation with teachers who love their content and want to teach it. The secret became more evident when I spent a year in a public residential high school for children with academic talent. In that setting, I observed a school culture that was different from other public high schools I have observed, characterized by an accelerated pace of learning and living.

The purpose of this chapter is to share insights about residential educational programs that provide enriched and accelerated learning opportunities to high school children with potential academic talent. More specifically, I discuss a public school program that is highly selective, is 2 years in length, and has a residential component. My insights come from living in that environment for a year while I conducted an ethnography (Coleman, 2005). Although I studied one school, I have learned from audiences at conference presentations, both nationally and internationally, that my comments are more universal than would seem warranted from the study of a single school. Nevertheless, my insights are my own. It is up to you, the reader, to make a judgment about the trustworthiness of my judgments.

In this chapter, I describe one residential high school to establish the background for my assertions about such programs. I summarize what I know about highly selective high school programs, describe what it is like being a student in such a program, describe what students learn nonacademically in such programs, and offer 11 insights into the culture of the school.

## Summarizing What I Know About Selective High School Programs

Children who participate in these highly selective enriched and accelerated high school programs learn more academic content than we normally expect of chronological peers (Kolloff, 2003). I am less certain about quantifying how much more they learn than peers who choose not to be in such programs. Doing that kind of research is difficult because of self-selection and the variation among American schools and the school populations. I know that children who attend selective high schools are quite successful in gaining admission to postsecondary schools. The students relish being in the company of high-ability peers (Coleman, 2001). They learn more than the academic material in these special programs (Coleman, 2002). Limited research has been done on the nonacademic effects of special programs (Csikszentmihalyi, Rathunde, & Whalen, 1993), yet anecdotal evidence suggests nonacademic outcomes might be powerful indicators of the worth of special programs (Coleman & Cross, 1993; Coleman, 1995). Summer programs of shorter duration report findings similar to mine (Enersen, 1993).

### What Is It Like to Be a Student in the School?

Entering the environment of a residential public high school means students encounter an institution organized around premises about them, about learning, and about educational outcomes. Some premises are explicit in the mission statement of the schools; others are tacit and embedded in the school culture. The premises capture the nature of the programs.

Explicit premises are:

- students are smart capable learners;
- students are committed to academic learning and eager for challenges;
- students are in a resource-rich environment;
- high achievement, creativity, and excellence are valued;
- postsecondary education is in the students' future;
- students are responsible for making good choices about the use of their time and coursework; and
- residential issues are complementary to academic issues.

These explicit premises make it apparent that much is expected of students. The students' strengths are to be nurtured. They are supposed to be active in their own learning. The school provides rich learning opportunities that the students are expected to seize and run with by studying hard, completing assignments and preparing for college, which is only 2 years or less away. The transition to college is on everyone's mind. Homework is ever-present as are the many nonacademic issues that emerge in a residential community. The days are filled with activities. Time moves quickly. One must manage time in the face of competing demands. Choices have to be made that fit the situation and are consistent with a student's values and personality. Both of these are in a state of flux. In short, students are changing, and life in these schools is very busy.

However, embedded in the culture are less obvious, tacit ideas that capture much about the *reality* of the program for students. They are:

- academics come first;
- the life of the mind is prized;
- you have no history—you can become what you want;
- homework advances learning;

- teachers value their own subject matter over others' content; and
- diversity in thought, actions, and values is desirable.

The tacit premises modify the meaning of the explicit premises. Giving oneself over to learning content and associated skills is valuable in its own right and worth the effort. Social interests and athletic activities are secondary. They take a back seat to academics. Homework is the way students acquire more information and skills than can be taught directly in a class. Amongst all the coursework, most teachers expect students to love their content as much as they do. My content comes first, teachers indicate.

Diverse ideas and lifestyles become apparent in residential life. Diversity is to be appreciated and actively supported. The range of variation in ethnicity, race, religion, and sexual orientation fuels the generation of a mixture of ideas that clash and, in conjunction with rigorous academics, propel students toward advanced learning, original ideas, and performances that demonstrate both.

What a student does in the present is preparation for the future. It makes no difference what your history was, now is the time to make something of yourself. College is where "the hard work pays off."

### What Do These Premises Mean in Terms of the Actual Life of a Student?

Life is filled with competing demands for your time. Attention is pulled in many directions by encountering new ideas, new content, and new values. Diversity adds more distractions that fuel the dissonance between one's own views and those of peers and admired teachers. The pace of life quickens under this onslaught of ideas and experiences. Nothing is really finished because more can be learned, and another assignment waits to be completed. Time becomes a precious commodity. Homework requires making decisions about what to do next and about how much time to devote to it. Meanwhile, reminders of future transition points are just around the corner—a second year, visiting colleges, applying to college, and graduation.

Living with strangers introduces more pressures. New strong friendships are made, often with others of diverse backgrounds one would not have associated with in the home school. The presence of minority peers enables students to experiment with more expanded social relationships. Life in the school is so involving, so interesting. Students ask, "Where do I fit into all of this? Do I belong here?" Some students answer these questions with apparent ease, others struggle with them, and still others are never quite comfortable with their place in the school. Most of the latter leave at some point, but some stay because they find something intoxicating about being in the school. They know that whatever "it" is will not be found in their home school.

### What Do Students Learn Nonacademically in Such Programs?

Obviously, students learn more than academic content and associated skills in these special residential programs. Some outcomes are positive, some less so. In a residential program, the academic and the residential become fused in the sense that the former is carried out and interpreted by students in the context of the latter. For 24 hours a day, a student is surrounded by academic activity, academic conversation, and high-ability peers. In this sense, academics are inescapable. A student's sense of self or agency is what is learned. This comes about because of the intense environment in which they have placed themselves.

When they graduate, students know they can adapt and survive in a high-energy, fast-paced environment. They have met many intellectual and social challenges and handled them successfully. The intellectual challenges have not only been in the form of new ideas, values, and people, but also a rigorous academic program and the volume of homework. Students learn how to interact and compete with bright peers in a rigorous academic setting. They learn how to study and how to adjust to the varying demands of teachers. The students have experienced living in a culture more diverse than most places. They have encountered ideas and values that conflict with their own, have had to examine their own views in light of those differences, and have been able to establish themselves as individuals within the culture. Furthermore, the students have left home, adjusted to living in an institutional setting, and made a new home. They have learned how to navigate rules, how to advocate for oneself in an institution, and how to meet one's own needs. As a result, they become different persons, special high school graduates who know they can deal with complexity and high demands and make choices that enable them to be themselves. I speculate that this outcome is most valuable for minority and low-socioeconomic students.

## Insights About the Culture

Characterizing the environment of a public residential school sets the background for insights about the school. My statements are not all that can be said, but represent my understanding of issues and experiences in this school. Any generalizations the readers draw from the text are their own.

### Insight #1: The Fast-Paced Nature of the School Is Co-Created by the Participants

The fast-paced nature of the school is the product of interactions between the nature of the institution and the nature of the students. By using the term *nature*, I intend no statement of why this is the situation; rather I am simply stating that is the way they are. Neither school nor student is solely responsible for the pace of the school. The school provides an enriched and accelerative curriculum. Experts with high standards teach the fast-paced classes. The demand to complete numerous homework assignments and meet deadlines increases the feeling of rapid movement in students.

The students arrive wanting to learn new material, possessing personal standards for performance, feeling dissatisfied with the lack of academic challenge of their home school, and being inexperienced in doing homework. These students' orientations intensify the total experience for them and contribute to the faster pace of the school.

I interviewed students to uncover their views of the sources of the accelerated pace. Many students welcomed the pressures, some were disoriented by it for a time, and a small minority struggled continuously. When asked how they would account for this accelerating pace, students surprised me by attributing the source to themselves. They recognized the school placed demands on them, but the quick pace was accelerated by their own desires and standards of performance. Thus, I regard the fast-paced setting to be co-constructed by students' desires and interests and the school faculty and administration's interest in promoting advanced learning.

### Insight #2: The Program Is Intoxicating and, in Some Ways, Addicting to Students

Certainly, this is a strange statement to make about a school, because the metaphor of addiction is normally disturbing. I have already asserted that the fast-paced nature of the school is fueled by the orientations to self and the school. Here, I introduce a new element to the story—the emotional lure of the school. The context of the school heightens student awareness of life. Various elements blend to intensify the experience. The academic classes excite students, as they feel engaged and overwhelmed with new ideas, many for the first time. The challenges presented by the curriculum and by living in close proximity with strangers produce emotional highs and lows as the students more or less successfully overcome the homework demands and confront their personal limits repeatedly. The thrill of late night and weekend bull sessions about the meaning of life and interpersonal relationships are special experiences that students mention. The openness and freedom of the school means almost everything is up for questioning. In a sense, so much is happening that students are often on the brink of a crisis. The intensity sometimes makes students want to escape, and at the same time they miss the school and eagerly return after holiday breaks. The school has become a special refuge where they can experiment in a protective environment. At graduation the students talk of how the school was so challenging, and graduates say proudly that "nothing comes close" to this place.

### Insight #3: New Students Are Shocked by What They Encounter

Students want to be at the school. They had to go to considerable effort to apply and believe they are ready for this different educational challenge. However, they are unprepared for three experiences.

The first is living together for 24 hours a day, 7 days a week in a relatively impersonal institution. Rules are promulgated for the group that would not apply back home. The familiarity of home is replaced by lack of privacy and the strangeness of roommates with unconventional ideas and tastes. The freedom and mobility of home, often with a car and flexible time limits, is traded for curfews and no car. Group think, well intended as it is, replaces personalization.

The second is the diversity of so many bright people, ideas, and values beyond what was anticipated. Many students came seeking more diversity and found more than they bargained for in the school. There is more diversity in this small public school than anywhere else in the state they reside. The openness of the environment to creativity, lifestyles, and attitudes is another aspect of the diversity that is disorienting and sometimes exhilarating.

The third shock is that academics come first; social concerns are less important. In the local high school, there was no conflict. There was a slower pace, enough time to do it all, and the demands were less rigorous. Decisions about prioritizing your activities did not create conflict. At the special school, the choices are everywhere.

Not all students feel as unprepared. Some who have been to camp or away from home in special programs may have an easier time with the residential component. Others who come from communities with more diversity are less amazed. But, having to place academics first is a shock to all.

## Insight #4: Being Stressed by the Demands of the School Is a Matter of Perception

Feeling stressed is endemic. Being unprepared for what you encounter contributes to the stress. However, the primary stressor is homework. A reasonable syllogism might be: The more homework one has, the more stress will be experienced. However, this idea is incorrect. Students of comparable ability with similar schedules and amount of homework experience stress differently. Furthermore, students who seem to have more homework than their peers are not always the most stressed students. Some students say the amount is about right; others claim there is too much work to ever finish. So, even the amount of homework is not an objective concept. The number of problems, number of pages to read, or the complexity of a project could be quantified. However, that misses the point. The students interpret the situation. There is not a simple algorithm that can state the relationship between feeling stress and the amount of homework. Trying to find the appropriate amount of stress for children at the school is a foolhardy enterprise because there is neither a universal definition of stress nor agreement about what is too much homework. In other words, perception is reality in judging the amount of homework that may contribute to stress.

## Insight #5: The Students and the Institution Are in Conflict With Mainstream America

The school values the life of the mind and diversity. American society is basically anti-intellectual and values material over abstract ideas. American society voices a diverse perspective, but the culture wars of 2004 reveal a deep disparity in the population. The school encourages diversity of thought and originality.

Questioning conventional thoughts and traditions encourages the students to find their own way. Novel ideas are appreciated. Going deeply into a topic so that the subtleties are revealed is a regular part of the students' conversations. Opinions are valued and are to be buttressed by data and reason. Originality is encouraged. Thus, conversations at the school converge at points where logic, emotion, and belief meet. The result is that the students are encouraged to question who they are, what they believe, and what they want. At the same time the school itself is under pressure to be as conventional as possible, even while the students are moving to a less conventional way of being.

### Insight #6: Incomplete Understanding of Advanced Development Distorts the Life of the School

I use the term *distort* to emphasize the idea that the school has policies and procedures that paradoxically work against the development of the students they serve. I trace this issue to the presence of naïve notions about development. Growth may be natural, but it is not harmonious and effortless. Development is episodic in that it lurches forward, plateaus, sometimes retreats, and then repeats the process. In the case of children with high academic potential, these episodes come faster and may be more irregular. These students achieve at advanced levels earlier than their age peers outside the school. The students often drive themselves toward these advanced levels. Their sharp focus and expenditure of energy unnerves adults who have not had similar experiences. A mismatch between intellectual under-standing and emotional understanding is often evident in these students.

The mismatch in level of functioning and the intense commitment to learning are worrisome and mysterious. The school's response is to put in place policies to "help" the chil-dren have a fuller life. The conventional meaning of those terms is at odds with who the students are. This is where distortion takes place. Resolving the problems of advanced development is neither to make children balanced nor to hide them from themselves, but rather it is helping them understand the inter-nal forces that drive them to excel and the resulting conflict in their lives. Being talented means students will be out of balance, because pursuing a talent takes one to the outer limits of know-ing or doing, where one is a minority. Being on the outer edge of a body of knowledge means the person is doing something that few others are likely to achieve. Having membership in a minority group is not an unnatural position, but rather the normal consequence of using your potential, following your interest, and developing a talent.

### Insight #7: Educational Malnourishment Is a Recurrent Issue

This issue has particular relevance for students of high potential who have had inadequate educational opportunities because of the schools they attend. *Educational malnourishment* is a term reserved for schools, not students, although the outcome is seen in students in the form of low achievement and inadequate preparation for advanced work. The students who frequently fit this category are members of culturally and linguistically diverse groups, students from impoverished homes, and rural students. Observable differences in academic achievement and functioning can be seen between students from advantaged and malnourished schools. The pernicious effect of educational malnourishment is that academic differences between students are interpreted as being a matter of ability rather than a matter of opportunity. Unfortunately, the students from malnourished schools, as well as other advantaged students and faculty, make this interpretation.

Two effects are real in this situation. The first is that ill-prepared students cannot handle the academic demands at the time they are expected. The second is that selection for special programs is hampered because students do not perform as well as they are capable. The latter is more of a concern for programs that try to be representative of the larger society.

The most obvious example of ill preparation is in courses such as math, which have a tight developmental sequence of skills and knowledge that requires mastery of the basics before one can do advanced work. Students must pass the prerequisites for admission into advanced courses. Two students of comparable potential may have completely different educational experiences, because one arrives with background skills and knowledge and the other is educationally malnourished. The special school has to decide how to deal with this divergence in educational readiness. The students from malnourished circumstances are not ready for advanced work, and the advantaged students are. Waiting for the groups to equalize makes no pedagogical sense. Yet, given the restricted time for being in a program, the malnourished students have a limited chance of catching up. At graduation, the advantaged group's members are ready to take on more advanced educational opportunities than the malnourished group's members. The result is that inequities of opportunity are perpetuated. Future opportunities are open to some, not all, and the interpretation that "those others are better than me" or "those others are not as smart" is continued and poisons the social fabric of our society. Procedures need to be put in place to remedy this situation.

### Insight #8: A Rigorous Academic Curriculum Is the Hallmark of the Program, Yet Its Definition Remains Unsettled

Academic rigor is bound up with concepts of challenge, learning rate, depth of inquiry, and choice. The relationship among these terms is fluid. The school asks students to complete large amounts of schoolwork in a relatively short period of time. The incessant deadlines challenge students to complete assignments. Students become more concerned with getting work done than learning the content. Students often regard the amount of homework as simply more work and devise strategies for dealing with the overload (Coleman, 2002). The amount of work creates the appearance of rigor, but this is not true for the students.

If academic rigor is not equivalent to the amount of work, then how does learning rate, depth of learning, and choice fit in? Speed of learning leads to rigor when students move on to more complex content. A faster rate of learning in itself is not rigor, but acceleration is useful in the early stages of mastering a domain because students move beyond the basics to the primary issues of a field where rigor resides. Dealing with primary issues moves students closer to depth of inquiry, but this depth doesn't occur unless the assignment requires students to analyze, synthesize, create, reinterpret, or evaluate complex information. Sometimes students are given choices of assignments as a way to increase rigor and as a way to be responsive to student interests. Choice only contributes to academic rigor when the alternatives are complex and the student academic products invoke the qualities of depth (Hertzog, 1997).

The faculty members deal with issues of academic rigor by the nature of their assignments, tests, and teaching strategies. In the special school, although it is not unanimous, the pattern differs for the natural sciences and mathematics versus the humanities. Faculty in mathematics and sciences use tests, often Advanced Placement tests, as the standard for rigor. The humanities use projects and papers where academic rigor is set by the kind of assignment and the standards for judging that kind of scholarship. Students often were confused by the two standards. The external standard of the natural sciences and math was easier for students to see than the internal standards embedded in the discourse of the humanities. Oddly, my interviews of students suggested that the math and science coursework was judged as more rigorous, yet the students reported the so-called less rigorous humanities courses made them think more deeply. Students seemed puzzled by this apparent paradox. How can thinking deeply not be a sign of rigor? Academic rigor is not easy to define. Establishing a clear easy standard is problematic, and that is why the meaning of rigor remains unsettled at the school.

### Insight #9: The Reason Students State for Learning Content Is Rarely the Intrinsic Value That the Faculty Wants to Foster

The reasons that students offer to describe why they learn waver among three points: instrumentality, personal growth, and getting it done. Instrumentality is the reason given when a student learns something because it helps her toward a distant goal, such as admission to medical school or winning a prize. Personal growth is the reason given when one is learning to fulfill a personal interest in the subject. Getting it done is the reason given when completion of the required assignment is the goal. All of these reasons produce observable achievements.

A student may also be learning for more than one reason. I see the three reasons as points in space with students gravitating to locations that are among the competing reasons rather than toward one reason. The students' reasons are supported by their view of the reality of the school. That is why when the reasons are ranked in terms of frequency from "most used" to "least often used," I found this pattern: getting it done, instrumentality, personal interest. Urgency is the most powerful force underlying the stated reasons. Getting it done is a realistic response to many assignments and deadlines. Students know that high achievement is their ticket to a good college and scholarships. Instrumentality is consonant with this view of reality. Learning for a personal interest is the third reason and the wild card reason, because it makes claim to the students' time in irregular ways.

Students see themselves as subject matter folks, that is they make statements such as: I am a science person; I am a humanities person; I am a computer person; I am a language person; I am a history person; I am a literature person; and so forth. These self-designations are indicators of students' preferences for content. The labels advertise the potency behind learning for personal interest. That force reveals itself in the selection of topics and the extent to which some students devote time to projects.

The school encourages students to follow their interests, but usually after the fact. If a child's schedule or class assignments permit it, then personal learning influences achievement. But, it is not the primary force. The school promotes all the reasons, but the fullness of the curriculum and the schedule promotes instrumentality and getting it done. The faculty prefers the learning of content for its own sake, but have difficulty advancing that goal within the structure of the program.

Some students make time to follow their own interest. They postpone required work to "do my own thing." I discovered two groups who did this. The first group basically accepted the school's intended outcomes but then ignored them. The

second group was more active in working against the school. I
call them the academic resistors. These students want to learn
and socialize with their peers, yet do not like the pressure to
make decisions about their unfinished future. The academic
resistors are successful students who will sacrifice the perfect
paper or the top grade to play and experiment with ideas and
peers. They seem to find the rush toward a career to be more
than what they want. They seem to have a love–hate relationship with the school in that they are attracted by the challenge
and activity, but resistant to academics that, in their view, push
them prematurely to making decisions about their future when
they are in the process of discovering who they are.

### Insight #10: A Special Residential High School Is Not for Everyone

This fact is evident by the withdrawals from the school,
as well as the way students talk about the place. Being smart
is a necessary quality but insufficient for staying at the school.
Students have to have several characteristics: persistence, shared
interests, and resilience. Persistence refers to being able to keep
working in the face of difficult competing assignments and
unsophisticated writing and study skills.

Shared interests means the students' interests are supported
by the school and peers, academically and nonacademically.
For example, if a student is interested in 4-H, football, or playing music, the school provides few mechanisms for supporting
those interests. It would be better for the student not to go to
the school.

Resilience means the ability to recover from mistakes. The
mistakes may be academic, such as not studying enough for a
test or misinterpreting an assignment, or nonacademic, such as
socializing too long or miscommunication with a peer about
their relationship. These mistakes can upset the student, but the
student must adapt in order to stay in the program.

The pace of the school impels students to move forward and
not dwell on shortcomings and mistakes. These three qualities
help the student live in the fast-paced environment, but they do

not guarantee a successful experience. The school could assist by communicating this information to potential applicants.

### Insight #11: "Who Owns the Kids?" Is an Issue Peculiar to Residential Programs

Two kinds of staff work in the school: academic and residential. Each staff has its own notion of professionalism and role. These notions translate into what is in the "best interests" of the children. The meaning of "best interests" is dissimilar. The teachers value content learning and the pursuit of knowledge at all costs and want to share their excitement with students. The counselors' values differ. They want students to have a full life in which the complexity of the human experience is appreciated and enjoyed. They offer a special program called wellness, which encapsulates this belief, and encourages students to have more "balanced" lives. These differences result in one group thinking the other encourages students in the wrong ways. Few members of either group seem to be able to understand the other's position. Teachers find it difficult to believe a child should stop studying, and counselors find it difficult to believe that a child could get joy out of studying. An interesting side note to this issue is that I have been told by attendees at conference presentations about life in the special school that the same problem happens in their academic year or shorter-term summer residential programs.

## Final Remarks

In this essay I have described the nature of a special residential and academic program and the insights I gleaned from living in that school. In my view, the tacit secret of gifted education is upheld again—ultimately what happens in this special program repeatedly is that students with academic potential and motivation meet masters of content who want to encourage learning of their content field. The student and master develop a relationship that feeds each of their needs, benefits both, and eventually may benefit the discipline by producing a new expert and benefit the society by producing new knowledge and solutions to intractable problems.

My account shows that placing children in special programs introduces new strains into their lives. The nature of the institution and the nature of the students interact to produce a fast-paced learning environment. Students learn academic content and nonacademic content. They graduate with a new sense of their agency by having been able to deal with diversity, deadlines, and dense curriculum. The special school resides in a matrix of people and institution where the purposes and goals of the school conflict and complement the values of our society. Life is rarely routine in the school. I recommend that more of these schools be created to enable more academically talented learners to face the challenges of self-creation.

## References

Coleman, L. J. (2001). "A rag quilt": Social relationships among students in a special high school. *Gifted Child Quarterly, 45,* 164–173.

Coleman, L. J. (2002). Adjusting to the shock of studying. *Journal of Secondary Gifted Education, 14,* 39–52.

Coleman, L. J. (2005). *Nurturing talent in high school: Life in the fast lane.* New York: Teachers College Press.

Coleman, L. J., & Cross, T. C. (1993). Relationships between programming practices and outcomes in a summer residential school for gifted adolescents. *Journal for the Education of the Gifted, 16,* 420–441.

Coleman, L. J. (1995). The power of specialized environments in the development of giftedness: The need for research on social context. *Gifted Child Quarterly, 39,* 171–176.

Csikszentmihalyi, M., Rathunde, K., & Whalen, S. (1993). *Talented teenagers: The roots of success and failure.* New York: Cambridge University Press.

Enersen, D. (1993). Summer residential programs: Academics and beyond. *Gifted Child Quarterly, 37,* 169–176.

Hertzog, N. (1997). Open-ended activities and their role in maintaining challenge. *Journal for the Education of the Gifted, 21,* 54–81.

Kolloff, P. (2003). State-supported residential high schools. In N. Colangelo & G. Davis (Eds.), *Handbook of gifted education* (3rd ed., pp. 238–246). Needham Heights, MA: Allyn & Bacon.

# Counseling Highly Gifted Students to Utilize Supplemental Educational Opportunities: Using the SET Program as a Model

*Linda E. Brody*

## Introduction

Jonah scored double 800s on the SAT as a 13-year-old eighth grader—a rare occurrence even among top talent search participants and an indication of extremely advanced cognitive abilities. While his parents and teachers had recognized that he was bright, the level of ability demonstrated by Jonah's scores surprised them, and they worried about how to meet his needs. It was clear that a typical high school program would not provide the level of challenge Jonah needed. At the same time, he did not feel ready to enter college full-time. Ultimately, with support from the Johns Hopkins Study of Exceptional Talent (SET), a program was developed that combined accelerated learning with a variety of rigorous supplemental opportunities.

For his core high school program, Jonah focused on Advanced Placement (AP) courses. By the time he graduated from high school, he had earned scores of 5 on 15 AP examinations. He accomplished this by bypassing prerequisites and supplementing AP courses offered by his high school with several others via distance education and summer programs. Accelerated in math, Jonah completed AP Calculus in ninth grade and followed it with college math courses for the next 3 years at a local university.

Jonah's learning was not limited to his coursework, as he also took advantage of a variety of extracurricular activities and supplemental programs. In school, Jonah was editor of his school paper, on the debate team, active in Model UN, had a role in the school play, and played violin in the orchestra. Not only did he enjoy these activities, he also took on responsibilities that honed his leadership skills and provided a way for him to relate to peers.

Outside of school, Jonah attended prestigious summer programs where he took courses not available in his school and engaged in research activities. He particularly valued the summer program that paired him with a mentor who guided him in doing original research in mathematics; now Jonah is preparing a paper for publication on his findings. He also participated in national and international math and science competitions, earning much recognition for his efforts. In addition to the challenges that these opportunities provided, Jonah met intellectual peers (i.e., other students who shared his abilities and interests) through these venues.

As a result of these experiences, Jonah entered college feeling that he had been well challenged during his high school years and had gained a solid background in a wide variety of content areas. In addition, his math knowledge and research skills rivaled that of many graduate students, and the university he chose to attend was willing to place him ahead appropriately in mathematics courses. He had also developed solid social skills and strong leadership abilities. Overall, the combination of in- and out-of-school educational opportunities that Jonah selected seemed to serve him extremely well.

## SMPY and the Growth of Opportunities

Jonah's scenario would not have been possible 35 years ago when Dr. Julian Stanley established the Study of Mathematically Precocious Youth (SMPY) at Johns Hopkins University, because few of the opportunities Jonah availed himself of existed then.

At that time, schools were extremely resistant to modifying their programs for academically talented students, the AP program was pretty much limited to high school seniors, distance education was confined to correspondence courses that were not widely respected, few summer programs existed that addressed the academic needs of advanced high school students, and rigorous competitions such as the Westinghouse Science Talent Search (now sponsored by Intel) were dominated by students who attended relatively few high schools. Because so few options existed for meeting their academic needs, the first prodigies identified by Stanley in the early 1970s entered Johns Hopkins University at extremely young ages, in some cases without attending high school at all (Stanley, 1974).

It was never Stanley's first choice to enroll his prodigies in college full-time, however, and, although follow-up studies attested to the success of these students in college and afterward (e.g., see Stanley, 1985), he remained concerned that radical acceleration might not be the best vehicle for meeting their social and emotional needs. He also worried that, while they could move ahead in their area of strength (e.g., mathematics), rapid grade advancement might limit radical accelerants from gaining the breadth of content knowledge important for ultimate satisfaction in life. So, Stanley set about to find ways to provide appropriate challenge for gifted students without having them enter college full-time at too young an age. He founded SMPY, as he said, to "find youths who reason exceptionally well mathematically and to provide them the special, supplemental, accelerative 'smorgasbord' of educational opportunities they sorely need and, in my opinion, richly deserve for their own optimal development and the good of society" (Stanley, 2005, p. 9). This smorgasbord, which includes a variety of ways for students to access advanced content, is described in numerous publications (e.g., Benbow, 1979; Lupkowski-Shoplik, Benbow, Assouline, & Brody, 2003; Southern, Jones, & Stanley, 1993).

Utilizing above-grade-level aptitude tests to identify students with advanced reasoning abilities, SMPY experimented with numerous program models. Research evaluating these programs demonstrated that students with advanced cognitive abilities could master content in much less time than is typically expected and also validated the importance of bringing students together with their intellectual peers (Stanley, 1996). In addition to providing direct services, SMPY counseled students to take advantage of challenging educational opportunities in their schools, communities, and elsewhere (see Stanley, 1989, for recommendations for counseling gifted students).

SMPY's counseling spurred participation, and participation increased the demand for programs. For example, students were advised to take AP classes before their senior year if they were ready earlier, and schools have gradually responded to these requests, allowing qualified students to take a greater number of AP courses before graduation and thus contributing to the growth in AP offerings at high schools around the country (Curry, MacDonald, & Morgan, 1999).

High-math scorers were encouraged to enroll in rigorous summer programs such as the Ross Program at Ohio State University, and many did so. Today, numerous summer math programs serve an increasing number of students seeking this form of academic enrichment. Similarly, students were encouraged to participate in contests and competitions, especially at the international level, and these events have been an important vehicle for intellectual stimulation for top students (Muratori et al., in press; Stanley, 1987). The number of available competitions and contests has also increased, as more students have recognized the value of these activities (see Karnes & Riley in this volume; also Karnes & Riley, 2005).

The scope of academic offerings grew dramatically with the establishment of university-based talent search programs at Johns Hopkins, Duke, and Northwestern Universities, the University of Denver, and elsewhere. Today, many thousands of students participate annually in residential summer programs or take distance education courses offered by the talent searches (see chapter by Olszewski-Kubilius in this volume; also Lupkowski-Shoplik et al., 2003; Touron, 2005).

Concern about young students entering college led to the establishment of early college entrance programs at a number of universities. These programs attempt to provide the social, emotional, and academic support considered to be crucial to the success of many young college entrants (Brody, Muratori, & Stanley, 2004; Sethna, Wickstrom, Boothe, & Stanley, 2001). Part-time college entrance has also been made more available to high school students through dual enrollment programs (McCarthy, 1999), and many gifted students have chosen this option in lieu of full-time early college entrance.

The growth in available opportunities during the past three decades—in the extracurricular activities, academic summer programs, distance education courses, part-time college courses, competitions, internships, and other learning opportunities that Jonah and students like him have been able to utilize—is clearly helping many gifted middle and high school students gain the experiences they need to achieve their potential. A key component to taking full advantage of these programs, however, is being knowledgeable about options and being encouraged to seek them out.

## The Study of Exceptional Talent

After founding the Center for Talented Youth (CTY) at Johns Hopkins University to administer talent searches and academic programs, Julian Stanley established a national search in 1980 for students who scored between 700 and 800 points on the math portion of the SAT before the age of 13. Believing that students with profoundly advanced reasoning abilities are most in need of a differentiated educational program and that they are at risk for social and emotional difficulties if they fail to interact with intellectual peers, Stanley hoped to provide the students who qualified for this group with the personalized counseling that he had offered to the early SMPY prodigies. He also felt strongly that it is important for the future of society that the talents of our most able problem solvers be developed.

In 1991, this initiative moved to CTY and became the Study of Exceptional Talent (SET). At that time, the program expanded to include high-verbal, as well as high-math scorers. More than 4,000 students have qualified for and joined SET since its inception, and approximately 300 new students qualify each year. Jonah's scores on the SAT made him eligible for SET, and the counseling and information he received helped guide his educational decision making. Research is also an important component of SET's work, as students are followed up and evaluated over time (Brody, 2005; Brody & Blackburn, 1996; Muratori et al., in press).

Although all of the students who qualify for SET exhibit extremely high cognitive abilities at the time they are identified, they differ in the profiles of their specific abilities, as well as in their interests, goals, values, maturity, and social skills (Brody & Blackburn, 1996). They also live all over the country (and, in some cases, in other countries) so that the resources available in their schools and communities vary tremendously. These differences result in SET students having differing educational needs and solutions, so that an individualized approach to counseling them is required (Brody, 2004, 2005).

While situations and solutions vary, some common elements are evident in SET's recommendations. The use of accelerative options is encouraged for these very bright students, particularly subject acceleration in the student's areas of strength (Colangelo, Assouline, & Gross, 2004; Southern & Jones, 1991). Articulation with school officials is important so that the student gets credit for any out-of-school experiences, not necessarily as credit toward graduation, but so that he or she does not have to repeat the course. Sometimes students decide a boarding school or full-time enrollment in college is the only solution for an unchallenging high school situation, but more often students stay in their home schools and request flexibility to be placed in more advanced courses, to be allowed to leave school early to take college courses, and/or to be granted credit for out-of-school experiences.

SET strongly encourages students to take advantage of supplemental programs outside of school, believing that these programs extend learning beyond the school day and school year, help develop talents, and can provide a way for students to meet and interact with intellectual peers. Thus, informing students about out-of-school programs is a key component of SET's services so that the students can then choose the programs most appropriate for developing their talents and achieving their goals. To this end, students are encouraged to increasingly take responsibility for their own education and make their own decisions. Thus, while SET does work with parents, counselors work directly with students as much as possible.

There are four components to SET's services: (1) providing individual counseling about educational options and choices, (2) providing information about supplemental opportunities and resources, (3) helping students connect with intellectual peers, and (4) exposing students to role models and mentors. These services combine to help students identify the strategies and resources they need to be academically challenged and socially and emotionally fulfilled during their precollege years, and to be prepared to excel in college and beyond.

### Educational Counseling

SET's staff provides counseling and advice to students and/ or their parents. This can take place in person or by phone or e-mail, and can range from answering specific questions to developing full learning plans. Jonah is one student who worked with a SET counselor throughout high school. Similarly, the student who wrote the following when she joined SET also received regular advice and support: "Because of the problems of language and culture, my parents can't give me any help. I am only 12 years old and have to make all decisions by myself. I really need SET's help with everything."

Some SET students request help in choosing a high school. For example, one student wrote in an e-mail: "My local school has such limited course offerings. Should I consider boarding school or go to college early? Or can I find enrichment opportunities so that I can stay home with my family during my high school years?" A SET counselor followed up with phone calls and helped her consider options. Ultimately, her choice was to supplement school offerings for the first 2 years of high school and then apply to her state's residential math and science magnet high school.

Another student struggled with a decision about whether to attend a prestigious New York City magnet school that required an hour's commute each way or to attend his local high school, which was good, but clearly did not have as many opportunities. SET helped him evaluate the pros and cons of both options, and he ultimately chose the magnet, although he was assured that he could supplement the local school program if he decided against the commute.

Once students choose their high school, they often still need help selecting courses and/or finding ways to access more advanced courses. For example, one student posed this question to SET: "My high school does not offer AP Computer Science or Calculus-based Physics. Is there a way I can learn such coursework on my own?" This student was encouraged to consider distance education courses in these subjects. Another student asked: "I am taking multivariate calculus as a 10th grader and my school has no more math courses; where can I get more math?" Online courses were an option for this student, but ultimately local college courses proved to be a better choice for him.

Students also seek advice with regard to accelerating in grade placement, and quite a few students who are identified for SET in seventh grade elect to skip eighth grade if they are particularly unchallenged by middle school and are socially and emotionally ready to be with older students. For example, one student inquired as follows, "I am a 7th grader but taking Algebra and Science with the 8th graders. What can I do about courses next year?" Skipping eighth grade and placing him in high school full-time gave him access to the more advanced high school curriculum.

Some students accelerate in subject matter until they ultimately run out of courses and enter college at younger-than-typical ages. One of these students reflected about her experience: "I was a 16 year old completing my sophomore year officially, but I was taking all AP courses with seniors that year. I was totally ready to move on to college with them and had no interest in staying behind with my age peers. I love college and it was the right decision for me."

SET members are invited to receive help with college selection, and this is particularly helpful to those whose parents are unfamiliar with the process such as the one who said: "My parents are immigrants and I am the first in my family to go to college . . . I need help with college planning." SET also puts students in touch with other SET members who attend the colleges under consideration, and provides letters of recommendations to colleges on behalf of its members.

Students often ask for help in finding particular programs or mentors. For example, one student said: "I am looking for a mentor in math who can prepare me for higher-level math competitions." A SET girl said, "I want to contribute more to society by doing community service but I don't know where to start," and a young man asked for help as follows: "I would like to do scientific research to prepare for science competitions, but my school does not even hold science fairs. How can I find opportunities on my own?" SET helped these students and others, including Jonah, who found his math mentor through a SET-recommended summer internship. SET's counselors talk knowledgeably to students about competitions, summer programs, study abroad opportunities, and other options they are considering, and/or put them in touch with others who have attended these programs.

Social and emotional issues arise often with this population. The need for peers is a major concern among new SET members who express a desire to meet other SET students or, as one student said, "I would like to meet others like myself." One of the girls asked, "How can I be gifted and also be cool and have friends and have a social life?" SET provides students with access to counselors who understand the difficulties many gifted students experience with such issues as finding peers, dealing with perfectionism, struggling with multipotentiality, and other concerns common to exceptional students (Neihart, 1999; Neihart, Reis, Robinson, & Moon, 2002).

Advice, reassurance, and resources are provided, and students are linked to peers and mentors for ongoing support. We have found that for many SET students, appropriate educational placement and access to intellectual peers through summer programs and extracurricular activities addresses many of their social and emotional needs. However, those who exhibit depression or more serious problems of any kind are encouraged to seek professional help in their home communities.

### Resources and Opportunities

In addition to recommending programs to students through its counseling efforts, SET provides them with much information about educational resources and opportunities through its print and Internet offerings. The hope is that when students learn about these opportunities, particularly from other students who have taken advantage of them, they will be encouraged to participate.

SET publishes *Imagine* magazine, which has been awarded a Parents' Choice Gold Award for content and design. Available by subscription, it is provided free of charge to SET members, because the information is a crucial part of SET's mission. Each issue spotlights a focus topic such as an academic discipline or content area and includes articles and resources related to this topic. Many of the articles are written by students, whereby they reflect on their personal experiences of participating in a program or activity. Nonfocus articles, college and career planning columns, a book review, and puzzles are also included in each issue. A parent shared this feedback about *Imagine*:

> We live in a small Midwestern town and my son is the first from his high school to be named an Intel and Siemens semifinalist and the first in 10 years to get into Harvard. Without *Imagine* we wouldn't know about such programs as Ross Young Scholars, CTY, RSI, Intel Science Talent Search, Siemens-Westinghouse, and MathCounts, let alone have thought to participate. Your magazine opened my son's ideas and gave him the motivation to reach his dreams.

A student said, "It was through *Imagine* that I first read about the National History Day competition, and this year my school's history club, of which I am the student coordinator, has entered students into the competition for the first time."

SET also publishes a newsletter, which spotlights members' activities and accomplishments. Rigorous programs in which SET students are well represented, such as the International Olympiads and the Research Science Institute, are given special attention in an effort to encourage other students to participate. Students have shared that they value this information, as this comment suggests: "I enjoyed reading the SET newsletter to see what the other students were doing. It encouraged me to try some of those things, especially the math competitions."

Supplementing the publications in this technological age are Internet resources, with the SET and *Imagine* Web sites providing links to a wide variety of programmatic options. Specifically, links to summer programs, competitions, distance education programs, and content related to topics profiled in *Imagine* are all available on the *Imagine* Web site. A new venture is http://www.cogito.org, a Web site that has been developed by SET's staff in cooperation with the regional talent search organizations and other partners in the gifted education field. This site, which plans to launch in September of 2006, provides a searchable database of programs, as well as articles and resources for profoundly gifted math and science students.

Jonah learned about educational opportunities through SET's publications and by following the *Imagine* online links. In particular, he found distance education programs where he could get the AP courses he needed and was inspired by the successes of other SET members to compete in rigorous math and science contests. He said that he enjoyed reading the content in *Imagine*, especially about topics he wasn't knowledgeable of, and used the information in the college reviews to help him choose a college to attend. Getting information about programs into the hands of gifted students is critical to their participation in these opportunities, and SET focuses much effort on being a clearinghouse of information for students.

## Peer Networks

Students who are exceptionally able compared to their age-mates can have difficulty finding peers who share their abilities and/or interests, so another important goal of SET is to develop a network of peers and encourage interaction among SET members. Students are invited to join SET's Peer Network by giving permission to have their identity shared with others who have similar interests. A student who requested being part of the network said: "I would like to interact with kids my age who know a lot about computers and want to talk about them." He was put in touch with several students who shared this interest.

SET also provides a listserv for its members, where they can freely interact with others in the group. A fair amount of discussion on the listserv relates to issues about being gifted; other topics include current events and politics, school issues, and even books and movies. One student shared that "The listserv was lots of fun . . . I loved learning about so many different points of view . . . the discussions challenged me and definitely sharpened my debating abilities."

Utilizing the Internet to build a vibrant community of bright math and science students is also a goal of the Cogito Web site. Numerous forums and discussion groups have been included to encourage students (SET members and other high-ability students) to connect with each other and share their interests and knowledge as they enhance their learning of science.

Articles in *Imagine* and the newsletter are also intended to engender the idea of being part of a peer group, even among students who don't meet each other. For students who feel isolated in their school or community because their interests are more intellectual than those of their classmates, it can be emotionally supportive even to read about the activities of other highly gifted students, to know that there are others like them out there somewhere. One student wrote: "I feel so different from my classmates. It is good to read about other SET students and I hope to meet some of them someday."

It is most desirable, however, for these high-ability students to meet each other. SET fosters social development by encouraging students to participate in challenging out-of-school opportunities where they are likely to meet other extremely able students. More than one student has shared comments like "I met my soul mates at CTY" or "RSI changed my life—the other 'Rickoids' were amazing!" Students who get involved in math activities often meet peers repeatedly through the wide variety of summer programs and competitions that attract top students in this discipline and become lifelong friends and colleagues. For example, Dr. Terry Tao, a former SMPY participant (see Muratori et al., in press), reminisced that "the competitions contributed quite a bit to my social life. I could hang out with kids with similar interests and I still keep in touch with a lot of people I met that way."

Occasionally, SET brings students together through regional meetings, sometimes with their parents. Typically, a SET counselor organizes and attends the first meeting with the goal of the group continuing to meet on their own. Of four group meetings that were organized in the past year, two have led to the creation of math circles that continue to meet on a regular basis, another has decided to meet regularly for social reasons, and the fourth has not gotten together since the initial meeting. The social needs and interests of the particular students who attend and the willingness of parents to organize subsequent events are factors in whether these network groups are successful in continuing to function (Muratori, 2004). The parent who hosted one of the more successful group meetings reported that: "We [the parents] chatted like old friends. The kids had a wonderful time, played board games, and engaged in interesting discussions. Everyone is eager for the next gathering, and several parents have offered to host it." The value of this exchange is reinforced when one remembers that a number of these students have had great difficulty making friends in their school environments.

Jonah had reasonably good social skills and friends when he was identified for SET, so his needs in this area were less than many SET students exemplify. However, his truly exceptional abilities demanded that he begin to find ways to be more challenged. As he began to participate in selective summer programs and competitions, he found joy in interacting with other high-ability students and engaging in intellectual conversations. He joined SET's listserv, was connected through the Peer Network to several students, and met highly able math and science students at competitions. He keeps in touch regularly with a number of the students he met through these programs and events.

## Role Models and Mentors

In addition to connecting SET students with intellectual peers, we try to link them to role models and mentors—individuals who were gifted young people themselves and who can help guide students toward their future goals. In *Imagine*, in particular, we spotlight individuals as writers or as the subjects of interviews who are accomplished in an area and can serve as role models for the readers. In the newsletters, as well, we hope to inspire students by portraying the accomplishments of older SET members. The Cogito Web site is also designed to embody this goal, as interviews with, and profiles of, scientists and mathematicians are an important component.

In addition to these informal efforts to provide role models, SET offers a Mentor Program whereby younger SET members are paired with older ones. The relationships vary; some are ongoing and long-term, while others serve a short-term need. However, students benefit from developing relationships with others who may have experienced and dealt with issues they now face. Jonah requested a mentor when he joined SET, at the time wanting to work with someone who could share his expertise in computer graphics. The individual he was paired with was a computer science major who encouraged Jonah's interest in computer science and also helped him with college selection, as Jonah ended up ultimately choosing the college this young man attended.

SET students sometimes request an adult professional as a mentor, such as a scientist who can advise them on a science fair project or an individual who can expose them to a career field. For example, one student requested help in meeting a university professor working in nanotechnology for expert guidance on his project in this area. SET's staff guides students in how to approach professionals who might serve as mentors and/or recommends programs that have mentoring components. Jonah found his math mentor through a summer internship program that SET recommended.

## Individual Pathways to Challenge

Jonah is just one of many highly gifted SET students who were challenged throughout high school as a result of flexible schooling and participation in supplemental out-of-school experiences. A few more examples may be helpful.

Drs. Terry Tao and Lenny Ng were considered by Julian Stanley to be among his greatest prodigies (see Muratori et al., in press). Although Terry lived in Australia and Lenny grew up in North Carolina, both were able to move through school at their own pace by being placed simultaneously at different levels such as taking high school courses while in middle school and college courses while in high school. However, Terry accelerated quickly in grade placement and entered college several years younger than is typical, while Lenny, not eager to go to college early, focused on part-time college courses during high school. Both young men supplemented schooling with summer programs and high-level math competitions, although Lenny did more of this, including winning two gold and one silver medal representing the United States in the International Mathematics Olympiad. Lenny has looked back very positively on the academic and social benefits that competitions provided him, and he said they were a factor in his decision not to leave high school too early (Muratori et al.).

Two other SET students, Thomas and James, have also been profiled to illustrate how different pathways can reflect the unique profiles of abilities and circumstances of the individuals (see Brody, 2005). These students were equally exceptional in math, but James had stronger verbal skills as evidenced by early language development, as well as his verbal SAT in seventh grade. Because he was so advanced across subject areas and with limited challenge in regular school classes, James accelerated rapidly in both subject matter and grade placement. In addition to moving ahead in math with distance education courses, he skipped several grades, took mostly college courses while he was in high school, and entered college full-time at age 16 with a great deal of college credit behind him. Thus, his solution to accessing more advanced work was to enroll in courses with older students. Because he spent little time in high school, he did not pursue the extracurricular math and science internships and competitions that many students with his math abilities do.

In contrast, Thomas was less advanced verbally and attended a selective and rigorous charter school that he found very challenging. But, Thomas was eager for more advanced experiences in math and science, which he sought through out-of-school opportunities. He took summer courses, worked with a mentor, and participated in math and science competitions, where he won awards at the international level. Both James and Thomas were well challenged during their high school years, but their specific abilities, interests, and the available offerings in their schools led to different choices and pathways.

A young woman in SET, Anna, chose to attend a prestigious boarding school in an effort to access more advanced courses than were available in her small community and to be where she could find a compatible peer group. Her talents were broad, not only mathematically and verbally, but also musically. The school did offer a full range of AP courses, but it was not willing to let her take college or distance education courses during the year. However, she enjoyed her coursework and used her summers to access courses she couldn't get in school. Her extracurricular time during the school year focused heavily on developing her musical ability, which was important to her. Though relatively few SET students choose to attend boarding schools, Anna was pleased with her choice and felt well prepared for a highly selective college when she left high school.

## A Counseling Model for Parents and Educators

Many of the components of what SET tries to offer its students can be found in other counseling-oriented programs for gifted students. In particular, two scholarship programs, the Davidson Institute Young Scholars Program and the Jack Kent Cooke Foundation Young Scholars Program, incorporate many of the SET components. Advisors in both of these programs work individually with students to guide their educational progress. They encourage students to take challenging courses and to excel in them, to take advantage of supplemental out-of-school educational opportunities, and to meet and interact with intellectual peers through a variety of venues.

Increasingly, knowledgeable parents also have taken on the role of finding challenging out-of-school educational opportunities for their children, and Internet resources such as http://www.hoagiesgifted.org and publications such as *Imagine* have made the task of identifying programs easier. The result of this involvement by parents has been more and more students taking advantage of supplemental opportunities and excelling in them every year.

If we look at descriptions of winning projects from competitions such as the Intel Science Talent Search, the Siemens-Westinghouse Competition, and the Davidson Fellows awards, the achievement exemplified by the participants is incredibly impressive. Large numbers of high school students are completing college-level coursework through summer, distance education, dual enrollment, and AP programs, and thus are entering college prepared to excel in a rigorous college environment. Numerous activities are providing opportunities for precollege students to develop and demonstrate leadership skills. And, equally important, students report on the positive social and emotional effects of meeting intellectual peers through these many programs and activities.

## Issues and Concerns

Unfortunately, many gifted students who would benefit from the opportunities described here fail to hear about them if they don't have knowledgeable counselors or parents advising them. Also, many of the supplemental programs are expensive and, while they may offer scholarship support, students and parents may assume they can't afford them. Equity issues clearly suggest that, if supplemental programs contribute to talent development as much as we believe they do, there is a need to broaden access to these opportunities. More systematic ways of informing students about supplemental programs are needed. More programs like SET would be desirable, but parents and schools also can do more to get information about supplemental programs into the hands of their students.

School counselors and gifted coordinators, in particular, need to reconsider their roles and think more "out of the box" —with the box being school. They need to be willing to place students where they will be appropriately challenged, even if it's in a class or another school with older students. They also must become knowledgeable about supplemental programs and resources outside of school, encourage students to participate, and help them obtain credit for out-of-school experiences when it's appropriate. They also must become conscious of the importance of helping students interact with intellectual peers and find ways for them to do so.

While there is much that schools and school systems can do to enhance their offerings for the gifted students they serve (e.g., provide advanced and rigorous curricula, support opportunities to do independent research, be flexible with regard to acceleration), they may lack the resources to provide all the opportunities truly advanced students need. They also may not have enough high-ability students to provide a supportive peer group for them. Out-of-school learning opportunities can help fill this void. Schools can embrace these opportunities as part of their advanced students' educational programs.

## Conclusion

Through a combination of accelerative strategies, flexible placement, supplemental programs, and out-of-school activities, Jonah and the other students described in this chapter found opportunities to be challenged and to meet intellectual peers. Their experiences kept their love of learning and motivation alive, enhanced their study skills, and prepared them well for the challenges that lay ahead for them in college and in life. If students with such *extremely* advanced cognitive abilities as the ones profiled in this chapter can be appropriately challenged throughout their precollege years, we should not have gifted students languishing unchallenged in classrooms anywhere.

## References

Benbow, C. P. (1979). The components of SMPY's smorgasbord of accelerative options. *Intellectually Talented Youth Bulletin, 5*(10), 21–23.

Brody, L. E. (2004). Meeting the diverse needs of gifted students through individualized educational plans. In D. Boothe & J. C. Stanley (Eds.), *In the eyes of the beholder: Critical issues for diversity in gifted education* (pp. 129–138). Waco, TX: Prufrock Press.

Brody, L. E. (2005). The Study of Exceptional Talent. *High Ability Studies, 16*(1), 87–96.

Brody, L. E., & Blackburn, C. C. (1996). Nurturing exceptional talent: SET as a legacy of SMPY. In C. P. Benbow & D. Lubinski (Eds.), *Intellectual talent* (pp. 246–265). Baltimore: Johns Hopkins University Press.

Brody, L. E., Muratori, M. C., & Stanley, J. C. (2004). Early college entrance: Academic, social, and emotional considerations. In N. Colangelo, S. G. Assouline, & M. U. M. Gross (Eds.), *A nation deceived: How schools hold back America's brightest students* (Vol. 2, pp. 97–107). Iowa City, IA: The Connie Belin & Jacqueline N. Blank International Center for Gifted Education and Talent Development.

Colangelo, N., Assouline, S. G., & Gross, M. U. M. (Eds.). (2004). *A nation deceived: How schools hold back America's brightest students* (Vol. 2). Iowa City, IA: The Connie Belin & Jacqueline N. Blank International Center for Gifted Education and Talent Development.

Curry, W., MacDonald, W., & Morgan, R. (1999). The Advanced Placement program: Access to excellence. *Journal of Secondary Gifted Education, 11*, 17–23.

Karnes, F. A., & Riley, T. L. (2005). *Competitions for talented kids.* Waco, TX: Prufrock Press.

Lupkowski-Shoplik, A., Benbow, C. P., Assouline, S. G., & Brody, L. E. (2003). Talent searches. In N. Colangelo & G. A. Davis,

*Handbook of gifted education* (3rd ed., pp. 204–218). Boston: Allyn & Bacon.

McCarthy, C. R. (1999). Dual-enrollment programs: Legislation helps high school students enroll in college courses. *Journal of Secondary Gifted Education, 11*, 24–32.

Muratori, M. C. (2004, November). *The meeting of the minds: Networks for the highly gifted.* Paper presented at the annual meeting of the National Association for Gifted Children, Salt Lake City, UT.

Muratori, M. C., Stanley, J. C., Gross, M. U. M., Tao, T., Ng, L., Tao, B., et al. (In press). Insights from SMPY's greatest former child prodigies: Drs. Terrence ("Terry") Tao and Lenhard ("Lenny") Ng reflect on their talent development. *Gifted Child Quarterly.*

Neihart, M. (1999). The impact of giftedness on psychological well-being: What does the empirical literature say? *Roeper Review, 22*, 10–17.

Neihart, M., Reis, S. M., Robinson, N. M., & Moon, S. M. (Eds.). (2002). *The social and emotional development of gifted children: What do we know?* Waco, TX: Prufrock Press.

Sethna, B. N., Wickstrom, C. D., Boothe, D., & Stanley, J. C. (2001). The Advanced Academy of Georgia: Four years as a residential early-college-entrance program. *Journal of Secondary Gifted Education, 13*, 11–21.

Southern, W. T., & Jones, E. D. (Eds.). (1991). *The academic acceleration of gifted children.* New York: Teachers College Press.

Southern, W. T., Jones, E. D., & Stanley, J. C. (1993). Acceleration and enrichment: The context and development of program options. In K. A. Keller, F. J. Mönks, & A. H. Passow (Eds.), *International handbook of research and development of giftedness and talent* (pp. 387–409). Oxford, England: Pergamon Press.

Stanley, J. C. (1974). Intellectual precocity. In J. C. Stanley, D. P. Keating, & L. H. Fox (Eds.), *Mathematical talent: Discovery, description, and development* (pp. 1–22). Baltimore: Johns Hopkins University Press.

Stanley, J. C. (1985). How did six highly accelerated gifted students fare in graduate school? *Gifted Child Quarterly, 29*, 180.

Stanley, J. C. (1987). Making the IMO team: The power of early identification and encouragement. *Gifted Child Today, 10*, 22–23.

Stanley, J. C. (1989). Guiding gifted students in their academic planning. In J. VanTassel-Baska & P. Olszewski-Kubilius (Eds.),

*Patterns of influence on gifted learners* (pp. 192–200). New York: Teachers College Press.

Stanley, J. C. (1996). In the beginning: The Study of Mathematically Precocious Youth. In C. P. Benbow & D. Lubinski (Eds.), *Intellectual talent* (pp. 225–235). Baltimore: Johns Hopkins University Press.

Stanley, J. C. (2005). A quiet revolution: Finding boys and girls who reason exceptionally well mathematically and/or verbally and helping them get the supplemental educational opportunities they need. *High Ability Studies, 16*(1), 5–14.

Touron, J. (Ed.). (2005). Special issue: The Center for Talented Youth model. *High Ability Studies, 16*(1).

# Competitions for Gifted and Talented Students: Issues of Excellence and Equity

*Tracy L. Riley & Frances A. Karnes*

## Introduction

Competitions provide opportunities for gifted and talented students to compete or perform, exhibiting their special abilities and talents, and as such, have long been a cornerstone of gifted education. Gifted and talented students, amongst all other participants, can take part in competitions that maximize their abilities in academics, fine and performing arts, leadership, service learning (Karnes & Riley, 1996, 2005; Riley & Karnes, 1998/1999; 1999), and athletics. Riley and Karnes (1998/1999) state that for gifted and talented students, competitions put their talents to the test, allowing students a chance to showcase their special abilities, and in doing so, receive recognition and acknowledgement. As Campbell, Wagner, and Walberg (2001) state, "One can create an arena where individuals are allowed to perform some task or set of tasks with those being selected as eligible whose level of performance is judged superior, by whatever definition or criteria" (p. 524). In this way, competitions may serve a dual role: the identification of special abilities and talents, as well as a provision for their development (Riley & Karnes, 1998/1999).

Competitions may be local, regional, national, or international and range from school-based to worldwide programs. Competitions may be designed for individual student participation or group entry. Campbell et al. (2001) describe three types of competitions: teams of talented students, long-term independent research projects, and tests to identify exceptional talent. Furthermore, competitions span many areas of talent and provide a platform for an array of creative challenges.

An example of a competition that meets many of these criteria is the Future Problem Solving Program developed by Dr. Paul Torrance in 1974 (Future Problem Solving Program, 2003). This creative problem solving program serves thousands of students throughout the world. It offers both competitive and noncompetitive options, including Team Problem Solving, Community Problem Solving, and Scenario Writing. The Future Problem Solving Program is open to all students in kindergarten to 12th grade and is incorporated into the gifted and talented curriculum in many schools. However, a school affiliation is not required for participation (Hume, 2001), and Future Problem Solving, like all other competitions, should not serve as the gifted and talented program in isolation of a continuum of accelerated and enriched approaches. Volk (2006), in her study of the FPSP in Australia, found that students who participated in the competition gained depth in their appreciation of the skills of problem solving and the transfer of those skills to everyday life. More than 81% of the students surveyed 5 years after participation suggested that the program had positively impacted their ability to think about societal problems as solvable. A replication of the study in the U.S. yielded similar results (Woythal, 2002).

A sample of other competitions that may be facilitated in the home, school, or wider community is shown in Table 8.1.

## Competitions as a Training Ground for Excellence

Competitions strive to celebrate, honor, and acknowledge excellence, while concurrently developing potential. Perusal of the verbs used in describing the purposes for the competitions

## Table 8.1
### A Sampling of Competitions for Gifted and Talented Students

**Biz Plan Competition**
Independent Means Inc., 126 East Haley St., #A16, Santa Barbara, CA 93101
http://www.independentmeans.com/imi/dollardiva/bizplan
   Gives teenage young women an opportunity to increase their understanding of the concepts, tools, and responsibilities of business ownership while putting their own entrepreneurial dreams on paper.

**Kids Philosophy Slam**
Kids Philosophy Slam, P.O. Box 406, Lanesboro, MN 55949
http://www.philosophyslam.org
   Gives kids a voice and encourages them to think using their creative potential through philosophical forums, and evidence their creativity in an original piece of work such as a painting, essay, song, or other artwork.

**John F. Kennedy Profile in Courage Essay Contest**
John F. Kennedy Library, Profile in Courage Essay Contest, Columbia Point, Boston, MA 02125
http://www.jfkcontest.org
   High school students write a compelling essay on the meaning of political courage, to learn about and be inspired by American's elected officials, past or present, who have tried to make a difference in the world.

**NewsCurrents Student Editorial Cartoon Contest**
Knowledge Unlimited Inc., P.O. Box 52, Madison, WI 53701
http://www.newscurrents.com
   Young people can showcase their complex thinking and communications skills through journalistic cartooning.

**The Lions International Peace Poster**
Lions Clubs International, 300 W. 22nd St., Oak Brook, IL, 60523–8842
http://www.lionsclubs.org/EN/content/youth_peace_poster.php3
   Youth are given the opportunity to express their thoughts about world peace in an original artwork.

*continued on the next page*

---

## Table 8.1 continued

**"Kids Helping Kids" Youth Action Greeting Card Contest**
United States Committee for UNICEF, 333 E. 38th St., New
York, NY 10016
http://www.unicefusa.org
   Children create greeting cards to depict the idea that even
though kids come from different countries, they all need the same
things to survive and grow.

**Prudential Spirit of Community Awards**
Prudential Spirit of Community Awards, 751 Broad Street, 16th
Floor, Newark, NJ 07102
http://www.prudential.com/community/spirit
   Students in middle and high school grades are recognized for
their exemplary community service.

---

listed in Karnes and Riley's book (2005) demonstrates these
twin goals: encourage, reward, support, recognize, increase,
enhance, honor, motivate, discover, test, and so on. Excellence
is also noted in many of the synonyms used in the judging criteria—outstanding, innovative, merit, distinction, accuracy, and
the like. Competition providers are striving to encourage excellence. Campbell et al. (2001) state that competitions operate on
five assumptions and these can be considered in light of excellence:

1. Students who are gifted and talented need to be identified early: Excellence is evidenced in youth and should
   be developed and celebrated.
2. Competitions are needed to supplement schools lacking in differentiated curricular experiences for gifted
   and talented students: Excellence is achieved through
   differentiating content, processes, and products across
   an array of approaches.
3. Competitions will attract students with extraordinary
   talent: Excellence is self-evident and gifted and talented
   youth are motivated to further develop their potential.

4.  Competitions will motivate early talent development: Gifted and talented students can set and reach standards of excellence.

5.  Once talents are developed, the expectation is that those talents will contribute to society: Gifted and talented students can make contributions of excellence for the betterment and future of today's world.

Competitions, therefore, assume excellence is attainable and desirable. Competitions recognize and develop excellence in our gifted and talented students, and in doing so they " . . . may help defuse any public antagonism towards gifted children and legitimise the making of appropriate provisions for them" (The Parliament of the Commonwealth of Australia, 1988, Section 4.67). Riley and Karnes (1999) agree that competitions can raise the public profile of gifted and talented students and their educational programs.

The successful outcome of a competition, or winning, is what athletes call performance excellence; but competitions also provide students with the chance to develop the qualities of personal excellence. Personal excellence requires competitors to focus not on the prize, but on the process: how one performs is a better measure of excellence than winning. Although winning first prize might be the ultimate goal, emphasis should be placed on the premise that participation in and of itself constitutes winning.

By being placed in a competitive environment with adequate supports, students learn to cope with differences, strive toward excellence, accept failure and frustration, and recognize their potential. Students who compete are given opportunities to experience a taste of what lies ahead in the challenges of the everyday world. Furthermore, students may reap the following benefits:

1.  satisfaction through goal-setting and management;

2.  enhancement of self-directed learning skills; sense of autonomy; cooperative team-work skills; content, process, and product development; and personal and interpersonal understandings;

3. opportunities to work with others of similar ability, confidentially exchanging ideas and enjoying new challenges; and

4. learning to set, assess, and recognize standards of excellence (Davis & Rimm, 1998; Riley & Karnes, 1998/1999, 1999).

Cropper (1998) argued for the use of competitions as an effective tool for short- and long-term motivational gains. Similarly, Riley and Karnes (1999) concluded that competitions can serve as a motivational spark plug. Gondek (2005) recommends competitions for girls, and particularly minority students, as a means of promoting gender equity in science and mathematics. It is important however, to note that these are all speculated benefits, for as Campbell et al. (2001), Rogers (2002), and Olszewski-Kubilius (2003) point out, there is a scarcity of research related to the effectiveness of competitions in meeting the unique social, emotional, and intellectual needs of gifted and talented students.

Nonetheless, competitions potentially offer students many opportunities for developing excellence. Students will learn more about themselves and their special abilities and talents by participating in competitions. For example, in retrospective studies of winners of the Mathematics, Physics, and Chemistry Olympiads, these high school students went on to enroll in prestigious universities, with many completing degrees and undertaking graduate study (Campbell et al., 2001). In fact, of the 229 students participating in the study, approximately half of those were enrolled in doctoral studies.

The majority of these students and their parents reported that their achievements and talents were enhanced through their participation in competitions. They also reported that the competitions helped raise their awareness of educational and career opportunities. For many of these students, their participation in competitions confirmed their gifts and talents, helping them objectively understand their outstanding potential.

Competitions can also serve as vehicles for self-directed learning, which makes students more responsible in planning and achieving their goals. Work and study skills can be enhanced through participation (Fletcher, 1995). These skills include: time management, following directions, punctuality, meeting new and different people, planning, and responsibility. Competitions can enhance the interests of students, giving them the opportunity to build on current interests and formulate new ones.

Students' understandings can be improved through opportunities to compete against and with one another. But, more importantly, their knowledge and skills are challenged and enhanced through competing against standards of content, process, and product excellence (Curran, Holton, Marshall, & Haur, 1991/1992). For example, students in mathematical competitions are competing against mathematical problems, striving to find accurate solutions. Students in competitions are assessed for their performances against criteria set and judged by teachers, as well as experts in the field, be they scientists, actresses, business people, or civic leaders (Riley & Karnes, 2005).

## Competitions as Breeding Grounds for Problems With Equity

The real-world experiences offered by competitions can, however, have potential negative outcomes. Davis and Rimm (1998) cited stress and feelings of failure as results of extreme competitiveness. Although success in competitions may serve to motivate students, thus leaving them wanting more, failure to succeed or a desire for perfectionism can be harmful. Cropper (1998) placed the blame for these negative effects upon poorly planned competitive goals and suggested a range of curricular strategies to deter or prevent negativity.

Rimm (1986) believes that competition may be a cause of underachievement, particularly for students who handle competitiveness poorly. Too much competition and too great an emphasis on winning can be destructive, so she believes students should be encouraged to compete against themselves for self-improvement. It is important, according to Rimm, that students are taught how to appropriately interpret wins and losses.

Another potential weakness is the costs involved in relation to entry requirements, travel, materials, sponsorship, and so on (Riley & Karnes, 1999). The availability of competitions and the time involved in seeking those out, adequately assessing their value, and working with students in preparation to compete could also prove to be a barrier (Riley & Karnes, 1998/1999). There are tensions surrounding equity of opportunity, funding, support, and recognition and development of excellence through competitive involvement.

For example, equity of participation in competitions moves along a continuum of opportunity. Competitions at a local level can provide equitable chances for participation, in that all students can be given an opportunity to take part. However, as students move through competitions at state, regional, national, and international stages, equity in opportunities for all students decreases, with the top competitors getting a greater slice of the pie, both in participation and benefits. Additionally, the age restrictions, costs, and entry requirements could prove prohibitive to some students' abilities to participate at these highly competitive levels.

All students should have the opportunity to participate to the best of their abilities, and the processes of selection should be transparent, clearly explained, and open to review. Unfortunately, many schools may limit competition participation to only those students who have been formally identified as gifted and talented—but the ability and motivation to do well in the competition arena is not the sole purview of intellectually or academically gifted students. It is also possible that a school or district will view competition involvement as the entire gifted program. This is inequitable to gifted and talented students who may have a very diverse range of abilities and skills, potentially not even addressed by the competition goals. The gifted and talented are not a homogeneous group, and therefore, there is no one-size-fits-all competition for meeting their unique academic, social, emotional, cultural, and creative needs.

To avoid these potential inequities, students who are participating in competitions obviously require human, physical, educational, and financial support, and their schools or districts should facilitate their involvement. Historically and today, athletic competitions have been highly supported by schools and communities. Despite the inequities in selection, participation, and levels of financial and physical support (by way of specialist coaches, equipment, scholarships, and awards), athletic competitions would seldom be labeled elitist. On the other hand, competitions in other areas, particularly in subjects such as science, mathematics, or spelling, have not always been viewed as favorably. Many times these competitions are considered to be bastions of academic elitism. This ironic situation points out our confused view of equity.

For example, a Texas media outlet's report describes one district's funding stipend for athletic coaches as nearly 10 times that of their academic counterparts, the existence of middle school athletic—but not academic—training programs in preparation for secondary competition, and a lack of balance in school and public recognition of academic competition winners (Schuhmann, 2002). The subtle message here is that competition in sports is fine, but the pursuit of excellence through competition in other areas is viewed with suspicion. The more direct message is that excellence in sports is highly valued and supported not only by spectators but also those holding the purse strings. Sadly, one of the academic competition directors described his team members as the unwanted stepchildren of the school, despite their first place ranking in two competitions after spending nine Saturdays in all-day preparation.

Unfortunately, just as there are disparities between athletic and other competitions, there are also inconsistencies within and across the range of academic competitions. For example, Karnes and Riley (2005) outline more than 100 competitions across a wide range of different content and skill areas, but an analysis of these shows that students with abilities and interests in traditional academic subjects have greater chances for participation than others. Of the 140 competitions listed, approximately 40% are for students with language arts abilities (including foreign languages) and 31% are for students interested in mathematics, science, and technology. Approximately 25% of the competitions are in the visual and performing arts, contrasted with 9% designed to support and recognize leadership and service. Furthermore, a closer examination of the competitions shows that many of the competition products are limited to essays, speeches, and posters/drawings. For example, of the 26 social studies competitions listed, half of those require students to write an essay.

In sum, competitions provide opportunities for students to develop their own personal and professional excellence. Additionally, they are designed as a means of recognizing, developing, and celebrating excellence, and therefore can enhance the profile of gifted and talented students and their special needs. By their very nature, competitions will not be equally inclusive of or appropriate for *all* students. Inequities in opportunity for competitive experiences operate along a continuum that varies, depending on the nature of the competition. Yet, striving for excellence *with* equity, especially for gifted and talented students in competition "showgrounds," is a worthy goal that requires thoughtful, well-planned facilitation by schools through curriculum alignment processes.

## School-Based Facilitation of Competitions

Schools and teachers should facilitate careful searching, collation, and distribution of competition information. When gathering information on competitions, the following factors must be considered: competition goals, age level, curricular area, entry requirements, deadlines, and costs. Students, of course, are often most interested in the potential winnings or awards. This type of information can and should be obtained prior to entry by contacting the competition sponsors or visiting their Web sites. Carefully reading all competition guidelines is crucial to ensure student success, as well as enjoyment. Gathering and collating this information into a competitions file, such as a computer database or hard copy notebook, is an advisable organizational strategy for teachers and counselors (Riley & Karnes,

1998/1999). The file should be made readily available to other teachers, students, parents, and community members.

Once the competitions have been located and information gathered, if schools make the decision to facilitate student involvement in competitions, it is very important that there is alignment between the competition goals and other educational or curricular goals. VanTassel-Baska and Stambaugh (2006) define the curriculum as "a set of planned experiences for a target population" (p. 19). This definition implies alignment but also highlights the importance of appropriate identification. There should be an interrelationship between the targeted students, their characteristics, and the competition, with identification serving as the mediating link (McAlpine, 2004).

Additionally, a curriculum requires a scope and sequence; thus, competitions should be planned and implemented in a coherent and comprehensive way. Finally, it is advisable that the curriculum experiences (in this case, competitions) " . . . be carefully planned, written down, and implemented in order to maximize their potential effect" (VanTassel-Baska & Stambaugh, 2006, pp. 32–33). If competition involvement is not carefully planned, there is a risk of providing gifted and talented students with indefensible, unsustainable, inappropriate, and fragmented educational experiences. As Borland (2003) points out, without such planning, competitions may masquerade as a defensible curriculum, but in fact be trivial.

So, for gifted and talented students, the cognitive, affective, and creative goals and objectives of their specialized or individualized program should match those of the competition(s). Furthermore, their educational program should be a continuum of qualitatively differentiated, enriched, and accelerated provisions, beginning in the regular classroom and stretching to opportunities outside of school. Competitions are just *one* part of that continuum, and their utilization as a stand-alone provision for meeting the needs of gifted and talented students is unjustifiable. In planning curricular experiences, the competitions selected should match or fit in with the rest of the student's educational program.

It is also recommended that gifted and talented programs be supported by a curriculum model specific to gifted and talented education (VanTassel-Baska & Brown, 2005) and several of these provide scope for the inclusion of competitions. For example, many competitions would fit with Renzulli's (1977) Enrichment Triad Model, particularly Type III enrichment and individual and small-group investigations of real problems. Competitions may also aid in the development of the content-based process skills described by VanTassel-Baska (1986, 1998; VanTassel-Baska & Stambaugh, 2006) in her Integrated Curriculum Model (ICM). Competitions could also be justified as part of the Stanley Model of Talent Identification and Development (Benbow & Lubinski, 1997). Table 8.2 shows the curriculum models in gifted education that support the facilitation of a range of competition goals.

Planning the curricular scope and sequence of competitions requires careful analysis of the age/grade requirements in relation to particular areas of ability to be developed or enhanced. Some sponsors have age-range categories for competitors of all ages; others are limited to students of certain ages. In the case of limited age requirements, several competitions may be selected that complement and build on one another throughout a student's school experience. This sort of planning would be preferable to singular competition experiences.

Additionally, as part of a curricular scope and sequence, schools may write goals related specifically to competitions. These might include the development of:

1. skills and attitudes related to different ways of competing constructively and responding appropriately to competitive situations (Udvari, 2000);
2. proficiency in setting and evaluating competition goals (Riley & Karnes, 2005) for personal and performance excellence; and
3. competence in locating competition opportunities, gaining sponsorship and/or funding, recruiting team members, and managing public relations (Riley & Karnes, 2005).

# Table 8.2
## Curriculum Models to Facilitate Competitions

| Curriculum Model | Curricular Goals | Competition Goals |
| --- | --- | --- |
| Enrichment Triad Model (Renzulli, 1977); Schoolwide Enrichment Model (SEM; Renzulli & Reis, 1985) | Types II and III enrichment: development of how-to skills and investigations of real problems | Development of process skills; individual or team products |
| Purdue Three-Stage Model (Feldhusen & Kolloff, 1978) | Stage II enrichment: development and application of creative problem solving | Application of creative problem solving strategies to real-world problems |
| Autonomous Learner Model (Betts, 1985) | Orientation, individual development, in-depth study: group and self-understanding, learning skills, projects and mentorships | Development of skills of teamwork and cooperation; thinking and learning processes; creating individual or team products; self-reflection |
| Stanley Model of Talent Identification and Development (Benbow & Lubinski, 1997) | Curricular flexibility | Introduction to career pathways; pursuit of topics beyond the traditional curriculum |
| The Integrated Curriculum Model (VanTassel-Baska, 1986, 1998; VanTassel-Baska & Stambaugh, 2006) | Advanced knowledge and higher order thinking and processes | Development of process skills embedded in advanced content |
| Parallel Curriculum Model (Tomlinson et al., 2002) | Curriculum of practice and curriculum of identity | Emulation of the roles, skills, thinking, and actions of professionals; self-reflection |
| Multiple Menu Model (Renzulli, Leppien, & Hays, 2000) | Knowledge, instructional products, and artistic modification menus | Developing skills of methodology; product development; sharing personal experiences, values, beliefs, and enthusiasm for a particular area of study |

Other curricular goals might be set based upon the specific competitions facilitated within a school or district. These might include specific content areas, teaching and learning processes, or product development skills needed for successful participation.

Given the goals of competitions, identification of students for competition involvement should be taken as seriously as identification for any other special opportunity. For gifted and talented students, their participation in competitions should be for the purpose of providing an optimal learning experience; therefore, the identification process should be seen as a means to an end, rather than an end in itself (McAlpine, 2004). In other words, during the identification process, information regarding students' exceptional skills and abilities should be documented and, as with educational goals, matched to competition goals. Multiple methods of identification should be used, including self, peer, parent, and teacher nomination. Nomination data can provide knowledge and information regarding the students' interests, strengths, personal skills, and dispositions. For some competitions, standardized test scores may be appropriate, particularly those that require students to have good numeracy and literacy skills. For other competitions, especially those in the visual and performing arts, portfolios and performances would be more appropriate methods of identification.

During the identification process, certain characteristics and behaviors of giftedness and talent may lend themselves well to involvement in different types of competitions. For example, students who demonstrate excellent leadership skills, or the potential to further develop them, may be well suited for team-based competitions. Those with good skills of communication and oratory talents would potentially perform well in speech competitions.

Students who have the potential to be successful competitors also need to be highly motivated self-starters who are able to set and maintain goals. On the other hand, students who do not enjoy competition or lack confidence, particularly in competitive settings, may not prove successful without some extra coaching and support. For some cultures, competition may not be appropriate or valued, particularly at an individual level (Riley, Bevan-Brown, Bicknell, Carroll-Lind, & Kearney, 2004).

Finally, in school or district-wide competitions, it is important that documentation of student participation in competitions is included as a part of the smorgasbord of educational experiences in which students are involved and provided. By documenting competitions, their alignment with curricular goals and identification processes, sustained support can be better assured. It is essential, too, that the evaluation of competition effectiveness in meeting the needs of gifted and talented children is undertaken as part of the program plan. Campbell and colleagues (2001) believe it is crucial for educators to determine the effects of competitions, explaining the lack of limited evaluations of students gifted. They also hypothesize that since many competitions are sponsored by community or business agencies, they may not have the resources or interest in funding evaluation.

In sum, for the successful implementation of competitions for gifted and talented students, schools and districts should consider:

- effective and coordinated planning and supervision of student participation in competitions, including curricular alignment, documentation, and evaluation; and
- careful selection of competitions based upon thorough understanding of their purposes and procedures, as well as the identified special abilities of individual students.

## Facilitating Individual Student Involvement in Competitions

Competitions may also be facilitated for students as an out-of-school activity. In these cases, teachers, parents, mentors, or community members should assist students in the selection of a competition in which to participate by having students assess their talent area. This can be facilitated using a standardized interest inventory or more informally by simply asking students "What talents do you have?" and having them list the areas in which they do very well. Some ideas might include math, science, history, reading, drawing, leadership, photography, playing the piano, creative writing, or singing. Students might also list their interests and the areas they would like to know more about. The interest and talent lists can be combined and ranked. The student ideally should select several competitions to consider initially. Each student should read the descriptions of the competitions, asking the following types of questions:

- Is this competition in my area of ability and interest?
- Can I do what is expected?
- Do I have the time and resources to participate?
- Do I need a sponsor? If so, how will I get one?
- If a team is needed, are there other students interested?

Students should discuss their ideas with their teachers, parents, and friends. Also, they should talk with students who have participated in the competitions of interest and ask them about their experiences. The students should then write the pros and cons of entering and check the deadlines to determine if there is sufficient time to participate. As Karnes and Riley (2005) remind students, it is important they prepare adequately for their involvement and use a competition planning calendar or diary.

Students should also reflect upon their participation, evaluating and celebrating their efforts, as well as setting new competition goals. Karnes and Riley (2005) advise students to reflect upon the following questions after a competitive experience:

- What did I learn?
- What did I do right?
- What could I have done better?
- What do I need to do in order to do better in the future? (p. 5)

Although these are very broad general questions, there may be a need for students to consider much more specific competition skills. The rubric shown in Figure 8.1 could be adopted or adapted for competitors as a tool for evaluation and self-reflection. For example, students might reflect on content, process,

| Competition Skills | Wow! I Competed Brilliantly. | I Competed With Excellence. | I Competed Pretty Well. | I Could Be a Better Competitor. |
|---|---|---|---|---|
| Time-management | I used my time well to make sure things got done on time and I met all my deadlines. | I usually used my time well, but procrastinated on one thing. I got everything done on time. | I tended to put things off and procrastinate, but I still met my deadlines. | I didn't meet the deadlines I had set for myself. |
| Planning | I developed a comprehensive competition plan and worked strategically. | I developed a good competition plan. | I did some planning, but I did not think of everything ahead of time. | I did not have a competition plan. |
| Teamwork | I was a cooperative and collaborative team member. I communicated well and supported others. | I was mostly cooperative and usually communicated with other team members. | I was fairly cooperative, but sometimes I was not a very good team member. | I was not very cooperative and did not really help the team the way I could have. |
| Preparedness | I had all the materials I needed to compete and was well-prepared. | I had most of what I needed to compete well and was pretty ready for the competition. | I wasn't as prepared as I could have been. | I wasn't ready for this competition. I didn't prepare well. |
| Pride | I competed to my best effort. I worked hard and it showed. | I competed with a lot of effort. | I tried to compete well, but could have put in more effort. | I didn't try my best and need to put in better effort next time I compete. |
| Attitude | I had a positive attitude throughout the competition. | I had a positive attitude most of the time during the competition. | I was usually positive about the competition. | I had a negative attitude about the competition. |
| Appearance | I looked my very best, was neat and tidy, and smiled a lot. | I looked good and appeared fairly confident. | I could have taken more care with my appearance. | I didn't look very nice and could have made my appearance better. |

**Figure 8.1.** Competition rubric

and product skills specific to the competition. Additionally, they may have others, such as parents, teachers, coaches, or team members, rate their performance.

The purpose of self- or peer evaluation should be to improve or enhance future participation, and this needs to be made clear to students. From the evaluation, individuals can set competition goals by identifying areas in which they would like to improve. However, when competitions are left purely to student initiative outside of school, the likelihood that students will participate is limited if they do not perceive themselves as outstanding in a given area. Thus, the value of competition as a learning experience is diminished. Moreover, in order to be successful in competitions of all types, having an advocate and/ or coach is desirable. For students from poverty, this possibility shrinks considerably if competition opportunities are separate from the school learning experience. The documentary *Spellbound* captures the differential effects of poverty on student performance in the National Spelling Bee, suggesting that practice and positive parental involvement is an important variable in success and the student's perception of success.

## Conclusion: Competitive Excellence With Equity

This chapter has explored issues of equity and excellence surrounding competitions as a provision for gifted and talented students, either inside of school or outside of school. There are potentially many benefits to competitions; however, these are more speculative than research-based. In order to attain excellence for our gifted and talented students who are involved in competitions, there is a need for quantitative and qualitative empirical research to determine their effectiveness. An obvious research question is "how effective are competitions in meeting the social, emotional, intellectual, creative, and cultural needs of gifted and talented students?" Other potential areas of research include:

- resolution of the rather speculative and controversial benefits and challenges of competitions, particularly the effects of competitive experiences upon self-concept;

- student, teacher, parental, and community perceptions of competitions; and
- longitudinal or follow-up studies of successful competitors.

It is important that such research be conducted and widely disseminated to practitioners, be they teachers, coaches, or parents. Any provision for gifted and talented students that is not supported by research demonstrating its effectiveness in meeting their unique needs is questionable.

One of the issues raised in this chapter has been the facilitation of competitions as part of a schoolwide approach to provision. Without documentation of a curricular scope and sequence, identification methods and approaches, evaluation processes, professional involvement, and support, competitions are in danger of being isolated, stand-alone experiences, inappropriate for achieving excellence in gifted and talented students. Furthermore, there are inequities in the support and resources for different types of competitions, which lead to inequitable opportunities. To remedy this situation, and to have competitive excellence with equity, schools and communities should:

- develop open, inclusive, and transparent criteria for selection of students for competitions, based on a match between the competition goals and methods of identification;
- secure human, physical, and financial support for competitions within the school and the wider community;
- ensure public recognition of all competitors, not just winners, through well-planned public relations campaigns;
- balance the opportunities, recognition, and support for competitors in all areas, from academics, to fine and performing arts, to leadership and service, to athletics;
- create a school environment that values excellence in all areas by raising expectations; and
- evaluate the effectiveness of competitions in meeting the needs of gifted and talented students.

Competitions have the potential to enhance educators' visions of excellence and equity, but *only* with planned, well-thought-out approaches to their implementation. Gifted and talented students, amongst all other competitors, can then enjoy competitive excellence *with* equity.

## References

Benbow, C. P., & Lubinski, D. (1997). Intellectually talented children: How can we best meet their needs? In N. Colangelo & G. A. Davis (Eds.), *Handbook of gifted education* (2nd ed., pp. 155–169). Needham Heights, MA: Allyn & Bacon.

Betts, G. (1985). *Autonomous Learner Model for the gifted and talented.* Greeley, CO: ALPS.

Borland, J. (Ed.). (2003). *Rethinking gifted education.* New York: Teachers College Press.

Campbell, J. R., Wagner, H., & Walberg, H. J. (2001). Academic competitions and programs designed to challenge the exceptionally able. In K. A. Heller, F. J. Mönks, R. Subotnik, & R. Sternberg (Eds.), *The international handbook of giftedness and talent* (2nd ed., pp. 523–535). New York: Elsevier.

Cropper, C. (1998). Is competition an effective classroom tool for the gifted student? *Gifted Child Today, 21*(3), 28–30.

Curran, J., Holton, D., Marshall, C., & Haur, P. W. (1991/1992). *A survey of secondary mathematics students.* Unpublished research report, University of Otago, Dunedin, New Zealand.

Davis, G. A., & Rimm, S. B. (1998). *Education of the gifted and talented* (4th ed.). Needham Heights, MA: Allyn & Bacon.

Feldhusen, J. F., & Kolloff, P. B. (1978). A three-stage model of gifted education. *Gifted Child Today, 3*(5), 53–57.

Fletcher, K. P. (1995, May). *International Chemistry Olympiad New Zealand team selection, training and evaluation.* Paper presented at Teaching Gifted Students at Secondary Level First National Conference, Palmerston North, New Zealand.

Future Problem Solving Program. (2003). *Information.* Retrieved October 15, 2003, from http://www.fpsp.org

Gondek, R. (2005). *Promoting gender equity in the science classroom.* Retrieved December 1, 2005, from http://www2.edc.org/WomensEquity/pdffiles/sciguide.pdf

Hume, K. (2001, March). The Future Problem Solving Program. *Parenting for High Potential,* 8–11.

Karnes, F. A., & Riley, T. L. (1996). *Competitions: Maximizing your potential.* Waco, TX: Prufrock Press.

Karnes, F. A., & Riley, T. L. (2005). *Competitions for talented kids.* Waco, TX: Prufrock Press.

McAlpine, D. (2004). Definitions. In D. McAlpine & R. Moltzen (Eds.), *Gifted and talented: New Zealand perspectives* (2nd ed., pp. 1–25). Palmerston North: Kanuka Grove Press.

Olszewski-Kubilius, P. (2003). Special summer and Saturday programs for gifted students. In N. Colangelo & G. Davis (Eds.), *Handbook of gifted education* (3rd ed., pp. 219–228). Boston: Allyn & Bacon.

Renzulli, J. S. (1977). *The Enrichment Triad Model: A guide for developing defensible programs for the gifted and talented.* Mansfield Center, CT: Creative Learning Press.

Renzulli, J. S., & Reis, S. M. (1985). *The Schoolwide Enrichment Model: A comprehensive plan for educational excellence.* Mansfield Center, CT: Creative Learning Press.

Renzulli, J. S., Leppien, J. L., & Hays, T. S. (2000). *The Multiple Menu Model: A practical guide for developing differentiated curriculum.* Mansfield Center, CT: Creative Learning Press.

Riley, T., Bevan-Brown, J., Bicknell, B., Carroll-Lind, J., & Kearney, A. (2004). *The extent, nature and effectiveness of planned approaches in New Zealand schools for providing for gifted and talented students.* Retrieved March 15, 2004, from http://www.minedu.govt.nz/goto/gifted

Riley, T. L., & Karnes, F. A. (1998/1999). Competitions: One solution for meeting the needs of New Zealand's gifted students. *APEX The New Zealand Journal of Gifted Education, 11/12*(1), 21–26.

Riley, T. L., & Karnes, F. A. (1999). Forming partnerships with communities via competitions. *Journal of Secondary Gifted Education, 10,* 129–134.

Riley, T. L., & Karnes, F. A. (2005). Problem-solving competitions: Just the solution! *Gifted Child Today, 28*(4), 31–39.

Rimm, S. B. (1986). *Underachievement syndrome: Causes and cures.* Watertown, WI: Apple Publishing Company.

Rogers, K. B. (2002). *Re-forming gifted education.* Scottsdale, AZ: Great Potential Press.

Schuhmann, S. (2002). *Balancing athletics and academics in AISD.* Retrieved December 1, 2005, from http://web.reporter-news.com/1998/2002/local/bal0804.html

The Parliament of the Commonwealth of Australia. (1998). *Report by the Senate Select Committee on the education of gifted and talented chil-*

*dren*. Retrieved June 1, 2003, from http://www.alphalink.com. au/~drednort/ssc.html

Tomlinson, C. A., Kaplan, S. N., Renzulli, J. S., Purcell, J., Leppien, J., & Burns, D. (2002). *The parallel curriculum: A design to develop high potential and challenge high-ability learners.* Thousand Oaks, CA: Corwin Press.

Udvari, S. J. (2000). Competition and the adjustment of gifted children: A matter of motivation. *Roeper Review, 22,* 212–217.

VanTassel-Baska, J. (1986). Effective curriculum and instructional models for talented students. *Gifted Child Quarterly, 30,* 164–169.

VanTassel-Baska, J. (1998). *Excellence in educating the gifted* (3rd ed.). Denver, CO: Love.

VanTassel-Baska, J., & Brown, E. F. (2005). An analysis of gifted education curriculum models. In F. A. Karnes & S. M. Bean (Eds.), *Methods and materials for teaching the gifted* (2nd ed., pp. 93–132). Waco, TX: Prufrock Press.

VanTassel-Baska, J., & Stambaugh, T. (Ed.). (2006). *Comprehensive curriculum for gifted learners* (2nd ed.). Boston: Allyn & Bacon.

Volk, V. (2006). Expanding horizons—Into the future with confidence! *Roeper Review, 28,* 175–179.

Woythal, D. (2002). Teacher, when will we ever use this? *ITAG News: The Magazine of the Iowa Talented and Gifted Association, 27*(3), insert.

## Competition Resources

**Karnes, F. A., & Riley, T. L. (2005).** *Competitions for talented kids.* **Waco, TX: Prufrock Press.**
More than 140 academic, fine and performing arts, service learning, and leadership competitions are shared in this book. Also featured is a competitions journal for students as they showcase their talents.

### Johns Hopkins University Center for Talented Youth—Link to Academic Competitions
http://www.jhu.edu/gifted/imagine/linkB.htm
This Web site provides direct links to competitions in the arts, debate, science, and much more.

### *Gifted Child Today*
http://www.prufrock.com/client/client_pages/prufrock_jm_giftchild.cfm
This magazine, published by Prufrock Press, features competitions in each issue.

# Distance Learning and Gifted Students

*Cheryll M. Adams & Paula Olszewski-Kubilius*

## Introduction

Distance education can be defined as the education and training resulting from the physical separation of student and teacher that keeps the student from having to travel to a specific location and time in order to experience learning (Keegan, 1995, as cited in Valentine, 2004). Although most researchers in the field agree with this definition of distance education, there is much debate over the origins of the field, although distance education courses were available in the 1700s when prospective clergymen were trained at a distance (Ludlow & Duff, 2003). Another author argues distance education began in 1873 when Anna Ticknor created the "society to encourage studies at home," a volunteer society based in Boston that encouraged women from all classes of society to improve their educational opportunities through home studies and provided correspondence education to more than 10,000 members during a 24-year period (Nasseh, 2004). Nasseh reports the first official recognition of distance education came between 1883 and 1891, when the Chautauqua College of Liberal Arts was authorized by the state of New York to grant degrees to students who completed coursework through distance education.

It is interesting that although distance education has a history of more than 100 years, researchers are unable to agree on its origins.

In the late 1800s and early 1900s, colleges and universities began to offer college correspondence courses, and in 1906, the Calvert School of Baltimore became the first elementary school to offer correspondence courses (Nguyen & Gattlin, 2004). In addition to these and many other correspondence courses offered in the United States, the University of Queensland in Australia established a Department of External Studies in 1911, and in 1969 the Open University was established in the United Kingdom. The Open University had a particularly influential impact on distance education because it used a multimedia (textbooks, audio, filmstrips, video, and radio and television broadcasts) approach to education, which was unheard of at the time. Since the opening of the original Open University, four other Open Universities have been established in Europe and more than 20 have been established around the world (Nguyen & Gattlin). Although this has been a brief review of the history of the field of distance education, there is one aspect of this field's history that is noticeably absent—distance education's use with gifted adolescents. Although gifted adolescents have benefited from distance education in the past, there is no mention of this population anywhere in the historical literature.

## Technologies and the Changing Face of Distance Education

The technologies used to deliver distance education can be divided into three categories: correspondence, telecommunications, and computers (Garrison, 1985). The earliest courses on distance education offered in the 1700s and 1800s relied solely on correspondence through the postal service, and this trend continued for 200 years of distance education (Jeffries, 2004). With the advent of new technologies, including radio, television, and telephone, a second technological category of distance education arose (Garrison). By the late 1940s, five universities were using television to teach distance education courses, and by the late 1950s, 17 universities used television to supplement correspondence courses. In the late 1960s, many schools began to use their own closed circuit television (CCTV) systems and experiment with Instructional Fixed Television Service (ITFS) microwave systems. By the early 1970s, there were 233 educational television stations, and several universities had the infrastructure in place to bring distance learning to a large number of students (Jeffries). The use of the ITFS technology allowed universities to connect with other campuses on their network and reach more students off campus. By the late 1970s and early 1980s, the use of videotapes became a popular way to transmit education at a distance. In addition, real-time interactions combining ITFS and telephones allowed students to communicate more effectively with the faculty teaching the courses, information could be transferred at a faster rate, students received more immediate feedback, and students developed a better relationship with their teachers (Jeffries).

Although these improvements had an impact on the transmission of information, students still had to travel to a specific location to participate in the course, a barrier to some students (Garrison, 1985). In the 1980s, the use of e-mail, computer teleconferencing, and Computer Assisted Learning (CAL) enabled students to become virtually independent while being able to maintain the quality and frequency of communication between student and teacher (Garrison), thus effectively eliminating the travel barrier. These advancements led to the first online undergraduate course being offered in 1984 at the New Jersey Institute of Technology, and the first online degree program being offered at the University of Phoenix in 1989 (Jeffries, 2004). With continued technological advancement, especially the use of Internet and broadband technologies, the face of distance education has continued to change. The majority of courses offered today are either provided online or through various forms of computer teleconferencing. In addition, because of the availability of computers and the Internet, many high schools and universities have moved beyond offering only a few courses and now offer complete degree programs and mentoring online (Jeffries). Obviously, the dramatic improvement in technologies has enhanced the delivery of distance education; however, technology has also spurred exponential growth in this industry. Americans spend more than $500 billion on distance education annually and enroll in more than 2 million classes each year (Shea & Boser, 2001).

Distance learning is now widespread, especially at the college level. It is being utilized for transmitting instruction across geographic boundaries and extending unique educational opportunities nationally and internationally (Timpson & Jones, 1989). Researchers and educators assert that distance education can enable schools to expand their standard curricula and offer courses for different levels of learners (Ravaglia & Sommer, 2000). Distance learning transcends the constraints of time and space by using media such as computer- or Internet-based programs, which allow educators and learners to "interact," but not necessarily in face-to-face situations ("Accessing Distance Learning," 1995; Hofmeister, 1994; Washington, 1997). Researchers and educators emphasize that distance learning programs may never replace existing classrooms and schools but can be used to compensate for educational deficits and lack of advanced coursework in regular schools or a limited array of offerings (Adams & Cross, 1999/2000; Ravaglia & Sommer; Washington; Wilson, Litle, Coleman, & Gallagher, 1997/1998) or as part of a homeschooling program (Ravaglia & Sommer; Washington).

## Other Critical Issues

As with any course, materials for distance learning classes must be carefully chosen and prepared. Although some hands-on assignments used in a traditional classroom may have to be modified for distance learning, there are a variety of resources such as the National Library of Virtual Manipulatives (http://www.nlvm.usu.edu/en/nav/vlibrary.html) that can assist with overcoming this problem.

Although virtual laboratories are often used in conjunction with science classes, there is some controversy about their use. Currently, the College Board requires any course using the Advanced Placement (AP) designation to be approved prior to receiving that designation. In addition, the College Board insists that any student taking an AP science class must have a hands-on, not virtual, laboratory experience. Consequently, students taking an online AP science class must be supervised by a science educator during their laboratory work.

Building community in an asynchronous environment is another critical issue to the success of distance learning classes. Collaborative learning that allows students to work together to solve a problem is an important part of learning (Dillenbourg & Schneider, 1995; Johnson & Johnson, 1996). Both providing and sustaining opportunities to collaborate and build community among class members and the instructor are aspects of distance learning that must be addressed (Curtis & Lawson, 2001; Swan & Shih, 2005). When initiated, sustained, and managed appropriately, these online interactions can lead to learning outcomes that are comparable to in-class interactions (Harasim, Hiltz, Teles, & Turoff, 1995; Hiltz, 1998). Self-introductions, discussion board postings, sharing personal experience, and student home pages are ways to begin building community in distance learning courses (Walling, 2003).

## Distance Learning and Gifted Students

Historically, distance learning was designed primarily for students who were not succeeding in a traditional school setting or were unable to attend a regular school (Olszewski-Kubilius & Limburg-Weber, 2002; Timpson & Jones, 1989). As a result, studies on the effectiveness of distance learning have been limited to these groups of students (Adams & Cross, 1999/2000; Belcastro, 2001; Lewis, 1989; McBride & Lewis, 1993; Ravaglia & Sommer, 2000; Threlkeld, 1991). Due to the lack of literature or research regarding the role and effectiveness of this type of program for the gifted, there are only a few distance learning programs designed specifically for the gifted population (Adams & Cross).

## Learner Characteristics

There is little research on the characteristics of gifted learners who take distance learning courses, nor their reasons for doing so. However, Olszewski-Kubilius and Lee (2004) studied 99 students who took high school honors-level courses and 87 students who took Advanced Placement courses through a distance learning program called LearningLinks (LL) sponsored by Northwestern University's Center for Talent Development. This program is specifically designed for gifted students in grades 4–12. One of the purposes of the study was to determine students' reasons for enrolling in the program. Most of the respondents attended public schools; specifically, 43% attended a public school in a suburban area, 28.7% in a rural area, and 10.3% in an urban area, while only 11.5% of students attended a private or parochial school, and 5.7% were homeschooled. Thus, for the majority of the students who participated, the distance learning courses were supplemental to their regular school programs.

Students had multiple reasons for taking a distance education course, but their own interest in the subject area and desire to enrich their learning (69.7%) was the most frequently given reason (Olszewski-Kubilius & Lee, 2004). A substantial proportion of students (42%) took a LearningLinks course because it was not offered by their local schools, while another 40.4% took the course because it allowed them to work through the material at their own pace. To accelerate and advance more quickly to the next level in the subject area was a reason given by 29.3% of students for taking the LL class, while 10.1% of students reported they took the course to get another high school credit and 6.1% said they took it to accumulate another AP credit for college. Less than 10% of the students took a course through LL because, although it was available at their school, the course was not open to them at their grade level (the total for this reason was 8.1%). Similarly, 7.1% of students took the course through LL because they could not fit it into their school schedule. For 5.1% of students, the LL course was part of their homeschooling curriculum. Thus, gifted students' reasons for taking a distance learning course were varied, and substantial numbers were taking such courses to fill in gaps in their school programs.

Several studies focusing on distance learning and gifted students have found promising results, including more autonomy in learning, an increase in critical thinking skills, improved communication skills, better collaborative learning skills, opportunities for unique challenges, and opportunities for students to be exposed to topics and instructors not available in their current environment (Cope & Suppes, 2002; Ewing, Dowling, & Coutts, 1997; McBride & Lewis, 1993; McLoughlin, 1999; Olszewski-Kubilius & Lee, 2004; Wallace, 2005; Wilson et al., 1997/1998).

### Rationale for Distance Learning Programs for Gifted Students

Although some programs around the country have been successful, the need to create more distance programming for the gifted is growing (Lewis, 1989). The shortage of qualified teachers (especially math and science teachers) continues to grow, and for many gifted students, distance courses are the only way to fill this gap (McBride & Lewis, 1993). Without the opportunity to take advanced courses, many gifted students may find themselves unchallenged or frustrated because they are forced to take courses not designed for their needs (Benbow & Stanley, 1996). This frustration often occurs because of the trend in education to treat everyone the same, or at least level the playing field. While services are provided for many lower ability students to assist them in increasing their performance, many gifted students are left without the challenges they need (Benbow & Stanley). If these students do not have access to advanced courses in their home school, distance education could fill this gap and ensure that these students reach their potential. Gifted residential programs are in a unique position to provide the courses that are lacking in many school systems. Gifted residential schools already have master teachers, a larger budget, and are in a better place to seek out additional funding, especially if this type of service becomes a focus of their out-reach efforts (McBride & Lewis).

Having access to the courses necessary to complete one's education empowers learners to take charge of their education and develop independence and autonomy in their educational experience (Bonk, Wisher, & Lee, 2004). In addition to fos-tering independence and autonomy, distance courses also teach new technological skills that are not always available in the tra-ditional classroom. Acquiring these skills not only increases stu-dents' self-confidence, but can also enhance their motivation to learn. This is especially true of introverted students. While many introverted students hesitate to participate in a traditional classroom, in a distance education environment these students are able to interact frequently with confidence because they feel less intimidated by other students when they take courses at a distance (Bonk & King, 1998; Chong, 1998; Cooney, 1998).

Schools benefit by being able to serve more students with-out having to create more "space" to serve them and can offer a more comprehensive curriculum than would otherwise be available (Russell, 2004; Turoff, Discenza, & Howard, 2004). Ravaglia and Sommer (2000) viewed distance learning as a way to provide advanced instruction for highly gifted students with-out having to remove them from their regular school environ-ment. Schools can provide elementary students with middle and high school level classes without having to consider transport-ing these students to other schools or deal with the social/emo-tional issues that often arise when younger students are placed in classes with students who are several years older.

### Distance Learning May Not Be Appropriate for All Gifted Learners

Not every gifted student will be successful in a distance education course, however. Wilson and colleagues (1997/1998) suggest there are four characteristics of a successful gifted dis-tance education student: prerequisite course knowledge, desire to take a distance education course, ability to work indepen-dently, and motivation to persevere when things are difficult. Lacking any or all of these could severely hinder a student's successful completion of a distance education course and could consequently hinder his or her educational experience. In addition, the structure of the course itself may be unattractive to students if they feel their independence or autonomy is being reduced through required group work (Dirkx & Smith, 2004). Therefore, instructors should take into consideration these criteria before suggesting distance education as a way to enhance a gifted adolescent's educational experience (Wilson et al., 1997/1998).

## Distance Programs for Gifted Students

It is difficult to gauge how many gifted students are participating in distance education programs. A national study of four talent search programs found that 33,644 students in grades 3–12 had participated in distance education courses through the talent search programs since their inception in the 1990s and 7,468 had participated in 2003–2004 (Lee, Matthews, & Olszewski-Kubilius, in press). For the year 2003–2004, males (53.9%) surpassed females (45.9%) in their participation in distance education. More than half (54.2%) of the students were 7th–9th graders, 43.1% were 3rd–6th graders, and 2.8% were 10th–12th graders. Many other gifted students may be participating in distance education programs through state-supported virtual high schools. A recent book aimed at helping high-school-aged students find an online high school lists 113 programs (Kiernan, 2005). Although the overwhelming majority of these are not geared specifically toward gifted learners, individual programs may have courses appealing to or appropriate for them.

Despite the scarcity of research on distance education for the gifted, gifted educators continuously indicate their interest in distance education and believe that distance learning programs can potentially increase their ability to serve gifted learners who can particularly benefit from technologically mediated instruction. Researchers and educators also assert that distance learning programs can be helpful to gifted students who want to accelerate their learning or supplement and enrich existing educational resources (Adams & Cross, 1999/2000; Olszewski-Kubilius & Limburg-Weber, 2002), thereby enabling students to learn at a level commensurate with their capabilities (Adams & Cross; Threlkeld, 1991; Timpson & Jones, 1989; Washington, 1997). Distance learning programs may be a good option for a variety of types of gifted students, including students who attend rural schools where advanced courses and gifted programs are limited, students who cannot obtain "early" access to advanced courses, students who want to take additional advanced courses but cannot fit them into their school schedules, students who are not thriving in a typical school setting (Goodrich, 1994; Lewis, 1989; Lewis & Talbert, 1990; McBride, 1991; McBride & Lewis, 1993; Ravaglia & Sommer, 2000; Savage & Werner, 1994; Wilson et al., 1997/1998), and/or homebound learners (Ravaglia & Sommer).

Many of the more than 90 institutional members of the National Consortium for Specialized Secondary Schools of Mathematics, Science and Technology, as well as other schools and colleges, offer distance learning courses for precollege students. Following is a sample of such programs.

### The Louisiana School for Math, Science, and the Arts

Despite very little actual data on how successful gifted students are in distance education, researchers have documented evidence about the positive effects of distance learning programs on gifted and talented students academically and socially. Lewis (1989) studied a telelearning program at the Louisiana School for Math, Science, and the Arts (LSMSA) in which classes were offered to gifted students in rural areas via computers, electronic blackboards, modems, and phone lines. During 1987 and 1989, the Louisiana school offered courses such as Precalculus, Survey of the Arts, and Trigonometry to about 200 students. Surveys of the students showed that participants in the program became more independent learners, taking more responsibility for their academic experience. The study also found that relationships with fellow peers in the program became close-knit through small-group learning assignments and a shared experience of becoming active explorers in a new learning area. In a later study, McBride and Lewis (1993) utilized the distance learning program to provide special classes for gifted and high-achieving students from more than 100 rural locations. Using audiographic computer technology for advanced-level courses in the areas of math, foreign language, science, and the arts, surveys showed that the academically gifted high school students became more independent and interactive with other students by not having teachers for their courses. The distance learning courses also enabled some students to take advanced-level classes such as calculus, thereby making them more attractive college candidates.

### The North Carolina School of Science and Mathematics

Wilson and her associates (1997/1998) found benefits for distance learning programs for high school students at the North Carolina School of Science and Math (NCSSM). With the use of multiple sources of data such as student and teacher questionnaires, interviews with students and distance learning staff, focus groups, observations, document review, and student products (e.g., journal entries, videos, computer communications, essays, and test scores), the distance learning program was extensively evaluated over the course of 3 years. Findings revealed that the program enabled the mathematically and scientifically talented students to develop independent study and thinking skills and to better prepare for college. Students' comments on the advantages of the program included that they learned a great deal and more in depth, learned and experienced more than in their regular classes, developed better study skills, learned new means of communication, and developed better skills at using graphing calculators. Other benefits perceived by students were challenging and interesting coursework, improved communication skills, and opportunities for interactions with other intellectual peers from different geographical regions. Students also expressed that they obtained an idea of where they stand in comparison to other students from different schools, a common finding for gifted students when placed in appropriately challenging courses.

### The Indiana Academy for Science, Mathematics, and Humanities

The Indiana Academy at Ball State University is a public residential academy for gifted juniors and seniors from across Indiana. The Office of Outreach Programs extends the school's mission to schools and students using the most economical and innovative technologies available. They provide advanced high school courses including AP Biology, AP Calculus, AP Chemistry, AP Physics, AP Statistics, Astronomy, Japanese I, Japanese II, Russian I, Russian II, and Physics I. The courses can be taken via computer at home or school and a toll-free number is provided to enable students to talk with their instructors. A site coordinator is needed to communicate with the Academy offices and to grade assignments. Students who have taken the courses at the Academy find them challenging and an appropriate substitute for less rigorous classes at their regular school. In addition, students from small schools, rural schools, and those who are homeschooled have appreciated the opportunity to have access to coursework that is not generally available to them elsewhere.

### Superhighways Teams Across Rural Schools

Combining multimedia resources with communication networks, the Superhighways Teams Across Rural Schools (STARS) program was developed in northern Scotland. Ewing et al. (1997) studied 127 STARS students, most of whom were gifted, from 18 primary and two secondary rural schools and found that the distance education program increased these students' problem-solving abilities, logical thinking skills, and collaborative learning skills by enhancing their interactions with peers from different schools. Results also demonstrated that the program promoted students' motivation, task commitment, leadership ability, and responsibility for learning.

### Australia

McLoughlin (1999) implemented a "telematics" classroom, defined as teaching contexts using audiographic technology and computer graphics, as a way to enrich the learning experience of gifted students. This study involved five teachers who had 8–10 years of teaching experience and 30 secondary-school-aged gifted students from Western Australia. It examined the effectiveness of audiographic conference technology on the development of gifted students' cognitive thinking skills in the areas of math, science, English, Italian, and social science and on the promotion of communicative interactions between learners. Based on classroom observations and discourse analyses, data suggested that the teachers' use of technology to support verbal and visual expression (e.g., presenting and discussing ideas, resolving problems, etc.), enhanced students' collaborative and higher order thinking skills such as logical explanation, critical inquiry, interpretation, and reflection over three phases of intervention. In this electronic classroom, teachers became less controlling, but more focused on students' written responses, while the gifted students became more involved in collaboration and discussion in their learning during the program than before. The author noticed that the role of technology changed from a tool for displaying and introducing new concepts to a tool for achieving collaborative dialogue within and/or between learners and instructors.

## OWLink

Although Miller and Kumari's (1997) study was not specifically designed for gifted learners, a dozen teachers from third grade to the high school level participated in an electronic community named OWLink. The purpose of the program was to provide better education to students in grades K–12 using video conferencing and Internet technologies. By linking Rice University to five schools in Texas, an electronic community was developed using two-way audio/video and high-speed Internet connectivity. Examples of courses offered to students and teachers in grades K–12 included writing, Macbeth, algebra, AP Statistics, viruses, preventive medicine, reptiles, and "local heroes." Positive outcomes found in this study were that students not only enriched their learning in the subject areas they studied, but also gained interdisciplinary, historical, and cultural perspectives across various subjects and took more initiative and responsibility for their learning. For instance, some students created afterschool Internet clubs and classes on their own and contributed to operating the OWLink site voluntarily.

### The Center for Talented Youth

The Center for Talented Youth (CTY) program at Johns Hopkins University offers computer-based multimedia courses in mathematics, computer science, and writing, and also Advanced Placement courses. Math and computer science classes are individually paced and students can begin at any time and enroll for 3, 6, or 9 months (Wallace, 2005; Ybarra, 2005) Math courses cover the entire elementary and high school curriculum and include college-level courses, as well. Mathematics classes enable students to accelerate through the typical mathematics sequence or to take enrichment classes. Writing classes are available for students beginning in grade 5 and have set beginning and ending dates. AP classes prepare students to take the College Board AP exams and earn college credit. Students interact with their instructors using e-mail, telephone, or by means of an interactive Internet-based whiteboard. Students can earn high school credit for high-school-level classes.

### The Talent Identification Program

The Talent Identification Program (TIP) at Duke University offers distance education courses to gifted students in grades 8–12 through their E-Studies program. Courses are Web-based and use Blackboard, a course management software system (Putallaz, Baldwin, & Selph, 2005). Students read course materials, post assignments, and interact with their instructor and peers through online discussions, virtual lectures, and real-time collaborations. Currently, eight courses are offered, including Anatomy and Physiology, JAVA for Video Games, Macroeconomics, Psychology, Short Fiction Workshop, and others. Classes are 15 weeks in duration and require 5–7 hours per week of independent study. Duke does not grant credit for successfully complete E- Studies courses, but students may seek this on their own from their local school.

### The Center for Talent Development

The Center for Talent Development (CTD) at Northwestern University has offered a distance education program, LearningLinks (LL), for gifted students for more than 20 years. The LL program offers distance education classes to students in grades 4–12. Classes range from 3–9 months in duration. Classes for younger students include 22 enrichment classes such as The Wonders of Ancient Egypt, Classic American Novels, Writing Workshops, Latin, Topics in Math, Detective Science, and The Business of Marketing. Thirty or more high school honors-level classes are offered including Creative Writing, Literary Analysis, Journalistic Writing, Economics, U.S. History, Biology, Chemistry, and JAVA. Nineteen different AP classes are offered including AP Environmental Science, AP U.S. History, AP Economics, AP Statistics, and more. Students receive textboxes, which include introductory course materials, textbooks, and course syllabi. Students connect with teachers via e-mail, but all courses are available to students in traditional correspondence by mail format if needed. Courses use Blackboard Course Management System, which enables them to participate with other students in online discussions. Some honors-level courses are available in the summer in a 6-week option, and all high-school-level courses carry high school credit. In addition, through an association with the Education Program for Gifted Youth at Stanford University, elementary-school-level mathematics classes and college-level mathematics and physics classes are available.

## The Education Program for Gifted Youth

The Education Program for Gifted Youth (EPGY) offers multimedia computer-based distance learning courses in mathematics, English, humanities, physics, and computer science (Cope & Suppes, 2002; Gilbert-Macmillan, 2000). The mathematics sequence covers kindergarten level through the advanced undergraduate level. Writing classes are offered from the fourth-grade level through the AP level. Most English courses require a weekly meeting in a virtual classroom where students and instructors discuss aspects of their work. Humanities classes are available to juniors and seniors in high school and are offered in conjunction with the Alliance for Lifelong Learning. Physics classes are offered from the secondary level through the advanced undergraduate level. Computer science classes are offered at the secondary level. Students receive Stanford University credit for successfully completing undergraduate-level courses.

## Other Distance Learning Providers

In the for profit sector, the major providers are http://K12.com, http://class.com, and Apex Learning. At the elementary and middle school levels, K12.com offers math, science, history, language arts/English, and art (grades K–4), plus three other art courses, as well as several music courses. At the high school level, they offer 14 Advanced Placement classes (core content areas plus French and Spanish). Class.com offers high school classes only. In addition to the same 14 AP classes found at K12.com, Apex Learning offers physical education/health and music appreciation.

## Final Thoughts

In summary, research studies on distance learning have scarcely dealt with gifted learners, but the findings concerning effects on gifted students are inspiring. Across studies, positive effects for students include better cognitive skills, increased personal responsibility for learning, and exposure to a greater diversity of people and perspectives. There are also concerns about distance learning, which include the inability to use students' body language as an indication of student engagement and understanding (Gallagher, 2001) and unexpected technological problems (Lewis & Talbert, 1990). Lack of contact with other students, potential for isolation and separation, and lack of emotional support from peers and tutors in person are other concerns about distance education programs (University of Plymouth, 2002).

## References

Accessing distance learning. (1995, November/December). *Imagine, 3*, 1–4.

Adams, C. M., & Cross, T. L. (1999/2000). Distance learning opportunities for academically gifted students. *Journal of Secondary Gifted Education, 11*, 88–96.

Belcastro, F. P. (2001). Electric technology and its use with rural gifted students. *Roeper Review, 25,* 14–16.

Benbow, C. P., & Stanley, J. C. (1996). Inequity in equity: How "equity" can lead to inequity for high-potential students. *Psychology, Public, Policy, and Law, 2,* 249–292.

Bonk, C. J., & King, K. S. (1998). *Electronic collaborators: Learner-centered technologies for literacy, apprenticeship, and discourse.* Mahwah, NJ: Lawrence Erlbaum.

Bonk, C. J., Wisher, R. A., & Lee, J. (2004). Moderating learner-centered e-learning: Problems and solutions, benefits and implications. In T. S. Roberts (Ed.), *Online collaborative learning: Theory and practice* (pp. 54–86). Hershey, PA: Information Science Publishing.

Chong, S. M. (1998). Models of asynchronous computer conferencing for collaborative learning in large college classes. In C. J. Bonk & K. S. King (Eds.), *Electronic collaborators: Learner-centered technologies for literacy, apprenticeship, and discourse* (pp. 157–182). Mahwah, NJ: Lawrence Erlbaum.

Cooney, D. H. (1998). Sharing aspects within aspects: Real time collaboration within the high school English classroom. In C. J. Bonk & K. S. King (Eds.), *Electronic collaborators: Learner-centered technologies for literacy, apprenticeship, and discourse* (pp. 263–287). Mahwah, NJ: Lawrence Erlbaum.

Cope, E. W., & Suppes, P. (2002). Gifted students' individual differences in distance-learning computer-based calculus and linear algebra. *Instructional Science, 30,* 79–110.

Curtis, D. D., & Lawson, M. L. (2001). Exploring collaborative online learning. *Journal of Asynchronous Learning Networks, 5*(1). Retrieved May 14, 2006, from http://www.aln.org/alnweb/journal/Vol5_issue1/Curtis/curtis.htm

Dillenbourg, P., & Schneider, D. (1995). *Collaborative learning and the Internet.* Retrieved June 19, 2006, from http://tecfa.unige.ch/tecfa/research/CMC/colla/iccai95_1.html

Dirkx, J. M., & Smith, R.O. (2004). *Learning to see through the invisible: The problem of process in online collaborative learning.* Retrieved June 22, 2004, from http://idea.iupui.edu/bitstream/1805/251/1/DirkxSmith.pdf

Ewing, J., Dowling, J., & Coutts, N. (1997). *STARS: Report on Superhighways Teams Across Rural Schools project.* Dundee, Scotland: Northern College. (ERIC Document Reproduction Service No. ED421319)

Gallagher, J. J. (2001). Personnel preparation and secondary education programs for gifted students. *Journal of Secondary Gifted Education, 12*, 133–138.

Garrison, D. R. (1985). Three generations of technological innovations in distance education. *Distance Education, 6,* 235–241.

Gilbert-Macmillan, K. (2000). Computer-based distance learning for gifted students: The EPGY experience. *Understanding Our Gifted, 12*(3), 17–20.

Goodrich, B. E. (1994). Creating a "virtual" magnet school. *T.H.E. Journal, 21*(10) 73–75.

Harasim, L., Hiltz, S. R., Teles, L., & Turoff, M. (1995). *Learning networks: A field guide to teaching and learning online.* Cambridge, MA: MIT Press.

Hiltz, S. R. (1998). *Impacts of college-level courses via Asynchronous Learning Networks: Some preliminary results.* Retrieved June 19, 2006, from http://www.aln.org/alnweb/journal/issue2/hiltz.htm

Hofmeister, A. (1994). Technological tools for rural special education. *Exceptional Children, 50*, 326–331.

Jeffries, M. (2004, October). *Research in distance education.* Retrieved June 22, 2006, from http://www.digitalschool.net/edu/DL_history_mjeffries.html

Johnson, D. W., & Johnson, R. T. (1996). Cooperation and the use of technology. In D. H. Jonassen (Ed.), *Handbook of research for educational communications and technology* (pp. 1017–1044). New York: Simon & Schuster.

Kiernan, V. (2005). *Finding an online high school.* Alexandra, VA: Mattily Publishing.

Lee, S. Y., Matthews, M. S., & Olszewski-Kubilius, P. (in press). A national picture of talent search and talent search educational programs. *Gifted Child Quarterly.*

Lewis, G. (1989). Telelearning: Making maximum use of the medium. *Roeper Review, 11,* 195–198.

Lewis, G., & Talbert, M. (1990). Telelearning: Reaching out to the gifted in rural schools. *Educating Able Learners, 15*(1), 2–3, 10.

Ludlow, B. L., & Duff, M. C. (2003). Distance education and tomorrow's schools. In D. R. Walling (Ed.), *Virtual schooling: Issues in the development of e-learning policy* (pp. 15–30). Bloomington, IN: Phi Delta Kappa Educational Foundation.

McBride, R. (1991). Strategies for implementing teletraining systems in education K–12. In C. Steinfield & T. Ehlers (Eds.), *ITCA teleconferencing yearbook.* Washington, DC: ITCA.

McBride, R. O., & Lewis, G. (1993). Sharing the resources: Electronic outreach programs. *Journal for the Education of the Gifted, 16*, 372–386.

McLoughlin, C. (1999). Providing enrichment and acceleration in the electronic classroom: A case study of audiographic conferencing. *Journal of Special Education Technology, 14(2)*, 54–69.

Miller, L. M., & Kumari, S. (1997, January). *Project OWLink: Distance learning in electronic studios.* Paper presented at the Annual Distance Education Conference, Corpus Christi, TX.

Nasseh, B. (2004). *A brief history of distance education.* Retrieved June 19, 2006, from http://www.seniornet.org/edu/art/history.html

Nguyen, T., & Gattlin, L. (2004). *Distance learning.* Retrieved June 19, 2006, from http://www.bol.ucla.Edu/~pinkachu

Olszewski-Kubilius, P., & Lee, S. Y. (2004). Gifted adolescents' talent development through distance learning. *Journal for the Education of the Gifted, 28*, 7–35.

Olszewski-Kubilius, P., & Limburg-Weber, L. (2002). *Designs for excellence: A guide to educational program options for academically talented middle and secondary school students.* Evanston, IL: The Center for Talent Development, Northwestern University.

Putallaz, M., Baldwin, J., & Selph, H. (2005). The Duke University Talent Identification Program. *High Ability Studies, 16*, 41–54.

Ravaglia, R., & Sommer, R. (2000). Expanding the curriculum with distance learning. *Principal, 79(3)*, 10–13.

Russell, G. (2004). Virtual schools: A critical view. In C. Cavanaugh (Ed.), *Development and management of virtual schools: Issues and trends* (pp. 1–25). Hershey, PA: Idea Group.

Savage, L., & Werner, J. (1994). *Potpourri of resources to tap gifted education in rural areas.* Reston, VA: ERIC Clearinghouse on Disabilities and Gifted Education. (ERIC Document Reproduction Service No. ED369601)

Shea, R., & Boser, U. (2001, October 15). So where's the beef? *U.S. News & World Report*, 44.

Swan, K., & Shih, L. (2005). On the nature and development of social presence in online discussions. *Journal of Asynchronous Learning Networks, 9(3)*. Retrieved May 14, 2006, from http://www.aln.org/alnweb/journal/Vol9_issue3/Swan/swan.htm

Threlkeld, R. (1991). Increasing educational options through distance learning. *Communicator, 21(1)*, 12–14.

Timpson, W. M., & Jones, C. S. (1989). Increased education choices for the gifted: Distance learning via technology. *Gifted Child Today, 12(5)*, 10–11.

Turoff, M., Discenza, R., & Howard, C. (2004). How distance programs will affect students, courses, faculty, and institutional futures. In C. Howard, K. Schenk & R. Discenza (Eds.), *Distance learning and university effectiveness: Changing educational paradigms for online learning* (pp. 1–20). Hershey, PA: Idea Group.

University of Plymouth (2002). *Distance education: Why distance learning?* Retrieved March 12, 2003, from http://www.fae.plym.ac.uk/tele/vidconf1.html

Valentine, D. (2004). *Distance learning: Promises, problems, and possibilities.* Retrieved from http://www.westga.edu/~distance/ojkla/fall53/ valentine53.html

Wallace, P. (2005). Distance education for gifted students: Leveraging technology to expand academic options. *High Ability Studies, 16*(1), 77–86.

Walling, D. R. (2003). Virtual schooling and the arts: Potential and limitations. In D. R. Walling (Ed.), *Virtual schooling: Issues in the development of e-learning policy* (pp. 99–112). Bloomington, IN: Phi Delta Kappa Educational Foundation.

Washington, M. F. (1997). Real hope for the gifted. *Gifted Child Today, 20*(6), 20–22.

Wilson, V., Litle, J., Coleman, M. R., & Gallagher, J. (1997/1998). Distance learning: One school's experience on the information highway. *Journal of Secondary Gifted Education, 9*, 89–100.

Ybarra, L. (2005). Beyond national borders: The Johns Hopkins University Center for Talented Youth reaching out to gifted children throughout the world. *High Ability Studies, 16*(1), 15–26.

## Authors' Note

Portions of this chapter were taken from: Olszewski-Kubilius, P., & Lee, S. Y. (2004). Gifted adolescents' talent development through distance learning. *Journal for the Education of the Gifted, 28*, 7–35.

# Developing Personalized Learning Experiences: Mentoring for Talent Development

*Annie Xuemei Feng*

## Introduction

Why do we need mentoring programs for gifted students? What are effective mentoring program practices? What are key features of successful mentor–mentee relationships? What is a feasible framework for mentoring programs for gifted students? In what ways can we help gifted students to boost their confidence and utilize their potential through a mentor–mentee relationship?

This chapter will review the historical evolution of mentoring programs, examine the research literature on effective mentoring program practices, review extant mentoring programs, and propose a mentoring model for best developing gifted students' potential, particularly for those who are scientifically talented.

## A Brief Review of the History of Mentoring Programs

Mentoring is an intense interpersonal relationship where a more senior individual (the mentor) provides guidance and support to a more junior individual (the protégé or mentee;

Kram, 1985, as cited in Eby & Lockwood, 2005). A mentorship is a dynamic and shared relationship in which values, attitudes, passions, and traditions are passed from one person to another and internalized (Boston, 1976, as cited in Berger, 1994).

The term and concept of *mentor* can be traced back as early as Homer's *Odyssey,* when Odysseus entrusted his friend Mentor with the care of his son Telemachus in the time of the Trojan War. The broader application of mentorship started in the early 20th century, where several major purposes served the origin and development of mentoring programs. Mentoring programs have been widely developed in the United States, Canada, Australia, and England, as well as in Western Europe and Israel for different social reasons and in different political contexts (Miller, 2002).

The widespread use of mentoring programs emerged in a number of social and political contexts in modern America. Big Brothers Big Sisters, the first in a wave of large-scale mentoring programs, emerged in the early 1950s to alleviate the social problems brought about by poverty and economic depression. The fundamental purpose of the Big Brother/Sister movement was to prevent social breakdown through socializing, guiding, and building personal relationships (Beiswinger, 1985). Propelled by the Civil Rights Movement, the second wave of mentoring programs arose in the mid-1960s to 1970s and established different mentoring schemes to help minority and/or women employees to gain confidence in the work place and become a more productive person at relevant stages of their careers (Freedman, 1992). The third wave of the mentoring movement was probably sped up by the release of the 1983 report, *A Nation at Risk*, produced by the National Commission on Excellence in Education, which called for collaboration among schools, corporations, and universities to provide mentoring opportunities for young people in order to increase the academic achievement of youth, as well as to develop talent and increase productivity of the society (Guetzlow, 1997, as cited in Miller, 2002). The major purpose of the recent mentoring movement appears to give priority to a younger age cohort, focusing more often on children from disadvantaged families and/or minority backgrounds, as well as children or youth who are at risk for joining gangs or committing crimes.

All of these mentoring program efforts have been focused on alleviating social problems through early prevention by matching and building individual mentor-protégé relationships and finding a caring adult for younger children who are likely to be at risk for failure in many facets of their lives. The investment and endorsement by the federal government, private corporations, and philanthropic organizations, as well as local communities have helped mentoring programs continue to grow in different sectors of lives and for lofty reasons to improve the society as a whole (see Miller, 2002).

## Forms of Mentoring

There are mainly two forms of mentoring: informal and formal mentoring. The informal mentoring, or natural mentoring, often occurs coincidentally between a senior or peer member (the mentor) of a field of study, an organization, or the community, and a junior member (the mentee) who may or may not be in the same field of study or work as the mentor. The relationship is established without being facilitated by any programs; rather, a coincidental experience, shared interests, or the proximity of the work environment made the two befriend each other, whereby the mentor is willing to provide psychological support and personal advice, as well as career-related advice. Research suggests that informal mentorships often elicit high levels of satisfaction and comfort between the mentor and the protégé (Eby & Lockwood, 2005; Linnehan, 2003; Miller, 2002). Examples of natural mentoring include a friendship occurring between two people (one senior, one junior) at work, an undergraduate student working with a professor who was not assigned the advisory responsibility for that student, a high school female science teacher and one of her female students, and doctoral students who studied in the same program and developed a friendship. The natural mentorship may take many forms and may occur in many settings, but the commonalities of this type of senior-junior or peer-mentor relationship are the informal nature of the relationship, and the associated satisfaction, comfort, appreciation, friendship, and academic and career opportunities that emerge for the junior person over a long period of time.

The other form of mentorship is a formal mentorship program. There is typically a structure to the program that facilitates the mentor and protégé relationship according to specific goals and objectives. Examples of formal mentorships include all kinds of mentoring programs, such as school-to-work programs (Linnehan, 2003), the Big Brothers Big Sisters organization (Beiswinger, 1985), the different versions of youth drug and alcohol prevention mentoring programs (Freedman, 1992), and many of the mentoring programs in the business world, such as Wachovia Corporation, MTV Networks, Lockheed-Martin, American Airlines, Sarah Lee, Bank of America, and Proctor and Gamble, with the objective to attract, develop, and retain high-quality employees (Eby & Lockwood, 2005).

## A Review of the Literature

Extensive research evidence on mentorship and mentoring experiences suggests that mentorships have positively impacted people in a number of ways. It has been an effective way to increase one's self-esteem (Hébert & Olenchak, 2000; Linnehan, 2003); to enhance productivity in both academic and corporate settings (Berger, 1994; Campbell, 1996; Feng, Campbell, & Verna, 2001); and to elicit friendship, life satisfaction, self-fulfillment of the mentor, and a clear vision of the direction of the future career for the mentee (Miller, 2002).

In the gifted education literature, Clasen and Clasen (2003) asserted, "Mentoring is a time-honored means of educating the gifted and talented" (p. 218). Gifted students are deemed to be particularly suitable for mentorship experiences because of their ability to work independently and their degree of motivation (Clasen & Clasen; Ellington, Haeger, & Feldhusen, 1986). Mentorships geared to the particular needs of talented and precocious children can be used to provide opportunities for the talented to actualize their potential (Cox, Daniel, & Boston,

1985; Hamilton & Hamilton, 1992; Lupkowski, Assouline, & Vestal, 1992; Stanley, 1979; Torrance, 1984; Wright & Borland, 1992). Mentorships allow gifted students opportunities to focus intensely on their area of talent and interest and explore it in a "ceilingless" environment (Purcell, Renzulli, McCoach, & Spottiswoode, 2002), because a good mentor establishes an environment in which the student's accomplishment is limited only by the extent of his talent.

The support and encouragement a protégé receives from the mentor greatly affects both his or her attitude and self-concept (Clasen & Clasen, 2003); mentoring experiences help to build up and solidify the mentee's self-esteem, influencing his or her interests in further research and helping his or her career orientations (Davalos & Haensly, 1997), eventually working toward eminence in fields of endeavor (Subotnik, Stone, & Steiner, 2001). Kaufman (1981), in her study of Presidential Scholars, found that mentors played significant roles in being a role model, providing support and encouragement, and offering intellectual stimulation, which had a long-lasting impact on academically exceptional people in the later stage of their lives. Hébert and Olenchak (2000) found that mentors who are open-minded and nonjudgmental and who are consistent and caring may reverse the pattern of achievement for gifted underachievers.

The literature suggests that there are three major dimensions of benefits mentorships can provide: (a) one-on-one individual advice and/or instruction on learning, career planning, time-management, and any other relevant knowledge and skills; (b) psychological support to the protégé through personal conversations, the presence of the mentor himself, constant and consistent advice, and developed friendship between the two parties; and (c) career opportunities through the mentor's deliberate and associated networking effort, often paving the way for job promotion and a long-term career path for the protégé (Freedman, 1992; Jacobi, 1991; Subotnik & Olszewski-Kubilius, 1997). Mentorships also benefit the mentor in different ways, including bringing life satisfaction, moments of self-reflection, and an opportunity to develop long-term friendships and collegial relationships with the mentee (Berger, 1994; Linnehan, 2003; Miller, 2002).

## The Role of a Mentor

In the mentor-protégé relationship, the mentor plays a critical role toward fostering a beneficial, productive, and long-lasting relationship. Mentors serve different roles in the mentor and protégé relationship. Pleiss and Feldhusen (1995) cited research about children with exceptional talent and the development of prodigies who had demonstrated the importance of intense relationships with adults, including nonfamily mentors in the lives of people who successfully transform their gifts into talents and achieve eminence. Mentors, according to Pleiss and Feldhusen, "introduce students to ideas, theories, tools, activities or careers in their own fields of expertise" (p. 159). The process of collaboration between mentor and mentee is an important aspect contributing to early productivity of scientists (Long, 1990). Students in mentorships are also socialized to the mentor's work habits, attitudes, values, and lifestyle (Pyryt, 2000; Subotnik & Olszewski-Kubilius, 1997), because the mentor is also expected to provide guidance for the mentee's life and lifestyle (Casey & Shore, 2000).

Mentors also serve as role models. The gifted learner can see in the mentor "an idealized self and in that sense realize possibilities for future accomplishments" (VanTassel-Baska, 1998, p. 493). In a longitudinal study of highly talented science students (i.e., 1983 Westinghouse/Intel winners), Subotnik and her colleagues (2001) found that highly regarded mentors imparted tacit knowledge about a domain of science to their protégé, an important factor in helping scientifically talented people to retain, excel, and contribute in research and applied science. A successful person who has achieved outstandingly in a field often cites a number of excellent coaches or mentors in his life who played a critical role in his path toward eminence (Bloom, 1985).

*Traits of Good Mentors*

Given the multiple roles that a mentor can play in a student's life, what counts as a good and effective mentor? Miller (2002) summarized more than 10 attributes of good mentors: enthusiasm, accessibility, sensitivity, self-awareness, discretion and trust, willingness to learn and experience, nonjudgmental, patience, positive expectations, kindness, and tolerance (p. 190). A good mentor listens carefully and patiently, builds a relationship, nurtures self-efficiency and curiosity, facilitates interests, finds a fit for a motivated student (resourceful), shares his- or herself, provides critical and constructive feedback, and acts as a role model in terms of commitment, work ethic, self-discipline, and personality. These qualities of a good mentor also matched with findings in other studies of mentorships (Arnold & Subotnik 1995; Dondero, 1997; Farmer, 1999; Jacobi, 1991; Withers & Batten, 1995). Quek (2005), in her study of mentorship programs for high-ability science students, found that the most highly ranked qualities of effective mentors were "genuine interest in the mentee as an individual," "well-versed in his field," and "passion for the subject/field" (p. 199). A good mentor also "knows when to help and when to let [a] mentee work independently," and "creates opportunities to give [the] mentee more exposure in the field" (Quek, p. 199).

These traits of effective mentors have important implications for developing a sustained and effective mentor-mentee relationship and for the successful development of mentorship programs. Although the expertise and prestige of a mentor might have been the initial attraction to the mentee, research findings suggest that the affective and emotional attachment between the mentor and the protégé was the real impetus that made the long-lasting impact on the life and work of the mentee.

## Mentoring Programs
## for Scientifically Talented Youth

In the United States, many off-campus special programs exist, serving as additional learning venues for students with talents in a specific domain. These programs often provide or facilitate more individualized learning experiences for their attendees, bridging mentoring opportunities for highly motivated and talented students. The following section examines a few such programs, presenting research evidence on effective mentoring experiences on program participants.

Three major types of special programs might shed light on developing effective mentoring models for scientifically talented students: the structured summer residential program model (e.g., the Research Science Institute), the competition-driven mentoring model with a focus on research (e.g., Intel Talent Search Program), and the competition-driven and semi-structured mentoring model with a focus on problem solving (e.g., the Academic Olympiad programs).

### The Research Science Institute

In the field of gifted education, the Research Science Institute (RSI) program sponsored by the Massachusetts Institute of Technology (MIT) and Center for Excellence in Education (CEE) is a model of a mentoring program in the sciences. The RSI students are selected on the basis of research projects they conducted in combination with an extended essay on goals, experiences, and insider knowledge of the research enterprise in math and science, as well as their superb performance in their science classes. Selected students are invited to participate in a summer residential program where they have accessibility to a first rate professor and/or his lab work and study. In this program, students will work under the apprenticeship of a prestigious professor conducting scientific research in biology.

Subotnik & VanTassel-Baska (2004) found that the RSI mentoring program has been an important experience for those who have participated. Participants commented that the program provided them a great opportunity to apply their interest in research, learning real science at a much more comfortable speed and at the right level of breath and depth of knowledge than they could have at their high schools. One participant noted, "Having great/passionate teachers" was the most crucial factor for the development of scientific talent. They felt they benefited a great deal from the research opportunities at RSI in comparison to what they learned in school settings. An RSI student noted, "In the past I have gone to many math and science summer camps, which were all very fine and well. But at RSI, I met many students from so many different fields that I never even knew existed. RSI has definitely increased my appreciation of the sciences in general."

The RSI participants encouraged and advised their peers to take every opportunity to pursue their passion and to prepare for a career in science through acceleration and contests, while finding a learning community of shared interests. One participant suggested the following:

> Take as many advanced classes as you can as early as possible; don't listen to others when they try to tell you what you can and cannot do. Try to earn recognition in science, competitions, and seize [each] research opportunity you can find. If you get discouraged because your school's scientific community is a community of one, see refuge in your studies until you can find peers you identify with, but never compromise who you are to fit in with your school community.

Another participant said, "Seize your own opportunities—create a niche for yourself and above all, do not let the dogma of the educational system encumber your interests, talent, and dreams." By contrast, the RSI participants criticized the lack of opportunities in school settings for their advanced ability and knowledge in science. Participants commented that "inability to accelerate [at school]," "parents' belief in more fun than hard work," "lack of advanced courses before high school," and "lack of opportunity to do extensive research near home" were all perceived barriers to developing science potential.

These findings suggest that a residential mentorship program like the RSI broadened the scope and interests of scientifically talented students, providing them an environment unlike the regular school setting.

## Singapore Research Program

Following the model of the RSI in the United States, the National University of Singapore established a mentoring program for high-potential science students called the Science Research Program (SRP). A recent study of SRP participants (Quek, 2005) covering a span of 17 years found that the SRP mentoring program was very effective in "deepening participants' knowledge of science beyond what the school curriculum could offer, and sharpening their research skills, and further stimulated their interest in science" (p. 205). The impact on participants' interest and confidence in doing science was more powerful and salient for female than male participants. Similar to findings from the study of the RSI participants, the SRP mentoring program was also highly praised for the interaction opportunities with other high-caliber participants who shared similar interests in science. The cohorts who had the experience of the residential component of the program ranked this component of the program as a special highlight.

Another benefit of such a mentoring program was to expose the students to the real life of a scientist, which helped participants have a clearer vision of what doing science as a college major or future career would be like, and whether he or she would relish the lifestyle and work of a scientist. Such an exposure at an early stage might well serve as a reality check to students for their further pursuit of a career in science.

However, a deeper examination of the SRP participants' insights revealed problems in the program, as well, including a mismatch between mentor and the mentee in terms of both interest and personality, the aloof attitude of some professors toward high school students, the lack of an accurate estimation of participants' abilities, as well as a conflict with school schedules during the school calendar year (Quek, 2005).

Overall, the study found that a mentoring program for scientifically talented youth such as the SRP can make a great impact on its participants. One SRP participant summarized well the impact of the experience on her personally by contrasting her experience at school and in the SRP:

> The scientific method is not well taught, practical experiments require an almost mindless following of instructions. Experiment materials and procedures are all prepared for students. Observations and deductions can be made by rote. This gives the impression that science is a manufactured, generate-out-of-thin-air study. (Quek, 2005, p. 130)

Of her SRP experience, however, she said that:

> If I had not been in the SRP, I would not have experienced a comprehensive study of the scientific process, which the SRP gave me, because it focused not just on the results, but also the process of achieving it. It has strengthened my interest in science, and my desire to pursue research as a career. (Quek, pp. 130–131)

Such a comment was echoed by many of the others who had similar experiences in the program.

Together, the RSI and SRP studies suggest that regardless of cultural settings, a well-structured mentoring program may make a long-term impact on student interest and further pursuit in the science field. It may also serve as a reality check at an appropriate time for those students who find a lack of fit in science so that they can make an early decision to opt out of a science career.

## Competitions That Require Mentoring

In the United States, there exist many competitions at different school levels, and in various domains, that require strong mentoring and coaching as a prelude to successful participation. The two types of competitions, research-oriented and problem-solving-oriented competitions (often in the form of the Intel Talent Search and the Academic Olympiads, respectively), are among the most prestigious contests in the country. A result of these competitions has been the development of preparatory programs including mentoring programs, albeit in an informal manner in many instances. These programs often facilitate the development of the most brilliant students in a specific scientific or mathematical domain, providing a bridge between the needs of talented students who desire advanced learning and university professors and research scientists who are very often solely immersed in the world of science at an institute of higher learning.

## Research-Oriented Competitions

There is a type of semistructured mentoring program popular in places where highly selective math and science schools are located and where there is also a high density of research institutes and/or university research facilities available, such as in New York City, Chicago, and Washington, DC. This mentoring relationship is informal in the sense that there is neither a specific program provided nor a designated staff member assigned. The mentor–protégé relationship is developed to meet the demands of competitions such as the Intel Talent Search or the Junior Science and Humanities Symposium held each year. Such a mentorship is often self-initiated by a faculty member at a local high school where the teacher may also serve as the mentor. However, the mentoring relationship is often intentional and undergoes a system of selection to match the mentor and mentee in terms of their shared interests, based on the potential of the young student. Despite a lack of a formal structure, however, once the mentor and mentee relationship is established, it may endure from 1 or 2 years to a lifelong friendship and colleagueship.

One example is an endeavor of the science department at a highly selective secondary school, Bronx Science High School, in New York City. Several major faculty members formed a system to help their students develop strong research skills and products for the purpose of winning the Intel competition, as well as to fulfill course requirements. These faculty either served as mentors for one or two students in an area of expertise every year, or more often, they served as the conduit and liaison between highly gifted students and university professors or scientists in prestigious research entities in the New York metropolitan area (e.g., Cornell Medical Research Center, Rockefeller Research Institute, New York University, Columbia University, City University of New York, and State University of New York; Berger, 1994), based on students' interest and ongoing research projects of the scientist. The high school teacher kept an updated list of scientists in those institutions, updating their research expertise and ongoing projects and maintaining a good rapport with these labs and the research faculty there.

During junior year, every student at Bronx High is expected to conceive a research topic of interest. The research topic can be in math, science, or the social sciences. Every student is expected to produce a research product at the end of his or her senior year as part of the course requirement. The research product is expected to meet the criteria for a scientific publication expected by the field of study, which is consistent with criteria set by the competition sponsors. Therefore, it is not unusual for a junior high school student from Bronx High to spend many afterschool hours per week, including the weekends, in an outside campus research lab for one or more years in order to produce a high-quality research product in preparation for the Intel competition (Berger, 1994). These talented high school juniors have already stepped into the forefront of cutting edge scientific research at a much younger age than students who would otherwise follow the college and graduate school routine of postsecondary education.

Subotnik and Steiner (1994) conducted a longitudinal study of the 1983 cohort of Intel winners and found quality mentorship (or having a mentor who cares, supports, and advises along the road) was perceived as the crucial factor in sustaining students' interests in science, and often became the driving force for them to choose a career in science. In the fourth follow-up study with the same cohort of participants, Subotnik and her colleagues (2001) found mentors played a critical role in helping their elite science protégé succeed through communicating tacit knowledge of the field, integrating the norms and expectations of the profession together with content expertise and cutting edge research skills.

### Problem-Solving-Oriented Competitions

Parallel to the research-oriented competitions represented by the Intel Talent Search is the problem-solving-oriented Academic Olympiad program. The Academic Olympiad competition is an analog to the athletic Olympics in the intellectual arena. Each year, brilliant high school students are selected from each country to compete at the International Academic Olympiad in different academic domains, ranging from math, physics, chemistry, biology, and informatics, to the most recent competition in astronomy. The math, physics, and chemistry Olympiads attract contestants from more than 60 countries every year to compete. While each country has its own mechanism of selection, the most common method employed is to select highly able students through domain-specific advanced assessments at local, state, and national levels. In the United States, the selection process goes through teacher recommendations and a series of screening tests sponsored by the American Mathematical Society, The American Chemical Society, and the American Association of Physics Teachers.

This type of competition produces another form of short-term "mentoring" programs, through domain-specific summer camps sponsored by the above-mentioned organizations and societies. There are about 20–25 students who are annually selected for the summer training camp within each subject matter from high school students all over the United States. The top mathematicians and scientists are often invited to give lectures and provide intensive coverage of topics in specific domains. The Olympiad summer camp lasts from 10 days to 2 weeks, thus it is hard to evaluate the mentor-protégé relationship based on such a short-term experience. In addition, the model of Olympiad summer camp is not a one-on-one model like the research product-driven mentorship. The focus of the

Olympiad training camp is on problem-solving skills and intensive knowledge compacting.

However, in a study with U.S. math Olympians, Campbell (1996) found that the mentoring experience played a critical role in math Olympians' productivity. Ninety-two percent of the total published books, articles, and research papers were produced by those who had college mentors, compared with only 8% of the publications produced by those who had no mentors; with regard to patents registered, 80% of the registered patents came from those who had mentoring experiences, versus 20% of registered patents from math Olympians who did not. Furthermore, none of the math Olympians in other countries studied had comparable productivity in terms of publications and patents. Investigators from other cultures agreed that the lack of mentoring experiences was one of the main reasons for the paucity of published work of their Olympians (Hirano, 1996; Kukushkin, 1996; Wu, 1996; Zha, Liu, & Tal, 1996). Further studies with chemistry and physics Olympians corroborated the findings in math (Feng et al., 2001; Verna, Campbell, & Feng, 2002).

### The Impact of the Olympiad Program

Despite a lack of direct evidence on the impact of a formal mentoring program, the Olympiad study showed that the short-term training program has positively impacted participants in a number of ways in the long run (Campbell, 1996; Feng et al., 2001; Lengfelder & Heller, 2002; Tirri & Koro-Ljungberg, 2002; Wu & Chen, 2001). The Olympiad experience was both an affirming and humbling process to most American Olympians (78%), confirming their interests and abilities in math and science, and also allowing them to get to know other highly able peers.

The Olympian participants reported their experiences in participating in summer programs through the Olympiad camp, as well as at specific universities. They took courses together, were involved in the laboratory work with graduate students, and immersed themselves with other high-caliber peers. One

Olympian stated, "The availability of an institution with a mission to support academically talented growth was crucial" (Feng, 2001, p. 134). The program not only brings these students to higher levels of academic challenges, but also creates a chance for them to meet other peers of similar caliber. Participation in these programs led them into the world of science and made it possible for them to interact with other peers, sharing their interests and helping them to satisfy their curiosity.

Research has suggested that despite the lack of a formal mentoring program structure, this competition-driven mentor-mentee relationship is quite successful in terms of ongoing scientific productivity, affirming talent and sustaining pursuit of research interests.

## Effectiveness of Mentoring Programs and Issues With the Programs

The mentoring research suggests that effective mentoring programs can benefit young gifted and talented students in many ways. Using out-of-school resources to best serve the needs of gifted students of different populations appears to be a feasible venue to help them fulfill their potential and develop a positive attitude toward life and work. As there is no panacea in any field, there will not be a one-size-fits-all mentorship model for all gifted students. The effectiveness of a mentoring model depends on several characteristics in a formal mentoring program; by contrast, the lack of these features often becomes issues or barriers to successful mentoring.

### There Needs to Be a Good Match Between the Mentor and the Mentee

Abundant literature suggests that a successful and sustainable mentorship depends a great deal upon a "fit" between the two parties (Berger, 1994; Higgins & Boone, 2003). These fits and matches imply both surface matches, such as ethnicity and gender, and the deeper level matches of shared interests, hobbies, and personalities; a match often entails a mutually satisfying experience and long-term friendship. Ortiz-Walters and Gilson (2005) studied the experiences of protégés of color in academia, finding that the shared ethnic background often implied similar values, which was positively associated with satisfaction and support received. The interpersonal comfort and commitment, however, mediated between the relationship of surface-level and deep-level similarities.

### Identified Needs of the Mentee Should be Assessed

Establishing a mentoring program often carries specific goals and objectives for a targeted population (Miller, 2002). However, not everyone from the same population will have the same type of needs. As a program staff member or coordinator, he or she should identify with the potential mentee or the mentee's family what kind of mentorship the mentee wants to develop, why he or she chose to join a mentorship program, and what his or her expectations are for the program. A gifted underachiever might need a mentor who gives him or her more encouragement rather than a push for knowledge and achievement. A participant in a mentoring program such as RSI and SRP might need more input to develop a sufficient knowledge background, more independent work, or more face-to-face discussion with the mentor assigned.

### There Needs to Be a Clear Communication Mechanism in the Program

A successful mentoring program should have a clear communication mechanism at different levels. First, the program should be structured in such a way that the goals of the program and the expectations and responsibilities of both the mentor and the protégé should be clearly communicated through program orientation and parent communication, as well as a cordial exchange of opinions between the mentor and the mentee. Does each party really understand what the program is for? Does the mentor or the mentee want such a program, given the specified expectations and responsibilities? What are the needs of the mentee?

Literature on effective mentoring relationships suggests that regular meetings of substantial frequency are crucial to establish trust, friendship, and collegiality between the mentor and protégé (Eby & Lockwood, 2005; Hébert & Olenchak, 2000; Miller, 2002). Through frequent and regular meetings, the two individuals have the opportunity to discuss needs and expectations clearly and in a timely way, adjusting unrealistic goals, and having more opportunities to get to know and befriend each other. However, flexibility in terms of mode and frequency of communication should be honored. An agreement regarding communication needs to be developed and agreed upon by the mentor and the mentee.

### There Needs to Be a High Level of Commitment to the Relationship

The level of enthusiasm and commitment to a formal mentoring program is not always high. This is not difficult to understand, because such mentor and mentee relationships were matched, rather than occurring naturally. After the study of the SRP mentoring program, Quek (2005) argued that given the resource-intensive nature of the mentoring program, one could not assume that altruism would be a sufficient factor to attract the best mentors for the program. She further suggested that a structure of incentives be put in place in recognition of the contributions of mentors who are willing to share their expertise and time to mentor gifted students. Both the residential mentoring model and the competition-related semiformal mentoring program (e.g., Intel, Olympiad programs) appeared to show that external incentives, such as winning an award, played a positive role in students' drive for continuing long-term, sometimes mundane, scientific work in order to have research results. The willingness for participation in a mentoring program of both the mentor and the protégé may depend on both external incentives and up front acknowledgement of the reality of work and the type of responsibility held.

## There Needs to Be a Well-Conceived System of Sustainability

Developing and sustaining mentoring programs is a resource-intensive process. Selecting students, mentor recruiting, and sustaining a steady pool of mentors are challenging issues. Mentoring programs typically have an expectation for long-term relationships between the mentor and the protégé; such a goal requires the time commitment of both parties and the availability of the mentor. Due to the long-term nature of many mentoring programs, it is not unusual that there is a drain of mentors from the program. Efforts need to be spent in maintaining a constant pool of mentors to continue such programs. A list of potential mentor candidates should be constantly updated, regular contacts with both program mentors and potential mentor candidates need to be established, and efforts need to be spent in communicating with mentors about their availability and intentions for serving their roles for a relatively long time (i.e., one year and longer). Given the limited pool of available mentor candidates and the mobile nature of American society, it is crucial to maintain an already established mentorship. Providing and facilitating channels for long-distance mentorships through telementoring may prove to be an alternative venue for efficiently utilizing limited resources.

## Mentorships Need to Be Targeted to Specific Populations of Gifted Learners

Targeting a particular population to be served in a mentoring program has proven to be another challenging issue. Even within the gifted population itself, a great variation of needs coexist. The heterogeneous characteristics of the gifted population embody different kinds of needs by students labeled under different categories (e.g., gifted underachievers, twice-exceptional students, domain-specific gifted, etc.), which entails mentoring programs with different goals and responsibilities and expectations for mentors. Given the resource-intensive nature of any mentoring program, prioritizing a targeted population for service becomes critical. Identifying the urgent, yet ignored needs of a particular population can be a first step. For example, a mentoring program could make it a priority to select talented students who are from disadvantaged backgrounds; in turn, the mentor not only serves as a content expert, but also a role model and a caring adult, compensating for what might have often been missing from such students' families.

### Mentorship Programs Require Incentives

Although competitions and awards entail extrinsic motivation, it is also true that the nature of these events requires intrinsic motivation in order for students to experience high levels of achievement, be it in sports, music, or academics. Both the studies of the Intel Science Talent Search winners and the academic Olympians show that competition-driven mentorships bring with them the recognition of achievement and efforts. This recognition also causes a ripple effect, which enhances self-confidence and increases interests, self-actualization, more sensitivity to others, and a stimulating peer group, as well as further opportunities to pursue science in postsecondary institutions. Yet, participation in these programs is more than the recognition that occurs for winners. The effort spent, the experiential learning gained from the mentor, the life and scholarship principles inherited from the mentor, and a choice for furthering or discontinuing a career in the field of math, science, or engineering may far outweigh the meaning of losing or winning a competition.

## Conclusion

It is a great fortune to have a few good mentors during one's lifetime. A mentor becomes a rich resource of encouragement and inspiration and a role model, influencing the protégé's attitude, interest, work ethic, ways of thinking, values, and perspectives at different stages of a protégé's life, academically, socially, and personally. To have a good mentor at a younger age is even more critical, as the role of the mentor can be influential in the early stages of development. Thus, mentoring programs can play an important role in effectively utilizing available educational resources from both within and outside of the school system. A great reservoir of mentors can be found in schools, communities, libraries, universities, research institutes, museums, corporations, and many other resources in the society. Identifying the needs of gifted students at different developmental stages and finding and matching good mentors for these needs is a challenging, but worthy endeavor.

## References

Arnold, K., & Subotnik, R. F. (1995). Mentoring the gifted: A differentiated model. *Educational Horizons, 73*, 118–123.

Beiswinger, G. (1985). *One to one: The story of the Big Brothers/Big Sisters movement in America.* Philadelphia: Big Brothers/Big Sisters of America.

Berger, J. (1994). *The young scientists: America's future and the winning of the Westinghouse.* Reading, MA: Addison-Wesley.

Bloom, B. S. (Ed.). (1985). *Developing talent in young people.* New York: Ballantine.

Campbell, J. R. (1996). Early identification of mathematics talents has long-term positive consequences for career contributions. *International Journal of Educational Research, 25*, 497–522.

Casey, K. M. A., & Shore, B. M. (2000). Mentors' contributions to gifted adolescents' affective, social, and vocational development. *Roeper Review, 22*, 227–230.

Clasen, D. R., & Clasen, R. E. (2003). Mentoring: A time-honored option for education of the gifted and talented. In N. Colangelo & G. A. Davis (Eds.), *Handbook of gifted education* (3rd ed., pp. 254–267). Boston: Allyn & Bacon.

Cox, J., Daniel, N., & Boston, B. O. (1985). *Educating able learners: Programs and promising practice.* Austin: University of Texas Press.

Davalos, R. A., & Haensly, P. A. (1997). After the dust has settled: Youth reflect on their high school mentored research experience. *Roeper Review, 19,* 204–207.

Dondero, G. M. (1997). Mentors: Beacons of hope. *Adolescence, 32*, 881–886.

Eby, L. T., & Lockwood, A. (2005). Protégés and mentors' reactions to participating in formal mentoring programs: A qualitative investigation. *Journal of Vocational Behavior, 67*, 441–458.

Ellington, M. K., Haeger, W. W., & Feldhusen, J. F. (1986, March/April). The Purdue mentor program: A university-based mentorship program for G/C/T children. *Gifted Child Today, 9*, 2–5.

Farmer, D. (1999). *Mentoring: Meeting the needs of gifted students in regular classrooms.* Retrieved June 22, 2006, from http://www.austega.com/gifted/provisions/mentoring

Feng, A. X. (2001). *Isolating home/school factors contributing to or hindering the development of American Physics Olympians.* Unpublished doctoral dissertation, St. John's University, New York.

Feng, A. X., Campbell, J. R., & Verna, M. A. (2001). The talent development of American Physics Olympians. *Gifted and Talented International, 16*, 108–114.

Freedman, M. (1992). *Partners in growth: Elder mentors and at-risk youth.* Philadelphia: Public/Private Ventures.

Hamilton, S. F., & Hamilton, M. A. (1992). Mentoring programs: Promise and paradox. *Phi Delta Kappan, 73*, 546–550.

Hébert, T. P., & Olenchak, F. R. (2000). Mentors for gifted underachieving males: Developing potential and realizing promise. *Gifted Child Quarterly, 44*, 196–207.

Higgins, K., & Boone, R. (2003). Beyond the boundaries of school: Transition considerations in gifted education. *Intervention in School and Clinic, 38*, 138–144.

Hirano, T. (1996). Achieving mathematical excellence in Japan: Results and implications. *International Journal of Educational Research, 25*, 545–551.

Jacobi, M. (1991, Winter). Mentoring and undergraduate academic success: A literature review. *Review of Educational Research, 61*, 505–532.

Kaufman, F. (1981). The 1964–1968 Presidential scholars: A follow-up study. *Exceptional Children, 48*, 164–169.

Kukushkin, B. (1996). The Olympiad movement in Russia. *International Journal of Educational Research, 25*, 553–562.

Lengfelder, A., & Heller, K. (2002). German Olympiad studies: Findings from a retrospective evaluation and from in-depth interviews. Where have all the gifted females gone? *Journal of Research in Education, 12*(1), 86–92.

Linnehan, F. (2003). A longitudinal study of work-based, adult youth mentoring. *Journal of Vocational Behaviors, 63*(1), 40–54.

Long, S. (1990). The origins of sex differences in science. *Social Forces, 68*, 1297–1315.

Lupkowski, A. E., Assouline, S.G., & Vestal, J. (1992, May/June). Mentors in math. *Gifted Child Today, 15*, 26–31.

Miller, A. (2002). *Mentoring students and young people*. London: RoutledgePalmer.

National Commission on Excellence in Education (1983). *A nation at risk: The imperative for educational reform*. Washington, DC: U.S. Government Printing Office.

Ortiz-Walters, R., & Gilson, L. L. (2005). Mentoring in academia: An examination of the experiences of protégé of color. *Journal of Vocational Behavior, 67*, 459–475.

Pleiss, M. K., & Feldhusen, J. F. (1995). Mentors, role models, and heroes in the lives of gifted children. *Educational Psychologist, 30*, 159–169.

Purcell, J., Renzulli, J., McCoach, N., & Spottiswoode, H. (2002, December). The magic of mentorship. *Parenting for High Potential*, 22–26.

Pyryt, M. C. (2000). Talent development in science and technology. In K. A. Heller, F. J. Mönks, R. J. Sternberg, & R. Subotnik (Eds.), *International handbook on giftedness and talent* (2nd ed., pp. 427–437). Oxford, England: Elsevier.

Quek, C. (2005). A national study of scientific talent development in Singapore. Unpublished doctoral dissertation, College of William and Mary, Williamsburg, VA.

Stanley, J. C. (1979). How to use a fast-pacing math mentor. *Intellectually Talented Youth Bulletin, 5*(6), 1–2.

Subotnik, R. F., & Olszewski-Kubilius, P. (1997). Restructuring special programs to reflect the distinctions between children's and adults' experiences with giftedness. *Peabody Journal of Education, 72*, 101–116.

Subotnik, R. F., & Steiner, C. L. (1994). Adult manifestation of adolescent talent in science: A longitudinal study of 1983 Westinghouse Science Talent Search winners. In R. F. Subotnik & K. D. Arnold (Eds.), *Beyond Terman: Contemporary longitudinal studies of giftedness and talent* (pp. 52–76). Norwood, NJ: Ablex.

Subotnik, R. F., Stone, K. M., & Steiner, C. L. (2001). Lost generation of elite talent in science. *Journal of Secondary Gifted Education, 13*, 33–43.

Subotnik, R., & VanTassel-Baska, J. (2004, November). *A preliminary report of results of studies with RSI students and Biology Olympiad participants*. Paper presented at the annual conference of the National Association for Gifted Children, Salt Lake City, UT.

Tirri, K., & Koro-Ljungberg, M. (2002). Actualizing mathematical giftedness in adulthood. *Educating Able Children, 6*(1), 14–20.

Torrance, E. P. (1984). *Mentoring relationships: How they aid creative achievement, endure, change, and die.* New York: Bearly Limited.

VanTassel-Baska, J. (1998). Counseling the gifted. In J. VanTassel-Baska (Ed.), *Excellence in educating the gifted* (pp. 489–510). Denver, CO: Love.

Verna, M. A., Campbell, J. R., & Feng, A. X. (2002). Chemistry Olympians' academic development and productivity. *Tempo, 22*(3), 15–22.

Withers, G., & Batten, M. (1995). *Programs for at-risk youth: A review of the American, Canadian and British literature since 1984.* Melbourne, Victoria: Australia Council for Educational Research.

Wright, L., & Borland, J. H. (1992). A special friend: Adolescent mentors for young, economically disadvantaged, potentially gifted students. *Roeper Review, 14*, 124–129.

Wu, W. (1996). Growing up in Taiwan: The impact of environmental influences on the math Olympians. *International Journal of Educational Research, 25*, 523–534.

Wu, W., & Chen, J. (2001). A follow-up of Taiwan Physics and Chemistry Olympians: The role of environmental influences in talent development. *Gifted and Talented International, 17*(1), 16–26.

Zha, Z., Liu, P., & Tal, X. (1996). Nurturing factors that promote mathematics achievement in Mainland China. *International Journal of Educational Research, 25*, 535–543.

## Author's Note

I would like to give my sincere thanks to three colleagues whose work inspired me in completing this chapter: Drs. Chwee Quek, Rena Subotnik, and Joyce L. VanTassel-Baska.

# Learning to Serve and to Lead: Empowering Gifted Youth to Make a Difference Through Service Learning

*Ai Lian Chee*

## Introduction

Many educators assume that leadership development is implicit in general education. Greenleaf (1991) questioned this assumption: "If that is true, how can it be that we are in a crisis of leadership . . . in which there is so little incentive for able and dedicated servants to take the risks of asserting leadership?" (p. 4). If gifted individuals are to be future leaders and given that they are a nation's most rare and precious resource, the values that they hold are important. This is based on the assumption that values form beliefs; that values may influence future decisions and predict actions (Piirto, 2003). One approach to nurture gifted individuals for the fulfilment of self and the betterment of society is via service learning. Service learning provides a theoretical perspective that simultaneously addresses affect and cognition, service and learning, and personal and interpersonal (including leadership) development. Its interdisciplinary nature inspires students to view an issue of interest through the lens of multiple disciplines. Because students *"experience issues* instead of simply reading about them" and "learn by constructing meaning as they research, plan, volunteer, engage in authentic problem solving and decision making," service learning provides a window for students to see the real-life applications of what they have been taught in school (Pleasants, Stephens, Selph, & Pfeiffer, 2004, p. 17). Service learning is therefore a method to overcome separation of a theoretical world of education from a real-world context by integration and engagement (Speck, 2001). It also fosters creative thinking because:

> . . . for creative thinking to occur and to continue to occur, there must be ample opportunity for one thing to lead to another and to do something with the information encountered. Therefore, it is inevitable that any genuine encouragement of creative thinking in schools and colleges must take students beyond the classroom, textbook, and the teacher. (Torrance & Safter, 1990, p. 11, as cited in Terry, 2003)

In addition, service learning has been successfully employed as a *modus operandi* to impart leadership education. Leadership development embraces the philosophy that leadership consists of a set of skills that can be learned and that many gifted students demonstrate leadership potential (e.g., strong sense of social justice, commitment, perseverance, responsibility, and confidence) but may need additional guidance to grow into more effective leaders (see Table 11.1). Because leadership goes beyond being elected or appointed to a position and can be enhanced through practice and experience, service learning provides students with opportunities to lead, to reflect on their own personal style of leadership, and to hone lifelong skills of collaboration, verbal persuasion, goal setting, conflict resolution, planning, and prioritizing (Pleasants et al., 2004). Student reflections on the service learning experience, combined with their personal vision and internal values, form the basis of their leadership strategies and actions. Service learning therefore involves the empowerment of students to serve and to lead, through the cultivation of minds.

This chapter reviews and analyzes the research on service learning and leadership development programs. It explores the general theories of service learning, leadership, and gifted-

## Table 11.1
### Characteristics of Leadership Potential in Gifted Youth

| Cognitive Functioning | Affective Functioning |
|---|---|
| • High energy levels and motivation, enthusiastic<br>• Persistence<br>• Processes and retains vast amounts of information<br>• Able to see new relationships<br>• Able to think divergently, to solve problems creatively, and to reason critically<br>• Able to sequence tasks to complete a goal<br>• Preference for complex and challenging work<br>• Accelerated language development, high verbal capacity | • Able to tolerate ambiguity (i.e., flexibility in thought and action)<br>• Sensitivity to the feelings of others<br>• Likes to be in charge<br>• Demonstrates initiative<br>• Gets along with a variety of people<br>• Heightened self-awareness<br>• High expectations of self and others |

*Note.* Adapted from Manning (2005).

ness, as well as case studies of quality service learning/leadership development programs that meet the needs of gifted adolescents, being cognizant of the relationship among these four components. The curricular implications of the research findings have been used to formulate a service learning model for gifted programs.

## Service Learning, Leadership, and the Affective Development of Gifted Youth

According to Passow (1989), the advanced cognitive abilities and heightened intensity of gifted children predispose them to experience more profound social, ethical, and moral concerns quantitatively, as well as qualitatively. Active participation in well-conceptualized service learning projects can provide the differentiated educational experience necessary to develop these students into responsible citizens concerned with what happens in their nation, as well as in the world. Exposing gifted students to opportunities for community and civic engagement would also address their strong need for social justice. Appropriately challenging service learning projects can help schools create social conditions that support, and are directed toward, talent development (Olszewski-Kubilius, 1998). It also holds the promise of converting intellectually gifted students who are armchair critics into constructive and productive individuals (Eyler & Giles, 1999).

By allowing students the flexibility to pursue research study in their own areas of interest (Pleasants et al., 2004), service learning recognizes that gifted youth are typically committed to tasks that are personally meaningful. Moreover, empowering students to initiate their own projects imparts a sense of ownership and can further student commitment, although younger students may need scaffolding and adult guidance to identify their areas of interest.

Service learning and leadership programs should be offered to young gifted adolescents because, as Simonton (1984) pointed out, "the potential of a creator or a leader is almost entirely established in adolescence and early adulthood, the rest of the individual's life being dedicated to actualizing this potential genius" (p. 181). Simonton is not alone in his argument that adolescence is the optimal period of life for identifying and nurturing leadership potential. Other scholars (Black, 1984; Chauvin & Karnes, 1983; Plowman, 1981) have also maintained that many characteristics of gifted adolescents enable them to profit maximally from leadership development. Most gifted adolescents are believed to be mature enough to internalize their experiences, and at the same time, young enough to be open-minded and curious (Black). Moreover, adolescence is a critical developmental period that requires a delicate balance of individuality and integration in a community. By integrating service learning with a leadership component into the academic curriculum, schools will increase the likelihood that gifted youths will develop into adults who are imbued with an aspiration to excel not only in terms of academic achievement, but also in the areas of value-based and social excellence. A strong moral compass is necessary to guide the gifted on how best to use their talents. In his balance theory of wisdom, Sternberg (1998) termed such decisions to use one's intelligence, creativity, and experience for a common good as *wisdom*.

Half a century earlier, Hollingworth (1939) had cautioned that we should not disregard Bertrand Russell's (1924) view that the highly gifted "might better be guided by educators to take up harmless games or live according to a do-nothing philosophy," because they have invented destructive things such as dynamite and poison, "which tend, in the hands of average men, to destruction and pain" (as cited in Hollingworth, 1939, p. 591). Hollingworth was insightful in realizing that "perhaps the suggestion emanating most insistently from the work of Bertrand Russell as a whole is that we need not to weaken scientific leadership, but to *strengthen moral leadership* in the modern world" (p. 591). These appeals to connect leadership education and moral education, and to provide leadership experiences that are morally educative are still very much echoed in more recent literature (Erez, 2005; Greenleaf, 1991; Haensly, 2001; Lindsay, 1988; Passow, 1988, 1989; Roeper, 1988).

Binet (1905, as cited in Hollingworth, 1939) and Terman (1925) concluded that gifted students were likely to be leaders in school. Hollingworth (1939) also suggested the relationship between leadership and giftedness by pointing out that despite the age-long discussion as to what a leader should be like, there is uniformity about leadership in one respect—that intelligence is an indispensable quality of leadership. In his review of 30 studies that investigated the relationship between leadership and intelligence, Stogdill (1948) cited the findings of Hollingworth (1926), which pointed out that leadership was inhibited by extreme discrepancies between the intelligence of leaders and that of the group. Hollingworth (1926) challenged Binet's (1905) and Terman's (1925) conclusion that gifted students were likely to be leaders at school. Based on her observation of children, she suggested that there was a direct ratio between the intelligence of the leader and that of the followers. According to Hollingworth (1939), generally,

> to be a leader of his contemporaries, a child must be more intelligent, but *not too much more intelligent*, than those who are to be led. This concept of an optimum which is not a maximum difference between the leader and the led, has very important implications for selection and training [of leaders]. (p. 581)[3]

Citing the work of Fiedler (2002) and Fiedler & Link (1994), Sternberg (2005) highlighted that:

> Intelligence matters to leadership under conditions of low stress but can actually impede performance under high stress. Experience is more helpful than intelligence to leaders under conditions of high stress, when they do not have the luxury of applying analytical techniques to the solution of problems and need to draw from experience to solve problems that confront them. (p. 41)

Sternberg's WICS (Wisdom-Intelligence-Creativity-Synthesized) theory of giftedness in leadership proposed that effective leaders demonstrate in their leadership a synthesis of three elements: creativity, intelligence, and wisdom. *Creativity* is used to generate novel ideas; *intelligence* is used to analyze the quality of those ideas (analytical intelligence), as well as to implement the ideas and persuade others of their worth (practical intelligence); while *wisdom* is used to skillfully balance the short- and long-term effects of those ideas on all possible stakeholders (Sternberg, 2003a, 2003b; Sternberg & Vroom, 2002, as cited in Sternberg, 2005). Recognizing that the environment strongly influences the extent to which we are able to use and develop whatever genetic potential we have, the WICS model is grounded on the premise that the "ingredients

---

3   Hollingworth (1926, as cited in Stogdill, 1948) reported that it was likely that the IQ of a leader would fall between 115 and 130 among a group of children with average intelligence. Exceptionally gifted children, with a high IQ of say 160, would have problems assuming a leadership position in this type of group, but might function as a leader of a group with a mean IQ of 130.

of gifted leadership" (i.e., giftedness in wisdom, intelligence, and creativity) are, to some extent, a form of developing competency and expertise in both leadership skills as well as attitudes (Sternberg, 2005).

## Review of the Literature

This review of the literature serves to explain the state of service learning and leadership in general, and in the field of gifted education in particular. It is based on the premise that understanding the literature and research on service learning holds important implications for structuring effective service learning opportunities with a leadership development component for gifted adolescents.

### Definitions and Theories of Service Learning

Identifying the effects of service learning seems as if it should be a straightforward task. However, research findings on the effects of service learning on youth are mixed, partly because of the wide range of service learning activities being studied, and the variability in the research methods employed from study to study (Terry, 2003). To date, few studies specifically examine the effects of service learning on gifted children (Keen & Howard, 2002; Lewis, 1996; Olszewski-Kubilius, 1998; Owens, 1982; Pleasants et al., 2004; Terry, 2000, 2003; Terry & Bohnenberger, 1999, 2003). This has resulted in a dearth of literature on this topic, and a lack of service learning curricular materials differentiated to meet the cognitive, as well as the affective, needs of young gifted adolescents.

Although the literature on service learning may not be in total agreement on the effects of service learning on youth, the general consensus is that service learning pedagogies can be effectively employed to enhance traditional modes of learning by actively engaging students in their own education through experiential learning in content-relevant contexts. It has also been reported that service learning exposes students to a wider network of friends, their communities, and the world beyond the classroom, thereby enhancing social connectedness and promoting a sense of being a part of a larger community.

The positive effects of quality service learning programs on youth include gains in intellectual development and the attainment of a greater depth of information processing skills (Brandell & Hinck, 1997; Conrad & Hedin, 1981, 1991; Follman & Muldoon, 1997; Hedin, 1987; Shumer, 1994), as well as gains in personal development such as leadership skills; responsibility for oneself, as well as others; self-esteem; self-confidence; intrinsic motivation; ability to take risks; real-life problem solving; organizational skills; communication skills; and concern for others (Astin & Sax, 1998; Brandell & Hinck, 1997; Conrad & Hedin, 1979, 1981, 1982; Eyler, Giles, & Braxton, 1997; Halsted & Schine, 1994; Hamilton & Fenzel, 1987; Harris, 1995; Hecht, Schine, Halsted, & Berkson, 1995; Mauricio, 1997; Melchior, 1997; Newmann & Rutter, 1983, 1989; Pleasants et al., 2004; Terry, 2003; Wang, 2000).

This growth may result either from direct participation in meaningful tasks, or indirectly from the knowledge that the service the students provided had either helped someone or contributed toward a worthy cause. Looking at the positive qualities that service learning has produced in youth, proponents have connected the effects of service learning to the developmental needs of young adolescents, maintaining that service learning can aid adolescents in their difficult transition into adulthood, as well as in their search for identity (Kohler, 1982; Schine & Harrington, 1982). In addition, Waterman (1997a, 1997b) reported that service learning in high schools has been found to foster growth in important areas such as career preparation, clarification of values, attitudes toward pressing social problems, and sense of self-efficacy, self-esteem, and civic responsibility.

Despite this impressive list, Terry (2003) observed that advocates of service learning still do not have much of a research base to support the effectiveness of their programming. Empirical research in service learning is low in quantity, lower in quality, and lower yet in unanimity. For any study that has shown positive effects of service learning on participating students, another study can be cited that has shown no effect, or even negative results (McLellan & Youniss, 2003). It is important to determine the reasons for inconsistent findings across studies. Methodological flaws in previous research include:

- lack of control groups[4] (Astin & Sax, 1998), or
- serious sample selection issues where the researcher only considered "high-quality" programs (Melchior, 1997), or where the researcher allowed students to self-select into the service learning project, ignoring the possible effects of previous volunteer experience (Conrad & Hedin, 1981; Hamilton & Fenzel, 1987) or the possibility that students who opt to be involved in service learning projects may differ substantially from students who decide not to be involved in service (Astin & Sax, 1998).

There have been relatively few attempts to discuss either negative or inconclusive results of studies because most of the literature has been prepared to bolster support for service learning, thereby representing value-laden positions adopted by advocates with stakeholder bias.

One reason for the lack of an appreciable amount of research on service learning, despite the growing interest in the topic, has been the lack of a clear conceptual framework for studies to identify with (Aiken, 1942; Conrad & Hedin, 1981; Furco, 1994; Hamilton & Zeldin, 1987; Newmann & Rutter, 1983; Terry & Bohnenberger, 1999). In fact, because service is not a single, easily definable activity, its definition has been stretched to include a range of experiential activities such as volunteerism, internships, and community service[5]. Because community service, service learning, and internships have very different orientations toward service and learning, their intended educational purposes also differ (see Table 11.2). It is crucial for educators to recognize these differences when implementing a

---

4    The lack of control groups could have resulted in the Hawthorne effect, thereby registering a positive effect among the subjects not because of the service learning experience but rather because of the subjects' knowledge that they are involved in a "special" study.

5    According to Jane Kendall, there were 147 different definitions of service learning in 1990 (Schine, 1997). The terminology that has been associated with service learning includes authentic learning, community problem solving, youth community service, community service learning, experiential learning, apprenticeship, internship, and community service. The formidable obstacle of finding a common operational definition of service learning has understandably made assessment of its impact problematic.

## Table 11.2
### Distinctions Among Three Types of Service Programs

|  | Community Service | Service Learning | Internship |
|---|---|---|---|
| Primary Focus | Service | Service and learning | Learning |
| Primary Link to Service Activity | Tied to a social cause; no explicit educational focus; civic development, and possibly personal and social development. | Tied to an academic discipline; projects designed and carried out with educational objectives in mind; academic, personal, and social development, and possibly civic development. | Tied to an industry or career; no explicit educational focus; career development, and possibly academic development. |
| Integration With Curriculum | Peripheral | Integrated | Cocurricular/ supplemental |
| Primary Beneficiaries | Recipient | Recipient and provider | Provider |

Note. Adapted from Furco (1997) and Morgan (2002).

service learning project, so that the intended educational outcomes are clear from the outset.

Eyler and Giles (1999) suggested that even though academic learning should be one of the key outcomes of service learning, the evidence of this is far from definitive. One of the common problems that researchers face in trying to discern the impact of service learning is that the nature of the projects and the age and circumstances of the students involved are varied (Morgan, 2002). Not only is the independent variable, service, difficult to operationally define, its wide range of possible outcomes (i.e., the uneven quality of students' experiences depending on the service learning design) complicates the process of determining the appropriate dependent variables to study (Aiken, 1942; Conrad & Hedin, 1981, 1989, 1991; Hamilton & Fenzel, 1987; Kraft, 1996[6]). Educators are still in search of universal principles for designing successful and sustainable service learning programs (Furco, 1994; Terry & Bohnenberger, 1999).

According to Yates and Youniss (1998), another possible reason for the weak and inconsistent findings could be because most service learning research is atheoretical (i.e., if researchers are not clear on the hypotheses that their study is testing and the process whereby service learning is likely to have an impact, they will ignore potentially important mediating factors). For example, if service learning is seen as having an impact because it allows students to recognize and embrace their unique leadership potential, then it is important for the programs and activities to provide opportunities for students to do so in a structured setting, such as an investigation into leadership theory.

To conclude, the quality of research on service learning is mixed and most of the answers are still far from clear. This is because the bulk of service learning research actually consists of evaluations where different standards are employed to study specific programs with important differences. Few studies on service learning have employed control groups, pretests and posttests, large samples, and multivariate analysis to control for background factors, and few have tested hypotheses, cited theoretical foundations of the program, and/or tracked whether the impact of service learning could be sustained over time (Billig, 2000; Myers-Lipton, 1996). The bulk of the literature on service learning is not empirical research, but rather process evaluation pieces written by practitioners, reporting what they did in their classrooms. Of the few studies that combine both quantitative and qualitative data, results are strong in the qualitative areas but reflect only modest quantitative impacts (Hamilton

---

6   For example, Kraft's (1996) review of the service learning literature included more than 30 studies. It was difficult to generalize findings because of the inconsistencies from study to study, and the variety in the grade levels where research has been conducted (15 studies involved high school students, 1 involved middle school students and elementary students, 4 involved college students, and 1 involved post-college-level students, while the rest of the studies reviewed did not mention the grade level(s) of the students involved).

& Fenzel, 1987). Although qualitative case studies inform us about the general effect of the service experience, as well as its unique impact on each individual, they tend to look at a smaller set of results or a select group of students, thereby raising questions about their external validity.

### Definitions and Theories of Leadership

Definitions of leadership, like definitions of service learning, are many and varied, and no single definition has won widespread acceptance. Generally, the definitions have evolved from simplistic, fixed, innate-trait definitions to more complex, multidimensional person-process-context interactive interpretations that treated leadership as a changeable entity (Karnes & Bean, 1996; Simonton, 1994). Although leadership is not a new topic to gifted education[7], it is one that has often been overlooked as an outcome incidental to the total educational experience (Karnes & Bean, 1991; Roberts, 2004). Comprehensive leadership education for gifted adolescents has yet to be systematically built into most curricula (Foster, 1981). Although classroom activities may coincidentally contribute to positive leadership development, ample emphasis may not have been given to discussion, debriefing, application, and mastery of leadership concepts and skills. The leadership literature is consistent in making the point that strong leadership development programs (capable of offering in-depth understanding of the significance of leadership roles and the personal development that can come from the experience of being a leader) are necessary to help gifted adolescents identify, develop, and fine-tune their leadership skills (Emmerich, 1983; Feldhusen & Kennedy, 1988; Foster; Hensel & Franklin, 1983; Johnson & Johnson, 1982; Karnes & Meriweather, 1989; Karnes & Bean, 1991, 1996; Maher, 1985/1986; Parker, 1983; Porter, 1981).

---

7   Leadership was listed as a category of giftedness in the Marland Report (Marland, 1972), the first national report on gifted education, and in *National Excellence: A Case for Developing America's Talent* (U.S. Department of Education, 1993), the second and only other national report on gifted education. Several states also include leadership in their state definition of children who are gifted and talented.

Despite the widespread acceptance of leadership as a critical component of talent development, there are limited well-designed effectiveness studies of existing leadership development programs for gifted adolescents. On the whole, the quality of leadership studies is inconsistent. This inconsistency across studies can readily be attributed to uncontrolled variability in definitions, key factors and dependent measures (e.g., different emphases in different leadership training programs), and the availability of valid and reliable instruments to assess students' leadership potential or the effectiveness of leadership development programs (Karnes & Bean, 1996).

### Connecting the Literature of Service Learning and Leadership

From the review of the literature, many parallels can be drawn between service learning and leadership education for gifted youth, including the lack of effective research, the availability of program models, the judicious timing of the programs at adolescence, and the potential of both types of programs for gifted students' personal, social, and academic development. It is therefore natural to incorporate a strong leadership component when designing service learning projects for gifted adolescents. No attempt yet has been made to generalize across service learning and leadership development programs for the purpose of deriving common lessons for the field of talent development.

The evidence from the existing literature suggests that carefully designed service learning and leadership development programs impact not only how much is learned, but the motivation to learn, the confidence that one can make a difference, and the development of the capacity to contribute, as well as the commitment to do so. Hence, careful program planning is critical.

### Implementing Service Learning With a Leadership Development Component for Gifted Adolescents

Thus far, the primary K–12 service learning typologies or classifications that have been developed can generally be defined by three key structural elements:

- the degree to which service is integrated within the school curriculum;
- the institution where the program is located and managed (Conrad & Hedin, 1981; Furco, 1994, as cited in Terry, 2003); and
- the varying degrees and levels of student learning and service to the community (Terry & Bohnenberger, 1999).

The three-dimensional model proposed here (see Figure 11.1) attempts to add a new dimension to the literature of service learning and leadership development by showing the integration of elements of effective service learning practice (with a strong leadership component) into the academic curriculum; and the intended cognitive and affective program outcomes.

This service learning/leadership development model was derived from a study of the:

- service learning and leadership literature;
- standards and guidelines for quality service learning projects (Alliance for Service-Learning in Educational Reform, 1995; Corporation for National & Community Service, 1990; Honnet & Poulsen, 1989);
- the National Service-Learning Cooperative's *Essential Elements of Service-Learning* (1998); and
- Duke University's Talent Identification Program's Leadership Institute (see Pleasants et al., 2004), John Hopkins University's Center for Talented Youth's Civic Leadership Institute, and Northwestern University's Center for Development's Civic Education Project.

Dimension 1 (D1) is *Curriculum (Subject Matter Content),* which is made up of language and literature, mathematics, science, social science, music, and art. Dimension 2 (D2) is *Elements of an Effective Service-Learning Practice With a Leadership Development Component.* The 10 elements are as follows:

1. *Service learning is not fully effective unless it is integrated into a framework of leadership theory.* Given that leadership is a dynamic concept that may require periodic modification to achieve the desired goals, students learn the value

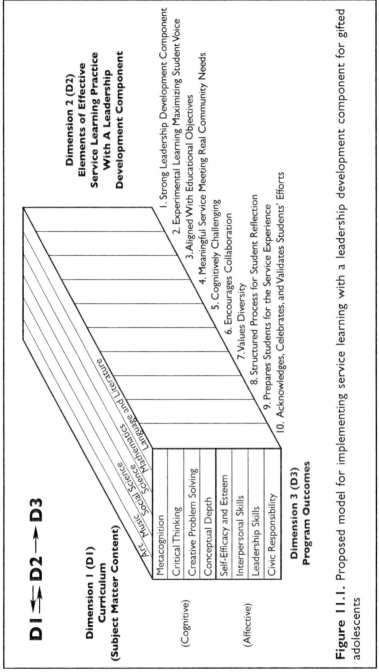

**Figure 11.1.** Proposed model for implementing service learning with a leadership development component for gifted adolescents

of receiving feedback regarding their projects to ensure that their established goals are achieved (Pleasants et al., 2004).

2.  *Effective service learning allows students to experience issues firsthand, providing students direct knowledge of, and an active interest in, the area of study.* It also seeks to maximize student voice in selecting, designing, implementing, and evaluating the service project. Morgan and Streb (2002) observed that a key mediating variable in employing service learning as a means of reforming society and preserving democracy would be the level of student leadership in designing and implementing the service project.

3.  *Effective service learning establishes clear educational goals that require the application of concepts, content, and skills from the academic disciplines.* It allows students to pursue their own interests and direct their course of study, recognizing that gifted students work particularly well when they are able to personalize and construct their own goals for learning.

4.  *Students are engaged in service tasks that have clear goals, meet real needs in the school or community, and have significant consequences that both the students and the community hold as important and worthwhile.* One theme that emerges from the empirical literature is the nature of the task and how the individual student experiences the task and the service or field setting. This factor has been found to impact the personal, social, and intellectual outcomes of the service learning experience, regardless of the general program type (Conrad & Hedin, 1981). Wade and Putnam's (1995) survey of gifted high school sophomores and juniors suggests that gifted students' willingness to participate in service learning and leadership activities will increase when they are provided with ample opportunities for making decisions, responsibility, and meaningful influence. Only when students do something with their experience does it become educative. In other words, experience becomes experiential

education when students are engaged in intrinsically worthwhile activities that awaken curiosity and stimulate reflection (Giles & Eyler, 1994).

5.   *Effective service learning engages students in tasks that challenge and stretch them cognitively and developmentally.* Students have to employ critical thinking skills and dispositions (Ennis, 1985) to fully identify salient problems (Getzels & Csikszentmihalyi, 1975) and appreciate the complexities and interrelationships within configurations of information that constitute those problems. Only with depth of analysis and understanding can students hope to successfully find creative solutions to real-world problems and issues. In order to identify salient problems and achieve a depth of analysis and understanding, a deep and well-articulated knowledge base in one or more academic disciplines is necessary (Glaser, 1984).

6.   *Effective service learning promotes communication and interaction with the community, encouraging partnerships and collaboration.* From the perspective of service learning, the school is more than a place where students go to learn. The school is a place where students go back into the community to apply what they have learned by solving community problems now. Students can simultaneously utilize their talents, skills, and energy to contribute today and develop skills and attitudes that will foster a more committed and involved citizenry tomorrow. Likewise, the community is viewed by the school as an educational partner with valued expertise and resources (National Service-Learning Cooperative, 1998).

7.   *Effective service learning values diversity through its participants, practices, and outcomes.* Sosniak (1999) highlighted that in contrast to schoolwork, "talent development tasks are linked with the lives and conversations of people of varied age groups, from many communities, institutions and organizations, even across historical time" (p. 169). Therefore, schools have to talk and work with the community if they want to achieve the optimal talent development of our gifted adolescents. Then and only

then can schools become clearinghouses for learning, thinking, and affective activities that would occur in a variety of other places (e.g., museums, playgrounds, hospitals, retirement homes, libraries, and business places). Teachers' expertise in subject-specific content knowledge would be complemented by community-based leaders' expertise in areas such as archaeology, environmental studies, life sciences, astronomy, art, theatre, drama, and sports. Adults from a wide range of public service agencies and businesses would assume responsibilities for extending the domains and the environments of students' learning (Heath, 1994).

8.    *Student reflection occurs before, during, and after the service experience, employing multiple methods that encourage critical thinking.* It forms a central force in the design and fulfilment of curricular objectives. Reflection is the window by which students see the difference their actions have made within the community, even when such actions had seemed insignificant at the time of service. Once students realize that they have the ability to make a difference, they are likely to feel inspired and empowered to do more. In addition, self-reflection also encourages students to critique their own leadership style and role within the school and/or community, providing them with opportunities to analyze and evaluate less successful efforts or instances when their projects failed to achieve intended goals (Pleasants et al., 2004). There is a growing body of literature to attest to the centrality of reflection to the process of learning through experience (Conrad & Hedin, 1982; Eyler, 1993, 2001; Eyler, Giles, & Braxton, 1995; Myers-Lipton, 1994; Rutter & Newmann, 1989). The empirical evidence suggests that not only is reflection important, the quality of that reflection is of equal importance.

9.    *Students need to be mentally prepared and equipped with the requisite knowledge and skills to effectively carry out the service tasks.* This is important as many of these service tasks are likely to involve unfamiliar situations (e.g., home-

less persons whose very appearance and demeanor may unsettle some students).

10.   *Multiple methods are designed to acknowledge, celebrate, and further validate students' service efforts.*

The review of the literature on the impact of service learning and leadership development programs on gifted adolescents highlighted that well-designed programs have the potential to develop gifted adolescents both cognitively and affectively. Dimension 3 (D3) is *Program Outcomes,* which consists of two main aspects: cognitive (metacognition, critical thinking, creative problem solving, and conceptual depth) and affective (heightened self-efficacy and self-esteem, interpersonal skills, leadership skills, and civic responsibilities).

We had earlier established that one of the distinct features of service learning is the fact that it is tied to an academic discipline with specific learner outcomes. This relationship is reflected by the formula $D1 \leftrightarrow D2$, which shows that curriculum content (D1) interacts with the elements of effective service learning practice and leadership development (D2). The result of the interaction between D1 and D2 is a set of cognitive and affective program outcomes (D3; i.e., $D1 \leftrightarrow D2 \leftrightarrow D3$).

## Issues in Developing Service Learning and Leadership Programs for the Gifted

One of the biggest issues that educators must confront in these programs is seeing them as beneficial for cognitive, as well as affective, purposes and thus finding a place for them in the school curriculum. Although the International Baccalaureate program requires service learning in order to complete the program, it is the only well-known academic program to have such a requirement. Thus, the chances that service learning will become a required part of schooling seems limited, given the current emphasis on high-stakes testing and the amassing of college credit for most high-school-age adolescents. Universities could help in the effort to enhance the chances of service learning being done in high school by offering academic credit or "points" toward admission for students who participated in such projects across multiple semesters and years.

Another issue in service learning projects is the rigor of the experience. Most of the projects lack even basic evaluation studies of effectiveness, let alone controlled studies of benefit. In order for these programs to gain legitimacy, they will need some stronger empirical evidence than they now have about their positive impacts. Current perceptions of such programs held by many educators suggest they see them as loosely organized and heavily dependent on context and the human resources in those contexts for successful implementation. A stronger role by school personnel in preparing students to participate in such projects, as well as carefully monitoring the implementation, will be necessary for enhanced benefits to accrue.

Finally, service learning needs a conceptual home. By linking it to leadership development, the field of gifted education stands to make a stronger case for its utility and purpose within the larger band of gifted program development. Depending on the nature of leadership, which can be determined within or across subject areas, students can initiate service learning projects that demonstrate academic, as well as personal and social learning. Thus, service learning can become a standard part of the high school experience for gifted students, not something separate from it.

## Conclusion

From her work on the Development of Talent Research Project directed by Benjamin Bloom and carried out by a team of scholars in the early 1980s (Bloom, 1985), Sosniak (1999) argued that the development of talent is directly related to what we do in our daily existence and who we associate with as we proceed with our lives. Instead of early discovery followed by development, Bloom's study found that its subjects "grew into their aptitudes and attitudes over time, in the context of supportive adults, peers, and societies of persons who valued and engaged in activity of a similar sort" (p. 166). Drawing inspiration from this finding, it is important that young gifted adolescents get "hooked" on service learning with a strong leadership development component early on. Such programs hold the promise of developing young adults who understand the value of knowledge, accept their social responsibilities, and are confident that they can effect positive change in their environments. The empowering impact of service learning/leadership development programs is perhaps best summed up by a participant of a John Hopkins University 2003 Civic Leadership Institute: "At the end of these three weeks, the world is exactly as it was [before]. But now the way I see it and myself is different." Service learning with a strong leadership emphasis is a promising avenue for gifted individuals to achieve not only self-actualization, but also self-actualization in service of humankind (Passow, 1988).

## References

Aiken, W. (1942). *Story of the eight-year study*. New York: Harper & Brothers.

Alliance for Service-Learning in Educational Reform. (1995). *Standards of quality for service learning. ASLER guidelines.* Alexandria, VA: Author.

Astin, A. W., & Sax, L. J. (1998). How undergraduates are affected by service participation. *Journal of College Student Development, 39*, 251–263.

Billig, S. H. (2000). Research on K–12 school-based service-learning: The evidence builds. *Phi Delta Kappan, 81*, 658–664.

Black, J. D. (1984). *Leadership: A new model particularly applicable to gifted youth.* Reston, VA: ERIC Clearinghouse on Disabilities and Gifted Education. (ERIC Document Reproduction Service No. ED253990)

Bloom, B. S. (Ed.). (1985). *Developing talent in young people.* New York: Ballantine.

Brandell, M. E., & Hinck, S. (1997). Service learning: Connect citizenship with the classroom. *NASSP Bulletin, 81*(591), 49–56.

Chauvin, J. C., & Karnes, F. A. (1983). A leadership profile of secondary students. *Psychological Reports, 53,* 1259–1262.

Conrad, D., & Hedin, D. (1979). Johnny says he is learning . . . through experience. *Journal of Experiential Education, 2*(1), 42–46.

Conrad, D., & Hedin, D. (1981). *National assessment of experiential education: A final report* (Report No. UD022614). Minneapolis: Center for Youth Development and Research, Minnesota University. (ERIC Document Reproduction Service No. ED223765)

Conrad, D., & Hedin, D. (1982). The impact of experiential education on adolescent development. *Child and Youth Services, 4*(3), 57–76.

Conrad, D., & Hedin, D. (1989). *High school community service: A review of research and programs.* Madison, WI: National Center on Effective Secondary Schools.

Conrad, D., & Hedin, D. (1991). School-based community service: What we know from research and theory. *Phi Delta Kappan, 72,* 743–749.

Corporation for National & Community Service. (1990). *Corporation for National & Community Service guidelines for service-learning.* Washington, DC: Author.

Emmerich, M. (1983). Teaching tomorrow's leaders today. *Educational Leadership, 40*(6), 64–65.

Ennis, R. H. (1985). A logical basis for measuring critical thinking skills. *Educational Leadership, 43*(2), 44–48.

Erez, R. (2005). Excellence and social responsibility. *Gifted Education International, 20,* 246–255.

Eyler, J. (1993). Comparing the impact of two internship experiences on student learning. *Journal of Cooperative Education, 29*(3), 41–52.

Eyler, J. (2001). Creating your reflection map. In M. Canada & B. W. Speck (Eds.), *Developing and implementing service-learning programs* (pp. 35–43). San Francisco: Jossey-Bass.

Eyler, J., & Giles, D. E., Jr. (1999). *Where's the learning in service-learning?* San Francisco: Jossey-Bass.

Eyler, J., Giles, D. E., Jr., & Braxton, J. (1995, November). *The impact of alternative models of service learning on student outcomes.* Paper presented at National Society for Experiential Education (NSEE) conference, New Orleans, LA.

Eyler, J., Giles, D. E., Jr., & Braxton, J. (1997). The impact of service learning on college students. *Michigan Journal of Community Service Learning, 4,* 5–15.

Feldhusen, J. F., & Kennedy, D. M. (1988). Preparing gifted youth for leadership roles in a rapidly changing society. *Roeper Review, 10,* 226–230.

Fiedler, F. E. (2002). The curious role of cognitive resources in leadership. In R. E. Riggio, E. E. Murphy, & F. J. Pirozzolo, *Multiple intelligences and leadership* (pp. 91–104). Mahwah, NJ: Lawrence Erlbaum.

Fiedler, F. E., & Link, T. G. (1994). Leader intelligence, interpersonal stress, and task performance. In R. J. Sternberg & R. K. Wagner (Eds.), *Mind in context: Interactionist perspectives on human intelligence* (pp. 152–167). New York: Cambridge University Press.

Follman, J., & Muldoon, K. (1997). Florida Learn & Serve 1995–96: What were the outcomes? *NASSP Bulletin, 81*(591), 29–36.

Foster, W. (1981). Leadership: A conceptual framework for recognizing and educating. *Gifted Child Quarterly, 25*, 17–25.

Furco, A. (1994). A conceptual framework for the institutionalization of youth service programs in primary and secondary education. *Journal of Adolescence, 17*, 395–409.

Furco, A. (1997). *School-sponsored service programs and the educational development of high school students.* Unpublished doctoral dissertation, University of California, Berkeley.

Getzels, J. W., & Csikszentmihalyi, M. (1975). From problem solving to problem finding. In I. A. Taylor & J. W. Getzels (Eds.), *Perspectives in creativity* (pp. 90–116). Chicago: Aldine.

Giles, D. E., Jr., & Eyler, J. (1994). The theoretical roots of service-learning in John Dewey: Towards a theory of service-learning. *Michigan Journal of Community Service-Learning, 1*(1), 77–85.

Glaser, R. (1984). Education and thinking: The role of knowledge. *American Psychologist, 39*, 93–104.

Greenleaf, R. K. (1991). *Servant leadership: A journey into the nature of legitimate power and greatness.* New York: Paulist Press.

Haensly, P. (2001). Creativity, intelligence, and ethics: Why do our gifted children need them? *Gifted Child Today, 24*(1), 33–35.

Halsted, A. L., & Schine, J. G. (1994). Service learning: The promise and the risk. *New England Journal of Public Policy, 10*(1), 251–257.

Hamilton, S., & Fenzel, M. L. (1987, April). *The effect of volunteer experience on early adolescents' social development.* Paper presented at the Annual Meeting of the American Educational Research Association, Washington, DC.

Hamilton, S. F., & Zeldin, R. S. (1987). Learning civics in community. *Curriculum Inquiry, 17*, 407–420.

Harris, M. A. (1995). *A descriptive study of selected high school service learning programs in California.* Unpublished doctoral dissertation, Pepperdine University, Malibu, CA.

Heath, S. B. (1994). Play for identity: Where the mind is everyday for inner-city youth. In J. N. Mangieri & C. C. Block (Eds.), *Creating powerful thinking in teachers and students: Diverse perspec-*

*tives* (pp. 215–228). Fort Worth, TX: Harcourt Brace College Publishers.

Hecht, D., Schine, J., Halsted, A., & Berkson, N. (1995, April). *Service learning: A support for personal growth during adolescence.* Paper presented at the Annual Meeting of the American Educational Research Association, San Francisco, CA. (ERIC Document Reproduction Service No. ED416428)

Hedin, D. (1987). Students as teachers: A tool for improving school climate and productivity. *Social Policy, 17,* 42–47.

Hensel, N., & Franklin, C. (1983). Developing emergent leadership skills in elementary and junior high students. *Roeper Review, 5,* 33–35.

Hollingworth, L. S. (1926). *Gifted children: Their nature and nurture.* New York: Macmillan.

Hollingworth, L. S. (1939). What we know about the early selection and training of leaders. *Teachers College Record, 40,* 575–592.

Honnet, E. P., & Poulsen, S. J. (1989). *Principles of good practice for combining service and learning: A Wingspread report.* Racine, WI: Johnson Foundation.

John Hopkins University Center for Talented Youth (2004). *Civic Leadership Institute Summer 2004 program.* Retrieved June 22, 2006, from http://www.cty.jhu.edu

Johnson, D. W., & Johnson, F. P. (1982). *Joining together: Group theory and group skills* (2nd ed.). Englewood Cliffs, NJ: Prentice-Hall.

Karnes, F. A., & Bean, S. M. (1991). Leadership and gifted adolescents. In M. Bireley & J. Genshaft (Eds.), *Understanding the gifted adolescent* (pp. 122–138). New York: Teachers College Press.

Karnes, F. A., & Bean, S. M. (1996). Leadership and the gifted. *Focus on Exceptional Children, 29,* 1–12.

Karnes, F. A., & Meriweather, S. (1989). Developing and implementing a plan for leadership: An integral component for success as a leader. *Roeper Review, 11,* 214–217.

Keen, C., & Howard, A. (2002). Experiential learning in Antioch College's work-based learning program as a vehicle for social and emotional development for gifted college students. *Journal of Secondary Gifted Education, 13,* 130–141.

Kohler, M. C. (1982). Developing responsible youth through youth participation. In D. Conrad & D. Hedin (Eds.), *Youth participation and experiential education* (pp. 5–12). New York: The Haworth Press.

Kraft, R. J. (1996). Service learning: An introduction to its theory, practice, and effects. *Education & Urban Society, 28,* 131–159.

Lewis, B. A. (1996). Serving others hooks gifted students on learning. *Educational Leadership, 53*(5), 70–74.

Lindsay, B. (1988). A lamp for diogenes: Leadership giftedness and moral education. *Roeper Review, 11*, 8–11.

Maher, R. E. (1985/1986). Learning leadership. *Educational Leadership, 2*(4), 26–28.

Manning, S. (2005). Young leaders: Growing through mentoring. *Gifted Child Today, 28*(1), 14–20.

Marland, S. (1972). *Education of the gifted and talented: Report to the Congress of the United States by the U.S. Commissioner of Education.* Washington, DC: U.S. Government Printing Office.

Mauricio, C. L. (1997). *Voices of personal growth: High school girls respond to community service and learning.* Unpublished doctoral dissertation, The Claremont Graduate University and San Diego State University, San Diego, CA.

McLellan, J., & Youniss, J. (2003). Two systems of youth service: Determinants of voluntary and required youth community service. *Journal of Youth and Adolescence, 32*, 47–58.

Melchior, A. (1997). *National evaluation of Learn and Serve America school and community-based programs: Interim report.* Waltham, MA: Brandeis University, Heller Graduate School, Center for Human Resources.

Morgan, W. D. (2002). *Building citizenship: Service-learning and student leadership.* Unpublished doctoral dissertation, Indiana University, Bloomington.

Morgan, W., & Streb, M. (2002). Service-learning: Promoting civic activism or civic apathy? *Politics and Policy, 30*(1), 161–188.

Myers-Lipton, S. (1994). *The effects of service-learning on college students' attitudes towards civic responsibility, international understanding, and racial prejudice.* Unpublished doctoral dissertation, University of Colorado, Boulder.

Myers-Lipton, S. J. (1996, Fall). Effect of a comprehensive service-learning program on college students' level of modern racism. *Michigan Journal of Community Service-Learning,* 44–54.

National Service-Learning Cooperative. (1998). *Essential elements of service-learning for effective practice and organizational support.* Roseville, MN: National Youth Leadership Council.

Newmann, F. M., & Rutter, R. A. (1983). *The effects of high school community service programs on students' social development.* Madison: Wisconsin Center for Education Research, University of Wisconsin.

Newmann, F. M., & Rutter, R. A. (1989). Organizational factors that affect school sense of efficacy, community, and expectations. *Sociology of Education, 62*, 221–238.

Olszewski-Kubilius, P. (1998). Developing the talents of academically gifted high school students: Issues for secondary school administrators. *NASSP Bulletin, 82*(595), 85–92.

Owens, T. R. (1982). Experience-based career education: Summary and implications of research and evaluation findings. In D. Conrad & D. Hedin (Eds.), *Youth participation and experiential education* (pp. 77–91). New York: The Haworth Press.

Parker, J. P. (1983). The leadership training model. *G/C/T, 29*(5), 8–13.

Passow, A. H. (1988). Educating gifted persons who are caring and concerned. *Roeper Review, 11*, 13–15.

Passow, A. H. (1989). Educating gifted persons who are caring and concerned. *Gifted Education International, 6*, 5–7.

Piirto, J. (2003, November). *"I live in my own bubble": The values of talented adolescents using the Rokeach Value Survey before and after September 11, 2001.* Paper presented at the annual meeting of the National Association for Gifted Children, Indianapolis, IN.

Pleasants, R., Stephens, K. R., Selph, H., & Pfeiffer, S. (2004). Incorporating service learning into leadership education: Duke TIP's Leadership Institute. *Gifted Child Today, 27*(1), 16–21.

Plowman, P. D. (1981). Training extraordinary leaders. *Roeper Review, 3*(3), 13–16.

Porter, P. D. (1981). We should be teaching leadership skills and competencies. *NASSP Bulletin, 65*(444), 76–80.

Roberts, J. L. (2004). Leadership is a "must" for children who are gifted and talented. *Gifted Child Today, 27*(1), 5.

Roeper, A. (1988). Should educators of the gifted and talented be more concerned with world issues? *Roeper Review, 11*, 12–13.

Rutter, R. A., & Newmann, F. M. (1989). The potential of community service to enhance civic responsibility. *Social Education, 53*, 371–374.

Schine, J. (Ed). (1997). *Service learning.* Chicago: The University of Chicago Press.

Schine, J. G., & Harrington, D. (1982). *Youth participation for early adolescents: Learning and serving in the community.* Bloomington, IN: Phi Delta Kappa Educational Foundation.

Shumer, R. D. (1994). Community-based learning: Humanizing education. *Journal of Adolescence, 17*, 357–367.

Simonton, D. K. (1984). *Genius, creativity, and leadership: Historiometric inquiries.* Cambridge, MA: Harvard University Press.

Simonton, D. K. (1994). *Greatness: Who makes history and why?* New York: The Guilford Press.

Sosniak, L. A. (1999). An everyday curriculum for the development of talent. *Journal of Secondary Gifted Education, 10,* 166–172.

Speck, B. W. (2001). Why service learning? In M. Canada & B. W. Speck (Eds.), *Developing and implementing service-learning programs* (pp. 3–13). San Francisco: Jossey–Bass.

Sternberg, R. J. (1998). A balance theory of wisdom. *Review of General Psychology, 2,* 347–365.

Sternberg, R. J. (2003a). WICS: A model for leadership in organizations. *Academy of Management Learning and Education, 2,* 386–401.

Sternberg, R. J. (2003b). *Wisdom, intelligence, and creativity, synthesized.* New York: Cambridge University Press.

Sternberg, R. J. (2005). WICS: A model of giftedness in leadership. *Roeper Review, 28,* 37–44.

Stogdill, R. M. (1948). Personal factors associated with leadership: A survey of the literature. *Journal of Psychology, 25,* 35–71.

Terry, A. W. (2000). *A case study of community action service learning on young, gifted adolescents and their community.* Unpublished doctoral dissertation, The University of Georgia, Athens.

Terry, A. W. (2003). Effects of service learning on young, gifted adolescents and their community. *Gifted Child Quarterly, 47,* 295–308.

Terry, A. W., & Bohnenberger, J. E. (1999, January). *Connecting community problem solving to service learning initiatives.* Paper presented at the meeting of the board of trustees of the International Future Problem Solving Program, Ann Arbor, MI.

Terry, A. W., & Bohnenberger, J. E. (2003). Service learning: Fostering a cycle of caring in our gifted youth. *Journal of Secondary Gifted Education, 15,* 23–32.

U.S. Department of Education, Office of Educational Research and Improvement. (1993). *National excellence: A case for developing America's talent.* Washington, DC: U.S. Government Printing Office.

Wade, R. C., & Putnam, K. (1995). Tomorrow's leaders? Gifted students' opinions of leadership and service activities. *Roeper Review, 18,* 150–151.

Wang, W. (2000, April). *Service learning: Is it good for you?* Paper presented at the Annual Meeting of the American Educational

Research Association Conference Roundtable, New Orleans, LA.

Waterman, A. S. (1997a). An overview of service-learning and the role of research and evaluation in service learning programs. In A. S. Waterman (Ed.), *Service-learning: Applications from the research* (pp. 1–22). Mahwah, NJ: Lawrence Erlbaum.

Waterman, A. S. (1997b). The role of student characteristics in service-learning. In A. S. Waterman (Ed.), *Service-learning: Applications from the research* (pp. 95–105). Mahwah, NJ: Lawrence Erlbaum.

Yates, M., & Youniss, J. (1998). Community service and political identity development in adolescence. *Journal of Social Sciences, 54,* 495–515.

## Author's Note

I am grateful to my mentor, Dr. Joyce L. VanTassel-Baska, for her encouragement and guidance in writing this chapter.

# Alternative Programs and Services: A Creative Response to the Unmet Needs of Gifted Students

*Joyce L. VanTassel-Baska*

This book has compiled a set of issues found to be critical in the development of talent for America's most gifted students. It has described in detail the history and nature of such programs and services as they currently exist, the evidence they present for their effectiveness, their contributions to spreading the efforts of gifted education more broadly to schools and other stakeholder groups, and the concomitant issues and concerns associated with running such programs, including concerns related to access and retention of students of poverty and color.

For summer programs for gifted learners, especially those based on the talent search model, major concerns arise over the responsiveness of schools in providing the articulation of appropriate coursework that matches students' demonstrated areas of advanced functioning. A related concern is the extent to which schools award credit or placement to students for faster paced summer classes they have taken. Yet, these programs are perhaps the most accountable in the field of gifted education, routinely collecting data on student progress through multiple modes of assessment including standardized tests and teacher-developed measures. Research studies have continued to demonstrate the effectiveness of student learning in fast-paced classes in most subject areas. Moreover, universities that run these programs also develop products for the field that are helpful to schools in the form of reports and guidelines for developing programs for gifted learners in various subject areas. All of the talent search programs are well institutionalized in their respective settings, having a history of operation since the early 1980s.

For students of color, the issue of out-of-school programs appears to be inextricably linked to issues of ethnic identity and peer group affiliations. Although research has shown that these students' success in life is inextricably linked to pursuing academic activities, it is equally true that they need to develop strong ethnic identities that promote the skills of bicultural competence. A supportive peer group with similar values and aspirations is a clear aid in this regard. Yet, access to out-of-school opportunities may be hindered by school district identification criteria or parental ignorance of the value of such options. Important longitudinal data on different ethnic groups are cited in Chapter 3 to support the contention of these targeted needs.

For university-based programs for gifted learners with an emphasis on finding and serving students of poverty and color and those that offer a full range of services including mentoring, parenting, peer activities, as well as academic year and summer opportunities, the central issue appears to be retaining students and finding ways to provide the personal and social supports these students need to stay in academically challenging programs beyond the school setting. These programs too have some evidence of effectiveness, especially evaluation data suggesting student and parent satisfaction with such programs in several dimensions including academic, social, and personal experiences. Tight linkages exist to school districts in respect to providing teacher training for the instructors of classes who are selected from the school district ranks. Evidence of products developed for use in school districts was not addressed. Programs like the one described in Chapter 4 have an even longer history of operation, going back to the mid-1970s for inception. Institutionalization of such a comprehensive model is often threatened by the limitation of funding or resources to carry out each component of the program, because such programs are costly to run, given the number of resources being provided to each student.

For public residential schools for the gifted, the major challenges would appear to reside in the question of how to promote their development in all states in the country. Although the chapter demonstrates the features of three different models for such schools, the point remains that only a few states have any such model at a time when school-based gifted programs are flagging. A second issue, of course, is the relative effectiveness of one model over another for which no data are available to date. Finally, several issues emerge over the organization of these schools, in respect to student selection, curriculum, selection of teachers, and accountability for reporting results to various stakeholders. The history of these schools dates back to the early 1970s and demonstrates the evolutionary development of the concept over the following decades in selected states. Institutionalization appears strong, yet these schools must contend annually with state legislatures to ensure adequate funding levels for continued operation. Research data are limited as to the effectiveness of the model, although relevant student performance indices from each school continue to be high enough to make the argument for continuation. Although each of the schools in Model 1 and 2 have as part of their mission to work with local school districts, little evidence of the impact of such work on traditional school change is available nor are products routinely disseminated to the field from the work of these schools.

Through an in-depth look at one residential school for the gifted, the issues appear to cluster around the interaction effect of the students who attend and the organization and operation of the school. How the themes of diversity, talent development, and socialization intertwine is presented in the chapter as central to the success of the residential enterprise. Questions about whether such schools would benefit all gifted learners is raised along with the question of student readiness for such rigorous expectations if they have not experienced them before, especially the expectation for homework and advanced product development. Students who leave the school do so primarily for reasons of the academic pressures being too great to manage. Yet, the ethnographic evidence on this school suggests that most students benefit greatly from an environment that clearly values individual differences, provides a supportive peer group, and provides intellectual challenge and stimulation as a regular diet.

For personalized counseling services for the gifted, the major issue would appear to be the paucity of them in this country. The chapter outlines well the needs for such services, summarizes the literature on the impact such services can have, and provides anecdotal commentary on one such program of services for highly gifted students. Yet, nowhere else can we find such a model being replicated, one that provides the psychosocial, academic, and career counseling so desperately needed by gifted students across a broader range of abilities. Research on effectiveness is limited by the lack of such models to study, as are viable products to be used in the development of talent. The SET program, however, has done a real service to the gifted community by the issuance of *Imagine* magazine, directed at college and career development issues for the gifted adolescent and their families. Longevity of the model described has passed the decade mark with strong roots in an existing talent search program and outside funding support, as well, guaranteeing its continuance.

For competitions and contests, the issues of excellence versus equity persist in respect to who competes and how they attained access to the information. The chapter also explores the inevitable issue of social comparison and whether competition benefits or impedes growth in an area. Does not winning a competition act as a catalyst for further talent development or merely confirm that talent in an area is mediocre at best? Research on highly talented individuals suggests that competition spurs them to develop intrinsic standards of excellence that motivate them to pursue a talent area over time. Yet, there is scant research on how students less talented in an area respond. Some studies have been done that document the effects of involvement in competitions over time, suggesting that participation was beneficial in skill development and, for collaborative competitions like the Future Problem Solving Program, in social skill development, as well. Products from many competitions are used in schools as a part of the curriculum or even the whole curriculum provided to gifted students. Because contest challenges are advanced, often problem-based, and require higher level thinking, they are also seen to contain the very elements of good curriculum for the gifted. Yet, Chapter 8 points out the criticality of linking contest work to a sound curriculum that provides an appropriate scope and sequence of skills in a talent domain over years. Contests and competitions are most often administered through outside organizations associated with domains of study and have a long and rich history of operation at local, state, and national levels.

For distance learning, the central issues of concern revolve around the translation of face-to-face courses to technological formats and the issue of which gifted students may be the best candidates for participation in this alternative format for learning. The history of distance learning is long and deep, although the technology of delivery has continued to advance and to influence the numbers of gifted students accessing online learning opportunities. Research evidence of effectiveness is emergent, and few products are available on a widespread basis due to the cost in development by different agencies. Distance learning clearly represents the most entrepreneurial form of alternative program at the moment, designed and marketed external to school districts and available typically at a per pupil cost. Yet, the future of distance learning for the gifted would appear to be very bright, given its potential for reaching groups of students from rural areas through telecommunications mechanisms, a strategy successfully employed by some of the country's residential schools for the gifted on a statewide basis. Its potential also rests with the flexibility in time and space provided by the venue for the highly gifted, many of whom prefer to learn independently.

For mentorships, the critical issues are associated with the organization and administration of the program, often a task that needs to be coordinated by schools or universities as opposed to content domains. Central to successful mentorships is the creation of an optimal match between mentor and mentee in respect to gender, ethnicity, area of specialty, and even socio-economic background in order to gain the dual benefits of role modeling and expertise for a mentee's further development in a field of study. However, other critical issues need attention, as well, including the processes for creating and maintaining a mentor bank, the preparation of mentors for their tasks, and the incentive system for both mentors and mentees to continue a formal relationship. Research on the success of mentorships comes mainly from the literature on developing scientific talent and suggests that mentors are critical to students' continuing to pursue scientific careers, especially at key transition points in schooling—after high school and after an undergraduate degree. Existing mentorship programs have produced little to guide school districts to develop such programs, yet several of them have become institutionalized, such as the Research Science Institute and the Singapore Research Program. Informal mentorships provided by teachers in top science schools also have been in place to help students compete in the Intel Science Talent Search, the premiere science competition in the country. The longevity of mentorships is timeless, going back to ancient times.

For service learning, the critical issues appear to reside in how to create coherence in the concept and link together loosely coupled existing programs under a single conceptual umbrella that might be used as a model for future program development in this area of learning. The chapter focuses strongly on the real connection between service learning and leadership development for the gifted, seeing this as a natural wedding of like goals and purposes. Although service learning is a relatively new emphasis in gifted education, it is firmly established in contexts like the International Baccalaureate program and some other secondary school programs, especially those that are self-contained in nature. Almost no research exists on the efficacy of the approach, and limited products have been developed to explicate its role in the talent development process; it has received much attention as a program model to promote prosocial behaviors in gifted students.

Table 12.1 provides an overview of the key aspects of each of these models for providing alternative programs and services to gifted learners. Ratings for evidence of effectiveness and demonstrable products are assigned, based on the evidence presented in the relevant chapter.

## A Model for a Coherent and Systemic Tapestry of Programs and Services for the Gifted

Although the programs for gifted students presented in this book represent both tested and promising directions for program development in the field of gifted education, they also raise disturbing questions about the systematic access of gifted learners to the potential benefits of any of them. Still, services to these learners in this country are not guaranteed, no matter how gifted they are or in what areas they are gifted. We have evidence that suggests we lose intellectual talent in this country after high school and after college entrance, with 38% of high-ability learners not finishing college. We also lose it in certain professions where we desperately need more highly qualified professionals—teaching, the sciences, and engineering. What could be done to provide a safety net for the gifted in America? As an advanced society with many resources available, can we not see the development of high-level talent as a priority, a clarion call to action on their behalf? If we are not willing to do it for the students themselves and their personal development, are we not willing to do it on behalf of our own enlightened self-interest?

Even as we do little to advance the learning potential of our brightest students, other societies are. Asian societies like Singapore, China, and Korea have major initiatives and clear-targeted emphases to find and serve their most talented students, especially those from poverty. European countries like Germany continue to invest in the development of talent, especially in the core areas of science and mathematics, through alternative programs at the secondary level. Middle Eastern countries like Jordan, Saudi Arabia, and the Gulf States have begun serious development of their human resources to the

# Table 12.1

Synthesis of the Major Types of Alternative Programs With Indicators of Longevity, Evidence of Effectiveness, Demonstrated Products, and Major Issues Identified

| Alternative Programs and Services for the Gifted Learner | Longevity | Evidence of Effectiveness and/or Research Agenda | Development of Models, Methods, and Materials to Benefit the Gifted | Major Issues and Concerns Identified by Authors |
|---|---|---|---|---|
| Summer Programs (Talent Search) (Olszewski-Kubilius) | 25 years | High | High | • Articulation of coursework with high schools<br>• Use of data by schools on high-scoring students<br>• Credit/placement for talent search students |
| Out-of-School Opportunities for Students of Color (generic programs) (Kitano) | Ageless | High | Moderate | • Ethnic identity<br>• "Fewness" of students of color in programs<br>• Self-perception<br>• Peer group identification |
| University-Based Enrichment Programs and Services (Johnsen, Feuerbacher, & Witte) | 35 years | Moderate | Low | • Retention of minority students<br>• Support needed for students of color and poverty |

*Note.* High = Programs and services have sustained evidence of a real contribution to the study and execution of talent development; Moderate = Some evidence of research of beneficial product development; Low = Little or no evidence of research or beneficial product development

| Program | Years | | | Issues |
|---|---|---|---|---|
| Residential Academic Schools for the Gifted (Cross & Miller; Coleman) | 25 years for science schools, 40 years for art schools | Moderate | Moderate | • Lack of prevalence in every state<br>• Lack of clear definitions of "rigor"<br>• Lack of impact on regular high schools |
| Personalized, yet Formalized, Academic Counseling (Brody) | 25 years | Low | High | • Issues of optimal match between student and program or service<br>• Continuous service based on differential developmental needs |
| Competitions (Riley & Karnes) | Ageless | Low | Moderate | • Equitable access<br>• Integration with school curriculum |
| Distance Learning (Adams & Olszewski-Kubilius) | 20 years (correspondence and other lower technical forms have been operating for more than 100 years) | Low | Low | • Lack of evidence of effectiveness<br>• Student qualities necessary for success<br>• Reorganization of curriculum to match modality of delivery |
| Mentorships (Feng) | Ageless | High | Moderate | • Optimal match of mentor–mentee<br>• Sustainability<br>• Target populations of students<br>• Qualities of the mentor |
| Service Learning (Chee) | 30+ years | Low | Low | • Linkages needed for leadership development<br>• Lack of effectiveness studies<br>• Need for curricular connection and scope and sequence |

highest level through a myriad of program opportunities, which are heavily subsidized by the rulers in these nations.

Can we as a nation not also take this charge seriously to develop our best human resources to optimal levels, using their peak performances as evidence of the next level to which more of the society should aspire? Evidence abounds that this has always been the way nations advance—through developing enlightened leaders in all intellectual spheres to serve as guideposts for the future. Carlyle saw history as a series of eminent biographies whose stories contain the evolution of human development. While other views of history abound, this one still has salience as a worldview. Daniel Boorstin, author and former librarian of Congress, writes of the discoverers, the creators, and the pioneers of the American experience who shaped our world. Surely we understand the power of one individual to shift our way of thinking, to advance our understanding of remedies for poverty, hunger, and disease, to create new models for discerning how the world works. Yet, our policies and practices in education suggest we care little for these things.

What would a system of talent development look like in this country if we took our cues from what works in these well-developed models of alternative options for gifted learners?

First of all, such a system would acknowledge the centrality of the individual differences of the learner, taking into account general abilities and specific aptitudes, as well as interests and predispositions, values and experiences in respect to cultural background, and the level of functioning in each area of learning. In order to do this efficiently and effectively, all students should have access to a thorough assessment of potential at critical stages of development—at ages 4, 10, 14, and 17. These data should become part of the statewide database on students, currently constructed in each state and correlated with comparable databases in local districts to respond to No Child Left Behind. The assessment process should be outsourced to talent search agencies who can handle large scale testing and analysis of data.

Second, the databases would be disaggregated according to geography, age level of the student, and areas of special talent. A profile of students then would be matched with an array of programs and services developed and available in their region of a state. Students and families would select relevant options each year that would provide sustained talent development in relevant areas. Each year's offerings would include academically challenging courses delivered face-to-face or online and counseling services related to individual needs and levels of educational attainment. Acceleration would be encouraged and triggered by contact with an academic counselor familiar with the student profile. All of the options for acceleration would be considered, from grade skipping, to telescoping, to tutoring. At appropriate stages of development for students who are highly gifted or those who demonstrate great need for extraordinary personalized support, mentoring should be provided. Universities, laboratories, and museums would constitute appropriate arenas to coordinate such efforts. Residential high schools would be available in every state and provide services to those in greatest need of advanced work in all areas of learning or in particular specialty areas designated by the school. The model of operation for such schools would combine the approaches of existing models and provide the first 2 years of high school according to Models One and Two, and then provide in every state a Model Three option where students attend courses on a university campus for their culminating secondary experience.

Third, personnel preparation for working with the gifted would be provided through at least two universities in each state, focusing on the development of teachers, coordinators, mentors, parents, and counselors who would show competency in the new NCATE standards upon completion of 12–18 hours of coursework. All personnel who would work directly with gifted learners in or out of schools would be required to participate in such structured learning opportunities. Practica placements would be in model programs where differentiation for gifted learners is standard practice.

Fourth, assessment and evaluation of student learning would be required at the end of each year, utilizing multiple data sources including relevant standardized test results, performance measures, and portfolio artifacts or special projects. Results would provide the database for a new round of academic counseling on next year's options, which would be open, based on the evidence from the assessment data available.

Fifth, the time frames for learning in the lives of gifted learners would necessarily shift from a predictable school-based agrarian model to a flexible schedule that would be conceived of as year-round continuous learning.

Sixth, the concept of place of learning would also shift to multiple venues in the community and beyond, to virtual learning contexts, and to independent contexts that enhance the possibility for reflection and revision in thinking.

Seventh, the coordination of gifted programs and services would occur outside of local schools in existing regional agencies, universities, or other community agencies equipped to manage the tasks associated with a comprehensive talent search and serve mechanism.

Eighth, the funding for gifted programs would be mandated in each state, guaranteeing services for up to 5% of its students, based on nationally normed measures. The funding base would be set aside from state lottery money, tax revenues, and other sources that would not take away existing dollars from other educational programs.

Such a vision of talent development suggests the importance of several interlocking elements that need to work together to create the tapestry suggested in the title of this section. In the absence of any of these elements, the likelihood of the success of the entire venture is put at risk. For too long, gifted education has settled for too little in respect to the large needs of the population. Table 12.2 delineates the system described above.

## A Policy Agenda for National Leadership

Just as a strong state system of talent development is crucial to address the needs of America's best students, there also exists a need to create policies at the national level that acknowledge the need to institutionalize processes to promote the development of human intellectual capital. Policymakers representing foundations, political appointees and elected officials, and organizations and societies all have a stake in the development of talent for the future. What can these entities do to lead the country on this issue?

First, policymakers can address the central problem of poverty in our society by assuring that children of poverty have access to early childhood programs and services by age 3 and sustained involvement in those programs until school entrance. These students could then be systematically screened for indicators of advanced development and provided additional value-added opportunities.

Second, policymakers can address the need for research and development of new models, programs, and services that would be most effective for different populations of gifted learners at different stages of development and in different areas of learning. As our society becomes more data-driven and the expectations for accountability rise, there is a real need to have Centers of Intellectual Development across the country that are actively pursuing a "what works" agenda. These nationally funded centers would focus on large-scale studies, using existing databases, including those from states, to answer important questions about gifted learners. They also would conduct controlled studies of effective interventions and do evaluations of existing models and programs of promise.

Third, policymakers can work together to provide the funding base for these national needs. Instead of competition among funding agencies on key societal issues to find the solutions, a consortium of such groups would go a long way to make the dollars stretch farther and demonstrate more impressive results.

## A Final Thought

A new paradigm is needed to address the needs of gifted learners in this country and in this century, one that acknowledges what has worked for these students in the last 20 years through opportunities crafted mostly outside of typical school settings. The new paradigm for gifted learning must take us outside the bounds of the schoolhouse with its set timeframes for learning and its set pacing guides, into a more flexible world of learning that values effort, sustained application of skills to

## Table 12.2
### A Model for a Coherent and Systemic Tapestry of Programs and Services for the Gifted

| | |
|---|---|
| **Thread 1**<br>Acknowledgment of the Centrality of Individual Differences | • Includes general abilities, specific aptitudes, interests and predispositions, values and experiences in respect to cultural background.<br>• Includes level of functioning in each area of learning.<br>• Students should have access to a thorough assessment of potential at critical stages of development. |
| **Thread 2**<br>Use of Data on Students | • Statewide databases should include relevant data on gifted students.<br>• Assessment process should be outsourced to talent search agencies.<br>• Databases should be disaggregated according to geography, age level of the student, and areas of special talent.<br>• Profile of students should be matched with programs and services available in their region of a state. |
| **Thread 3**<br>Structure of Programs and Services | • Students and families would select relevant options each year.<br>• Yearly offerings would include academically challenging courses delivered face-to-face or online.<br>• Counseling services would be provided related to individual needs and levels of educational attainment.<br>• Acceleration would be encouraged (e.g., grade skipping, telescoping, tutoring).<br>• Universities, laboratories, and museums would be used for coordination of services.<br>• Residential high schools would be available in every state (combining the approaches of existing models and provide the first 2 years of high school according to Models One and Two).<br>• Provision in every state for a Model Three option. |

| **Thread 4**<br><br>Personnel Preparation | • Provided through at least two universities in each state.<br>• Focus on the development of educators who would show competency in the new NCATE standards upon completion of 12–18 hours of coursework.<br>• Personnel working with the gifted mandated to participate in such structured learning opportunities.<br>• Practica placements would be in model programs utilizing differentiation as a standard practice. |
|---|---|
| **Thread 5**<br><br>Assessment and Evaluation of Student Learning | • Required at the end of each year.<br>• Utilizing multiple data sources (standardized test results, performance measures, portfolio artifacts and/or special projects).<br>• Results would provide the database for a new round of academic counseling on next year's options. |
| **Thread 6**<br><br>Time Frames for Learning | • Shift from a predictable school-based agrarian model to a flexible schedule.<br>• Could be conceived of as year-round continuous learning. |
| **Thread 7**<br><br>Place of Learning | • Multiple venues in the community and beyond.<br>• Virtual learning.<br>• Independent contexts. |
| **Thread 8**<br><br>Coordination of Programs and Services | • Occur outside of local schools.<br>• Include regional agencies, universities, or other community agencies.<br>• Must be equipped to manage the tasks associated with a comprehensive talent search and serve mechanism. |
| **Thread 9**<br><br>Funding | • Mandated in each state.<br>• Guaranteed services for up to 5% of student population.<br>• Be set aside from state lottery money, tax revenues, and other sources. |

worthy problems and projects, and competency-based progress. It is time we woke up to the realities that talent development will not happen if it is left to chance, to the accident of birth, or the serendipity of a caring teacher at a critical point in life. It will only happen if we have the will to work together and the insight to work smarter so that our efforts truly benefit the society and the high-potential individuals within it that we all care about so deeply.

# About the Authors

## About the Editor

**Joyce L. VanTassel-Baska** is the Jody and Layton Smith Professor of Education and Executive Director of the Center for Gifted Education at The College of William and Mary in Virginia, where she has developed a graduate program and a research and development center in gifted education. Formerly, she initiated and directed the Center for Talent Development at Northwestern University. She has also served as the state director of gifted programs for Illinois, as a regional director of a gifted service center in the Chicago area, as coordinator of gifted programs for the Toledo, OH, public school system, and as a teacher of gifted high school students in English and Latin. She has worked as a consultant on gifted education in all 50 states and for key national groups, including the U.S. Department of Education, National Association of Secondary School Principals, and American Association of School Administrators. She has consulted internationally in Australia, New Zealand, Hungary, Jordan, Singapore, Korea, England, Germany, The Netherlands, and the United Arab Emirates. She is past president of The Association for the Gifted of the Council for Exceptional Children, and the Northwestern

University Chapter of Phi Delta Kappa. She currently serves as the president of the National Association for Gifted Children.

Dr. VanTassel-Baska has published widely, including 20 books and more than 375 refereed journal articles, book chapters, and scholarly reports. Recent books include: *Comprehensive Curriculum for Gifted Education* (3rd ed.; 2006) with Tamra Stambaugh; *Curriculum for Gifted Students* (2004); *Designing and Utilizing Evaluation for Gifted Program Improvement* (2004) with Annie Feng; *Content-Based Curriculum for Gifted Learners* (2003) with Catherine Little; and *Curriculum Planning and Instructional Design for Gifted Learners* (2003). She also served as the editor of *Gifted and Talented International,* a publication of the World Council on Gifted and Talented, from 1998–2005.

Dr. VanTassel-Baska has received numerous awards for her work, including the National Association for Gifted Children's Early Leader Award in 1986, the State Council of Higher Education in Virginia Outstanding Faculty Award in 1993, the Phi Beta Kappa faculty award in 1995, the National Association of Gifted Children Distinguished Scholar Award in 1997, and the President's Award, World Council on Gifted and Talented Education in 2005. She has received awards from Ohio, Virginia, Colorado, South Carolina, and Illinois for her contribution to the field of gifted education in those states. She was selected as a Fulbright Scholar to New Zealand in 2000 and a visiting scholar to Cambridge University in England in 1993. Her major research interests are on the talent development process and effective curricular interventions with the gifted. She holds her bachelor's, master's, and Ed.D. degrees from the University of Toledo.

## About the Authors

**Cheryll M. Adams** received her bachelor's degree from the University of Georgia and her master's and doctoral degrees from the University of Virginia. She is director of the Center for Gifted Studies and Talent Development at Ball State

University. She also teaches courses on gifted education. Dr. Adams is a former member of the board of directors of the National Association for Gifted Children, is the current secretary of The Association for the Gifted of the Council for Exceptional Children, and the past president of the Indiana Association for the Gifted. In 2002, she received the NAGC Early Leader Award, and in 2005, the Indiana Association for the Gifted Service Award. She has published a book, several book chapters, and numerous journal articles, as well as presented internationally, nationally, statewide, and locally in the field of gifted education since 1990. She has coauthored and received two Javits grants from the federal government in partnership with the Indianapolis Public Schools. Dr. Adams was a classroom teacher for 15 years in public and private schools. Her research interests are in identification of gifted students, programming, and curriculum.

**Linda E. Brody** directs the Julian C. Stanley Study of Exceptional Talent (SET) and codirects the Diagnostic and Counseling Center at the Johns Hopkins University Center for Talented Youth (CTY). She also supervises counseling efforts on behalf of the Jack Kent Cooke Young Scholars Program for CTY, the development of the http://www.cogito.org Web site for top math and science students, and the publication of the award-winning *Imagine* magazine. Dr. Brody has counseled gifted students and their families for more than 30 years and has published widely in professional journals and books. Her research interests focus on the efficacy of strategies to serve gifted students such as acceleration, and on special populations of gifted students including the highly gifted, gifted females, and twice-exceptional students. She received her doctoral degree from Johns Hopkins University.

**Ai–Lian Chee** is a provisional curriculum specialist at the Gifted Education Branch in the Ministry of Education, Singapore. She graduated with a master's degree in curriculum and instruction with an emphasis in gifted education from the College of William and Mary in Williamsburg, VA.

**Laurence J. Coleman** is the Judith Daso Herb Chair in Gifted Studies at the University of Toledo, OH. Dr. Coleman is a special education teacher who became a professor. He notes that he is fortunate to be able to do work that he values, which is preparing teachers and doing research. He formerly served as the editor of the *Journal for the Education of the Gifted* and received the Distinguished Scholar Award of the National Association for Gifted Children in 2000. At present, he is principal investigator of Accelerating Achievement in Math and Science in Urban Schools, a Javits' sponsored program for economically disadvantaged children. His scholarly interests spring from his desire to capture the experience of gifted children and teachers. In 2005, he published *Being Gifted in School* with Tracy L. Cross for Prufrock Press, and *Nurturing Talent in High Schools: Life in the Fast Lane* for Teachers College Press.

**Tracy L. Cross**, George and Frances Ball Distinguished Professor of Gifted Studies, is associate dean for Graduate Studies, Research and Assessment for Teachers College at Ball State University (BSU). For 9 years, he served BSU as executive director of the Indiana Academy for Science, Mathematics, and Humanities, a public residential school for academically gifted adolescents. He received his graduate degrees in educational psychology from the University of Tennessee. Dr. Cross has published more than 70 articles and book chapters, a coauthored textbook, *Being Gifted in School: An Introduction to Development, Guidance, and Teaching*, and a supplemental book entitled *On the Social and Emotional Lives of Gifted Children*, both in their second editions. He is the editor of the *Journal for the Education of the Gifted* and editor emeritus of *Roeper Review*, *Gifted Child Quarterly*, *Journal of Secondary Gifted Education*, *Research Briefs*, and other publications. He served as president of The Association for the Gifted of the Council for Exceptional Children and is on the executive committee and the board of the National Association for Gifted Children.

**Annie Xuemei Feng** is the research and evaluation director of the Center for Gifted Education at the College of William and Mary. Her research interests include curriculum effectiveness studies, program evaluation research, gender-related studies, and cross-cultural research. She received her Ed.D. degree from St. John's University in New York.

**Sarah Feuerbacher** earned a bachelor and master's degree in social work and a doctoral degree in educational psychology from Baylor University. She is currently employed as the Battering Intervention and Prevention Program Intake Specialist/Counselor at Hope's Door in Plano, TX. In addition, she serves as associate faculty of psychology in Behavioral and Brain Sciences at the University of Texas at Dallas. Her previous social service experience has allowed her to work as a therapist in a family preservation program, as a school case manager for vulnerable students and families, and as a caseworker at a residential care facility. She has also taught in multiple positions of academia, including university, community college, secondary, and elementary educational levels. Dr. Feuerbacher has completed quantitative and qualitative research studies, presentations, and publications in the area of holistic approaches to working with at-risk, multicultural youth and their intrapersonal and environmental systems. Her current research and public outreach focuses on multifaceted themes of family abuse.

**Susan K. Johnsen** is a professor in the Department of Educational Psychology at Baylor University in Waco, TX. She directs the Ph.D. program and programs related to gifted and talented education at both the graduate and undergraduate levels. She teaches assessment courses at the graduate level and courses in exceptionalities at both the undergraduate and graduate levels. She has written more than 150 publications, including 9 books, 12 chapters, and teacher curriculum materials. She is the author of the *Independent Study Program, Identifying Gifted Students: A Practical Guide,* and three tests that are used in identifying gifted students: Test of Mathematical Abilities for Gifted Students (TOMAGS), Test of Nonverbal Intelligence, Third Edition (TONI-3), and the Screening Assessment for Gifted Elementary and Middle School Students, Second Edition (SAGES-2). She is a frequent presenter at international, national, and state conferences. She is editor of *Gifted Child Today* and serves on the editorial review boards of *Gifted Child Quarterly*, *Journal for the Education of the Gifted*, and the *Journal of Secondary Gifted Education*. She is past president of the Texas Association for the Gifted and Talented and currently serves on the board of The Association for the Gifted of the Council for Exceptional Children (TAG). She is the co-chair of the graduate program standards task force of the National Association for Gifted Children and serves on the Board of Examiners of the National Council for Accreditation of Teacher Education.

**Frances A. Karnes** is a professor in the Department of Curriculum, Instruction, and Special Education and director of the Frances A. Karnes Center for Gifted Studies at The University of Southern Mississippi, where she has been a member of the faculty since being awarded the Ph.D. degree by the University of Illinois in 1973. Dr. Karnes, who also directs the Leadership Studies Program at USM, has become widely known for her research, publications, innovative program developments, and service activities in gifted education and leadership training. She is author or coauthor of more than 250 papers published in scholarly journals, numerous monographs, and book chapters, and is coauthor of 38 books in gifted education and related areas.

**Margie Kitano** serves as associate dean of the College of Education and professor of Special Education at San Diego State University (SDSU). She codeveloped and works with the San Diego Unified School District collaborative certificate in gifted education and SDSU's graduate certificate and master's degree program in developing gifted potential. Dr. Kitano's publications address services to culturally and linguistically diverse gifted learners. Specific research interests include instructional strategies for gifted English language learners and methods for building academic resilience among gifted students from low-income backgrounds.

**Kimberly A. Miller** is a doctoral candidate in the counseling psychology department at Colorado State University. She is currently working on her dissertation which involves continuing to establish the psychometric properties of the Miller Needs Assessment, which is a measure of psychological well-being. Prior to attending Colorado State, she received her bachelor's degree from Auburn University and her master's degree from Ball State University.

**Paula Olszewski-Kubilius** is director of the Center for Talent Development at Northwestern University and professor in the School of Education and Social Policy. She earned her bachelor's degree in elementary education from St. Xavier University in Chicago and her master's and doctoral degrees from Northwestern University in educational psychology. Dr. Olszewski-Kubilius has worked at the Center for more than 20 years, during which time she has designed and conducted educational programs for learners of all ages, including summer programs, weekend programs, distance learning programs, and programs for underrepresented gifted students, as well as workshops for parents and teachers. She is active in national- and state-level advocacy organizations for gifted children in the Midwest. She currently serves on the board of directors of the Illinois Association for Gifted Children and on the board of trustees of the Illinois Mathematics and Science Academy. She has conducted research and published more than 80 articles or book chapters on issues of talent development, particularly the effects of accelerated educational programs and the needs of special populations of gifted children. She currently serves as the editor of *Gifted Child Quarterly* and formerly was a coeditor of the *Journal of Secondary Gifted Education.* She has served on the editorial advisory board of the *Journal for the Education of the Gifted* and *Gifted Child International,* and was a consulting editor for *Roeper Review.*

**Tracy Riley** is a senior lecturer specializing in gifted and talented education at Massey University in New Zealand. She teaches undergraduate and postgraduate students in the field, as well as supervises postgraduate research. Tracy is the coeditor of *APEX: The New Zealand Journal of Gifted Education* and serves on the editorial board of *Gifted Child Today*. An active advocate for gifted and talented students, Tracy has served on numerous Ministry of Education advisory groups and coauthored the Ministry handbook, *Gifted and Talented Students: Meeting Their Needs in New Zealand Schools*. She publishes and presents widely at both national and international levels.

**Mary M. Witte** is a senior lecturer in the School of Education at Baylor University. She directs the Center for Community Learning and Enrichment, which offers enrichment programs for gifted and talented students. As the administrator of the University for Young People Project, Dr. Witte has worked with at-risk gifted and talented students for 7 years, providing them with academic and fine arts enrichment opportunities during the summer and academic year. In 2006, the UYP Project won the Audrey Nelson Community Development Achievement Award from the National Community Development Association. Dr. Witte's research interests include at-risk gifted and talented students, interdisciplinary curriculum, differentiation in elementary classrooms, and the development of preservice teachers.